DEVELOPING YOUR
SPIRITUAL POTENTIALS

DEVELOPING YOUR SPIRITUAL POTENTIALS

The Christian and Religious Value Profiles

Rem B. Edwards,
David Mefford, and
Vera Mefford

To order additional copies of this book, contact:
Xlibris Corporation
1-888-795-4274
www.Xlibris.com
Orders@Xlibris.com
28631

CONTENTS

For Thomas Remington Edwards, the long desired
grandson of Rem and Louise Edwards, and
in loving memory of the mothers of David and
Vera Mefford, Margaret Mefford (1920-2002) and
Inge Mette (1930-2005), for their unwavering support,
encouragement, spiritual inspiration, and unconditional love.

PREFACE

Have you ever wondered where you are in your own personal spiritual development? Are you strong or weak in faith, knowledge, obedience, service, and love to God and to others? Have you been searching for a way to measure and further develop your spiritual values? Values give life meaning or significance; values make life worthwhile. Ideas, property, persons, principles, behaviors, and attitudes are examples of value. Do you really understand and appreciate your own religious values?

As often as possible, we should take inventories of what we think is worthwhile in ourselves, in our surrounding world, and in our ultimate environment. Our judgments about what is worthwhile, and what is not, are the keys to our personalities and to the stages of our religious and spiritual development.

Scientific value theory, known as "*formal axiology*," provides a more powerful, systematic, and general frame of reference for understanding religious development than anything previously available. Wouldn't it be nice if we had an instrument for measuring our "spiritual temperature" in something like the way thermometers measure physical temperature? The Religious and Christian Value Profiles, offered for the first time in this book, are based on formal axiology and should function as "thermometers of the soul" to help us measure our spiritual potential and development. They should be immensely helpful to people who want to know where they are now and where they can go in the future for improvement in moral and spiritual growth.

The Christian and Religious Value Profiles (CVP and RVP), along with their interpretations and applications, are offered as aids to spiritual and moral development. They are not intended to convert anyone from one religious outlook to another. We anticipate that non-

Christian believers in one God will want to take only the RVP, and we encourage Christians, who are also committed to one God, to take both the CVP and the RVP. Very few spiritual-minded people ever change from one religion to another; generally, people stay within the religious culture in which they grew up. All world religions and religious denominations agree that spiritual growth and development are desirable; they also recognize that such growth can be revolutionary and its results unpredictable. The Profiles offered here are designed to help people grow religiously and ethically, beginning right where they are now. The authors agree with the theologian Nels F. S. Ferré that "The way to help people become socially and religiously more adequate is not to uproot them from their historic faith and transplant them to a new ideology, but to nurture them in their accustomed soil."[1]

As explained in Chapter Seven, these Profiles are solidly grounded in a logical systematic frame of reference for identifying and ordering human values, spiritual or otherwise. A powerful formal system for measuring and structuring our values and value judgments has been developed over the last 50 years, beginning with the work of Robert S. Hartman, Ph.D. Dr. Hartman was the creator of scientific axiology (axiology = value science), as expressed in his 1967 book, *The Structure of Value*.[2]

This is a book on *Developing Your Spiritual Potentials*. Its religion-oriented Value Profiles are based on Hartman's work and on developments in value theory since his premature death in 1973. The RVP and the CVP are new and powerful tools designed to help you develop a clearer understanding of and appreciation for monotheistic religious and/or Christian values, and to clarify and further develop your own spiritual potentials. These new instruments are based on the formal axiological structure of the Hartman Value Profile (HVP), a personal values inventory developed by Dr. Hartman. The HVP has been used since the early 1960s to take value-based "snapshots" of personalities and lifestyles, and it is widely used today in business consulting, psychology, psychotherapy, and counseling.[3]

To get the greatest possible benefit from this book, you will find the following steps helpful.

STEPS TO TAKE IN USING THIS GUIDE

STEP 1: Take the Profile(s). Before you read beyond the Profiles in Chapter One, please take the CVP or the RVP or both. Just follow the instructions given on the Profiles. The CVP and the RVP are given at the beginning of Chapter One, but you should take them on the Internet website: *http://www.RVP-CVPautoscore.com.*

STEP 2: Get the Profile(s) scored. After taking the Profile(s), your next step is the numerical scoring. This complicated procedure is made easy for you on our Internet site. Automated scoring is available to you at no additional cost at *http://www.RVP-CVPautoscore.com.* All the scoring calculations and procedures will be done for you if you go to this website and follow the simple instructions. Although you can and should take the Profile(s) on the Internet, you may first want to do a practice ranking using the Profile(s) as they are given in Chapter One. When you go to the Internet site, you will be asked to order the items in Parts I and II by dragging and dropping each item according to the rank that you choose for it. After you enter your final selections, your scores will then be provided to you on three Result Forms. You should print out your three Result Forms when they first appear so you can use them with Chapters One, Two, and beyond.

Step 3: Interpret the Meaning of your Scores. Once you get your Result Forms from the Profile(s), then go to Chapters One and Two the for definitions of the key terms on your Result Forms. Then go to Chapter Three for further interpretations of the significance or meaning of your scores. You must correlate your ranking numbers on the Result

Forms with the interpretations given in those chapters. For example, lines 1, 2, and so on of Result Form 1 correlate with the definitions and interpretations that are so numbered in Chapters One and Two. We recommend that you read and think about only those sections in Chapter Two that correlate with your worst scores, that is, with your scores in the "average," "fair," and "weak" ranges.

Step 4: Pursue Your Own Spiritual Growth. After working through the sections of Chapter Two that relate to your scores, you will be ready to move forward with your own spiritual growth and development. Take your time with this, and do what follows at your convenience. With God's grace and help, and doing your part, you can be changed into the kind of person that you really want to be in the depths of your soul and that God wants you to be in the depths of God's love for you. Soul development and transformation involves interaction between you (or us) and God; and no matter how eager God is for us, soul development does not happen unless you (we) put some serious effort and time into developing and using the *gifts* of God's Spirit and into bearing the *fruits* of God's salvation.

Chapters Three and Four, "For Your Spiritual Growth and Development, Part I" and "For Your Spiritual Growth and Development, Part II," correlate with the positive values in Parts I and II of the Profile(s). These chapters contain exercises or meditations that will help you set working goals, actualize more of your own spiritual potentials, and achieve better balance among the various dimensions of your spiritual life. Read the relevant scriptures at the end of each section. Concentrate first on the areas in which you have weaknesses, but later try reading all the exercises as devotional meditations, perhaps at the rate of one per day from each of the three sections. Even if you did not take the Religious Value Profile, you are strongly encouraged to use its "General Religious Exercises" for devotional purposes. Problems associated with overvaluing or undervaluing the **positive** or good items on the Profiles are also identified and discussed in Chapters Three and Four.

Chapter Five, "Negative Values: Overvaluation or Undervaluation" will help you to recognize and correct any spiritual problems associated with the **negative** or disvalue items on the Profile(s). You may have no problems at all here, but if you overvalued or undervalued some of the negative or bad items, this chapter, along with its suggested Scripture readings, should be helpful to you. Your scores on lines 3, 5, and 7 on Result Forms 1 and 2 reflect your tendencies to overvalue (a positive score greater than 50%) or undervalue (a positive score less than 50%) the intrinsic, extrinsic, and systemic value items.

Chapter Six, "Being and Becoming All that You Can Be Before God," provides further information and gives broad guidance for setting, developing, and reinforcing your personal spiritual improvement goals. Do you know who you are before God? Is your relationship with God an integral part of your own self image and identity? Are you fully developing and using the gifts and talents that God has given personally to you? What can you do to overcome your neglect of some dimensions of spiritual value? Both internally and externally, is your life bearing the fruits of God's grace, love, and salvation? You may want to keep a personal spiritual journal, to write down your goals, to engage in spiritual disciplines and practices both alone and with others, to understand and live a morally good life, to set a time frame for achieving your spiritual goals, to record your progress, and to pray for God's help. If you need human help, please contact one or more of your religious leaders, counselors, or guides. Many of you may want to work on the Profile(s) within religious classes or group discussions. We strongly encourage you to read Chapter Six only after you have interpreted and thought seriously about your results from taking the CVP and/or the RVP.

Step 5: Understand the Theory: Reading **Chapter Seven**, "The Structure of the Religious a Christian Value Profiles," is not required for getting the most out of this book; but if you really want to understand the value structure of the CVP and RVP, as well as the value theory underlying them, you should read it. If you are a religious leader, counselor, or professional, you will greatly benefit from reading it, and it will be of great help to you in guiding others. Even if you do not read all of Chapter Seven, you should definitely read and think about the dimensions of selfhood discussed in the section on "Axiologically Structured Selfhood."

Step 6: What's Next? After completing the first 5 Steps, please consider taking the Profile(s) again to measure your actual spiritual growth. As a more scholarly companion volume for learning even more about how and what we value spiritually, we recommend: Rem B. Edwards, *Religious Values and Valuations*. This book is available for $22.50 plus $3.50 postage and handing from its publisher, Paidia Press, 17 Grayswood Hill Road, Chattanooga, TN 37377. You may also want to look at some of the books on stages of religious development mentioned at the end of Chapter Seven.

CHAPTER ONE

The Profiles and Result Forms

I. The Profiles

The Christian and Religious Value Profiles consist of two lists of 18 spiritual value items. When you take the Profile(s), you are asked to order or rank the 18 items from best to worst. On a scale from 1 to 18, please assign "1" to the item that you believe is the very best or most valuable thing on the list; assign "18" to the very worst thing on the list; assign the remaining numbers to all the other items. Good and bad things come in degrees, so you have to judge the degree of goodness or badness of each item in relation to all the others. Some things of spiritual significance are better than others, some less good, some bad, some even worse.

Part I of each Profile contains nine familiar good or desirable spiritual items—positive religious values (compositions), and nine familiar bad or undesirable spiritual items—negative religious values (transpositions). These are taken from your religious or Christian world and should be familiar to you.

Part I asks you to consider religious values that exist outside of yourself in your familiar religious world, including spiritual values in other people; you will also consider the ways that you present your own religious involvements to others. You must rank these 18 items from best to worst. Likewise, Part II contains nine good or positive and nine bad or negative commonplace spiritual values for you to rank. When taking Part II, you should focus on how you personally relate to those 18 religious items in your own spiritual life, on how they apply to you. You are asked to rank the 18 spiritual value statements from "most agreement" to "most disagreement." Which of these statements best describe your own spirituality, which least describe it, and which fall somewhere in between? When taking the CVP and the RVP, you express your own spiritual priorities. You rank the values inherent in monotheistic (one-God) religions generally and/or in Christianity more specifically. Both Profiles measure the degrees to which you have fulfilled your own spiritual potentials. They are not meant to be judgmental, and neither is a "test." You cannot pass or fail them. The Profiles will help you to know yourself and to understand your own spiritual strengths and weaknesses; with a clear view of this information you can build further upon your strengths and act to compensate for your weaknesses. The CVP and RVP are structured to help you (1) take a current "snapshot" of your own present level of spiritual understanding, involvement, and development, (2) better realize and prioritize your own religious and/or Christian capacities, (3) facilitate your personal spiritual growth, (4) express your convictions in greater resonance with others in your social world, and (5) improve your relationship with God.

When you take the CVP or the RVP, please follow the directions provided in each part. You may read and think about the Profiles as they appear next this book, but to take them, you need to go on the Internet to *http://www.RVP-CVPautoscore.com*. After you complete the CVP or the RVP on this website, your Profile(s) will be scored for you automatically, and you can and should print out your Result Forms for further use.

Your ranking of the profile items must be entirely your own. Do not ask for help from anyone else. If you do, the profiling process will not give you the spiritual self-knowledge that you would like to have. If working in a group, rank the items by yourself first; then you may discuss them with others after you have finalized your own ranking. An honest expression of *your own* religious values is essential. You need to establish a base line for where you are now in your spiritual development; later you can measure your future progress against this base line. To measure your improvements, please take your Profile(s) again *after you have completely worked through this book.*

THE CHRISTIAN VALUE PROFILE (CVP)

Part I, Christian World

DIRECTIONS FOR PART I: PHRASES

On the next page you will find 18 phrases. Each of these represents something on which individuals may place different "values" (good or bad)—depending on their own feelings about how good or bad it is.

Read all of the phrases carefully. (If there is a word you do not understand, ask what it means, or look it up in a dictionary.)

Write the number "1" in the blank by the phrase that has the highest (most) value as far as you are concerned—that is, the one you feel is the **best**.

Write the number "2" in the blank by the phrase that has the next best (second best) value.

Number **all** of the phrases in the same way, to show the order of their respective values to you. Use a **different** number for each of the 18 phrases (3, 4, 5, and so on). The number "18" should be in the blank by the phrase that has the lowest (least) value to you—that is, the one that you feel is the **worst**.

Judge the expressions **only by the goodness** or **badness** of their content.

Decide quickly how you feel about each of the phrases. There is no time limit, but most people are able to complete numbering all the phrases in about ten to fifteen minutes. You may begin.

After you have finished, please CHECK to make sure that you have used all the numbers from 1 through 18, without repeating any. (Start with your number 1 and find each number up through 18.)

Cross out numbers used: 1, 2, 3, 4, 5, 6, 7, 8, 9, 10, 11, 12, 13, 14, 15, 16, 17, 18

Practice   **Final**

_____   Participating in church activities   _____

_____   Christian beliefs that support one another   _____

_____   Misunderstanding a Bible verse   _____

_____   Telling lies   _____

_____   Burning a cross   _____

_____   Learning about Jesus   _____

_____   Despising Christian living   _____

_____   Maliciously perverting religious teachings   _____

_____   Doing what we know is wrong   _____

_____   Personal salvation expressed by good works   _____

_____   Jesus, our Redeemer   _____

_____   Absolutely rejecting Jesus   _____

_____   Rejoicing in Christlike living   _____

_____   Religious doctrines that depreciate   _____
          women, minorities, or outsiders

_____   Actions guided by Christian principles   _____

_____   Persecuting Christians   _____

_____   Loving scriptural truths   _____

_____   Witnessing about the Gospel   _____

Continue ➜

THE CHRISTIAN VALUE PROFILE (CVP)

Part II, Christian Self

DIRECTIONS FOR PART II: STATEMENTS

Please read these directions carefully. They differ from those of Part I.

On the next page you will find 18 statements. Each concerns something on which people may place different "values" (good or bad)—depending on their own feelings about how much they agree or disagree with it, that is, how true or false it is in their own lives.

Read all of the statements carefully. (If there is a word you do not understand, ask what it means, or look it up in a dictionary.)

Write the number "1" in the blank by the statement that you agree with most as it applies to you—the one that has the highest (most) value in your own life. The blanks to the left are for practice; the blanks to the right are for your final rankings.

Write the number "2" in the blank by the statement with which you agree next most (second most).

Number all of the statements in the same way, to show the order of their respective values to you. Use a different number for each of the 18 statements (3, 4, 5, and so on). The number "18" should be in the blank by the statement that has the lowest (least) value in your own life—that is, the one that you disagree with the most as it applies to you.

Decide quickly how you feel about each of the statements There is no time limit, but most people are able to complete numbering all the phrases in about ten to fifteen minutes. You may begin.

After you have finished, please CHECK to make sure that you have used all the numbers from 1 through 18, without repeating any. (Start with your number 1and find each number up through 18.)

Cross out numbers used: 1, 2, 3, 4, 5, 6, 7, 8, 9, 10, 11, 12, 13, 14, 15, 16, 17, 18

Practice   **Final**

_____   I support and attend my church regularly.   _____

_____   I understand God's covenant.   _____

_____   I am confused about God's plan.   _____

_____   I don't always know the right thing to do.   _____

_____   I work hard to undermine the church.   _____

_____   My Christian beliefs help me to understand myself   _____
and others.

_____   I hate doing God's will.   _____

_____   I despise religious rules.   _____

_____   I do what I know I shouldn't do.   _____

_____   To me, the heavens declare the glory of God.   _____

_____   I love Christ with my whole heart, soul, mind,   _____
and strength.

_____   I feel that God could never forgive me.   _____

_____   Christ's love is expressed in everything I do.   _____

_____   I have doubts about Jesus.   _____

_____   In religion, I put my money where my mouth is.   _____

_____   My actions dishonor Christ.   _____

_____   My life is centered around Christian principles.   _____

_____   I practice what I preach.   _____

RELIGIOUS VALUE PROFILE (RVP)

Part I, Religious World, For One-God Religions

DIRECTIONS FOR PART I: PHRASES

On the next page you will find 18 phrases. Each of these is something on which people may place different "values" (good or bad)—depending on their own feelings about how good or bad each is.

Read all of the phrases carefully. (If there is a word you do not understand, ask what it means, or look it up in a dictionary.)

Write the number "1" in the blank by the phrase that has the highest (most) value as far as you are concerned—that is, the one you feel is the **best**. The blanks to the left are for practice; the blanks to the right are for your final rankings.

Write the number "2" in the blank by the phrase that represents the next best (second best) value.

Number **all** of the phrases in the same way, to show the order of their respective values to you. Use a **different** number for each of the 18 phrases (3, 4, 5, and so on). The number "18" should be in the blank by the phrase that has the lowest (least) value to you—that is, the one that you feel is the **worst**.

Judge the expressions **only by the goodness** or **badness** of their content.

If you prefer not to use the word "God," where it occurs in the items, please substitute "Allah," "G-d," "The One," or whatever is appropriate for you.

Decide quickly how you feel about each of the phrases. There is no time limit, but most people are able to complete numbering all the phrases in about ten to fifteen minutes. You may begin.

After you have finished, please CHECK to make sure that you have used all the numbers from 1 through 18, without repeating any. (Start with your number 1and find each number up through 18.)

Cross out the numbers used: 1, 2, 3, 4, 5, 6, 7, 8, 9, 10, 11, 12, 13, 14, 15, 16, 17, 18

Practice   **Final**

_____   Attending a house of worship   _____

_____   Knowing God's commandments   _____

_____   False religious doctrines   _____

_____   Actions condemned by a religious belief   _____

_____   Defiling a house of worship   _____

_____   The principle of forgiving others   _____

_____   Loathing righteous living   _____

_____   Utter contempt for the idea of God   _____

_____   Mocking sacred teachings   _____

_____   Helping needy people   _____

_____   God's love for us   _____

_____   A person's eternal separation from God   _____

_____   The glory of God in creation or nature   _____

_____   Doubts about God   _____

_____   Health and healing resulting from religious beliefs   _____

_____   Oppressing God's people   _____

_____   Total devotion to religious truths   _____

_____   Living according to God's laws   _____

Continue ➜

RELIGIOUS VALUE PROFILE (RVP)

Part II, Religious Self, For One-God Religions

DIRECTIONS FOR PART II: STATEMENTS

Please read these directions carefully. They differ from those of Part I.

On the next page you will find 18 statements. Each concerns something on which people may place different "values" (good or bad)—depending on their own feelings about how much they agree or disagree with it, that is, how true or false each is in their own lives.

Read all of the statements carefully. (If there is a word you do not understand, ask what it means, or look it up in a dictionary.)

Write the number "1" in the blank by the statement that you **agree** with most as it applies to you—the one that has the highest (most) value **in your own life**. The blanks to the left are for practice; the blanks to the right are for your final rankings.

Write the number "2" in front of the statement with which you agree next most (second most).

Number **all** of the statements in the same way, to show the order of their respective values to you. Use a **different** number for each of the 18 statements (3, 4, 5, and so on). The number "18" should be in the blank by the statement that has the lowest (least) value **in your own life**—that is, the one that you **disagree** with most as it applies to you.

If you prefer not to use the word "God," where it occurs in the statements to the right, please substitute "Allah," "G-d," "The One," or whatever is appropriate for you.

Decide quickly how you feel about each of the affirmations. There is no time limit, but most people are able to complete numbering all the phrases in about ten to fifteen minutes. You may begin.

After you have finished, please CHECK to make sure that you have used all the numbers from 1 through 18, without repeating any. (Start with your number 1and find each number up through 18.)

Cross out numbers used: 1, 2, 3, 4, 5, 6, 7, 8, 9, 10, 11, 12, 13, 14, 15, 16, 17, 18

Practice   **Final**

_____   I actively help my religious group to grow.   _____

_____   My mind is in harmony with God's plan.   _____

_____   Some of my religious beliefs contradict each other.   _____

_____   God's commandments are too hard for me to keep.   _____

_____   Serving God is a waste of my time.   _____

_____   My religious beliefs strengthen my soul.   _____

_____   I detest organized religion.   _____

_____   I despise religious dogmas.   _____

_____   My actions often conflict with my religious beliefs.   _____

_____   My love for others is enhanced by my   _____
           religious group.

_____   I am fully devoted to God.   _____

_____   I blame God for all the evils people suffer.   _____

_____   Good works are very dear to me.   _____

_____   I have doubts about God.   _____

_____   I try to live by God's commands.   _____

_____   I curse God.   _____

_____   I love the words of God.   _____

_____   My actions reflect and support my religious beliefs.   _____

II. The Result Forms

When you have completed taking your profile(s) on the Internet website, you will be given three Result Forms that outline your own personal spiritual growth and development up to this point in your life. In many areas of spirituality, they will tell you whether your own spiritual development is excellent, strong, average, fair, or weak. Please print each of these three Result Forms. They will probably make very little sense to you at first, but the purpose of this chapter is to help you understand what they mean.

First, the basic terms on the left of each Result Form need to be defined or briefly explained. The next discussions will do just that. After that, the rest of this chapter will provide you with an opportunity to explore the meaning of your own specific spiritual strengths and weakness in greater depth. Upcoming chapters should help you with your own personal spiritual growth, beginning with where you are right now.

In the Result Forms, all dimensional scores (I, E, & S) and involvement (%) scores are derived from a combination of how you ranked the three positive and three negative phrases that relate to each of three value dimensions. These three dimensions will be explained later.

A. Result Form 1,
Social Spiritual Values, Definitions

1. **Values Judgment Capacity** (DIF 1): A measure of your capacity to discern and distinguish between different spiritual values. An excellent score indicates that you are using all or most of your spiritual capacity, while a fair or weak score indicates that you could benefit from spiritual guidance.

2. **Devotional Focus** (DIM-I_1): This score reflects your emphasis on a devotional relationship with God, personal salvation, the inspiration of God's Holy Spirit, and the loving communion of God's people.

3. **Intrinsic Orientation** (DIM-I$_1$%+): The positive percentage of the above Devotional score. A balanced score (50%) indicates excellence. A high positive (>65%) shows the degree to which you overvalue the devotional focus described above. A low positive (<35%) indicates the degree to which you undervalue these intrinsic spiritual values and presents you with a spiritual development opportunity.

4. **Practical Focus** (DIM-E$_1$): This score reflects your emphasis on the practical impact of your religion, including attending a house of worship, engaging in other spiritual activities regularly, recognizing God's presence in nature and the surrounding world, and appreciating the practical impact of spirituality, e.g. the health and healing that results from spiritual involvements.

5. **Extrinsic Orientation** (DIM-E$_1$%+): The positive percentage of the above Practical score. A balanced score (50%) indicates excellence. A high positive (>65%) shows the degree to which you tend to overvalue the practical focus of religion. A low positive (<35%) indicates the degree to which you undervalue practical spiritual values and presents you with a spiritual development opportunity.

6. **Conceptual Focus** (DIM-S$_1$): This score shows your degree of emphasis on spiritual truths, doctrines, rules, commandments, and rituals. An excellent score indicates a very strong emphasis on religious truths, God's laws, *etc.*

7. **Systemic Orientation** (DIM-S$_1$%+): The positive percentage of the above Conceptual score. A balanced score (50%) indicates excellence. A high positive (>65%) shows the degree to which you tend to overvalue religious truths, beliefs, and God's laws, and may indicate dogmatism. A low positive (<35%) reflects a lack of clarity about or the degree to which you tend to undervalue religious truths, laws, and knowledge.

8. **Dimensional Harmony** (DIM$_1$): This measures the distance separating the three DIM scores. When your focus is primarily on one spiritual dimension, your DIM score will be weak, indicating that the other dimensions are out of focus. An excellent

score reflects stability and balanced development among the three spiritual dimensions.

9. **Stress/Tension** (DIM$_1$%): This is number 8 above as a percentage of number 1 above; it indicates your level of spiritual comfort. An excellent score indicates very little spiritual tension, while a weak score reflects confusion and spiritual stress, discomfort, or disharmony.

10. **Spiritual Clarity** (DIS$_1$): When all positive items are ranked as positive and all negative items are ranked as negative, this score will be zero. If any positive items are ranked as negative, or conversely, your spiritual clarity decreases.

11. **Spiritual Balance** (DIF$_1$%): This score is a measure of your spiritual flexibility. A balanced score (50%) shows your emphasis on all aspects of your religion and your capacity to remain open and responsive. A negative % reflects varying degrees of rigidity such as lack of spiritual clarity, indecision, fear, passive withdrawal, and aggressive hostility.

B. Result Form 2,
Personal Spiritual Values, Definitions

1. **Personal Spiritual Judgment Capacity** (DIF 2): A measure of your capacity to discern spiritual values in your own life. An excellent score indicates that you are using all or most of your capacity, while a fair or weak score indicates you may need spiritual guidance to help you live a deeper and richer spiritual life.

2. **Being-Feeling Focus** (DIM-I$_2$): Your emphasis on the importance of your relationship with God, personal salvation through your spiritual involvements, and your full devotion to God and your religious group.

3. **Intrinsic Involvement** (DIM-I$_2$%+): The positive percentage of the above Being-Feeling score. A balanced score (50%) indicates excellent devotion, reaching out to others with love, empathy, compassion, and forgiveness, because you see yourself and others as children of God. A high positive (>65%) indicates an excessive

degree of devotional involvement. A low positive (<35%) indicates the degree to which you are not actively engaged in accepting and living intrinsic spiritual values.

4. **Doing Focus** (DIM-E $_2$): This score reflects how you act on your moral and spiritual convictions: living your life as an example to others, attending and supporting your house of worship regularly, and using your energy and initiative to be of service to others.

5. **Extrinsic Involvement** (DIM-E$_2$%+): The positive percentage of the above Doing score. A balanced score (50%) indicates excellence in *doing* religious works and acting out your spiritual roles. A high positive (>65%) reflects an excessive degree of active engagement. A low positive (<35%) indicates distance from actively engaging yourself in practical spiritual values.

6. **Thinking Focus** (DIM-S$_2$): Your focus on the structure of your religion, its doctrines, rules, commandments, and rituals. An excellent score indicates that you have developed a spiritual foundation of harmonious beliefs based on your knowledge of religious truths and God's words.

7. **Systemic Involvement** (DIM-S$_2$%+): The positive percentage of the above Thinking Focus score. A balanced score (50%) indicates excellence. A high positive (>65%) reflects an excessive emphasis on spiritual truths and laws, and it may indicate dogmatism and lack of flexibility. A low positive score (<35%) shows a lack of clarity or rebelliousness concerning spiritual truths, laws, and knowledge.

8. **Dimensional Harmony** (DIM$_2$): This measures the distance separating the three DIM scores. When you are involved primarily in one dimension, your DIM score will be weak, indicating a lack of involvement in the other dimensions. An excellent score reflects a balanced development among the three dimensions.

9. **Stress/Tension** (DIM$_2$%): This is number 8 above as a percentage of number 1 above; it indicates your level of spiritual comfort or discomfort. An excellent score indicates harmony and low or no tension, while a weak score reflects confusion and spiritual stress or disharmony.

10. **Spiritual Clarity** (DIS_2): When all positive phrases are ranked as positive and all negative phrases are ranked as negative, this score will be zero. If any positive phrases are ranked as negative, or conversely, your spiritual clarity decreases.

11. **Spiritual Balance** ($DIF_1\%$): This score is a measure of your personal spiritual flexibility. A balanced score (50%) indicates that your are a spiritually dynamic and versatile individual. A negative attitude reflects varying degrees of unhappiness with aspects of your spiritual life. A weak score indicates severe depression, and a low sense of personal spiritual worth.

C. Result Form 3,
Combined Spiritual Values, Definitions

1. **Social-Personal Spiritual Values**: Harmony-Irritability: This score measures how well you discern religious values in the social world around you, as opposed to how well you have internalized spiritual values in your own life. The numerical score for this measure is the absolute difference between the DIF 1 and the DIF 2 scores. Your score is an indication of the well being that results from the harmony of your social spiritual understanding and your personal spiritual identification. An excellent score reflects harmony between spiritual values outside yourself in society and culture, and spiritual values held by you personally. It also reflects your ability to make full and integrated use of your own spiritual potential within the world; it indicates a stable, clear, strong sense of spiritual self-identity that is firmly grounded in community. A relatively weak score indicates tension and irritability between spiritual values on the outside and those spiritual values with which you identify on the inside.

2. **Intrinsic Harmony**—Irritability ($DIM\ I_1 - DIM\ I_2$): This score indicates the degree of harmony or irritability between your social Devotional values (intrinsic social) and the personal Being-feeling values (intrinsic personal) with which you identify. An excellent score reflects a high level of harmony between your social and

personal intrinsic spiritual values. A relatively weak score indicates intrinsic tension and irritability.

3. **Extrinsic Harmony**—Irritability (DIM E_1-DIM E_2): This score indicates the degree of harmony or irritability between your social Practical spiritual values (extrinsic social) and the personal Doing values (extrinsic personal) with which you identify. An excellent score reflects a high level of harmony between the social and personal extrinsic spiritual values. A relatively weak score indicates tension and irritability between recognizing and understanding what other people actually do with spiritual values and how you, yourself, act on similar spiritual values.

4. **Systemic Harmony**—Irritability (DIM S_1-DIM S_2): This score indicates the degree of harmony or irritability between your social Conceptual spiritual values (systemic social) and the personal Thinking spiritual values (systemic personal) with which you identify. An excellent score reflects a high level of harmony between social and personal systemic spiritual values. Relatively weak scores show degrees of systemic tension and irritability.

CHAPTER TWO

The Profiles and What They Mean

The following discussions will help you to interpret in greater depth your scores on Result Forms 1, 2, and 3. These scores are derived from how you ranked the Profile items when you took them on the Internet at *http://www.RVP-CVPautoscore.com*. You should now have Result Forms 1, 2, and 3 that you printed out from this website before you.

This chapter provides a more detailed analysis of the meaning of each of the 26 Result Form items (11 for Result Form 1, 11 for Result Form 2, and 4 for the combined scores on Result Form 3), but **it is not necessary to use or read all of the following. We suggest that you focus primarily on your scores that show average, fair, or weak development even though looking at the entire range of development scores may also be helpful to you.**

The profiles are based on the system of formal axiology, and the interpretive language is similar and repetitious for each of the five gradations from excellent to weak. To achieve greater spiritual understanding and improvement, you need to concentrate on your weakest scores. Your best scores, strong or excellent, need only be reinforced and your strengths put to use. Keep in mind throughout that good scores are expressed in small numbers; large numbers, suggesting weaknesses, indicate opportunities for further spiritual growth.

Review now the results on your Result Forms. You will recognize that Lines 2 and 3, Lines 4 and 5, and Lines 6 and 7 are similar.[4] Focus on your scores in the average, fair, or weak ranges; these show your least developed areas. **First go to the corresponding interpretation pages in this chapter; then go to the corresponding "Exercises" in the two following chapters.** If you prefer, however, you may work on all twenty-six areas, and at some point you should read all relevant exercises in the following chapters. Christians should consider them all; non-Christians will probably want to consider only the "General" exercises.

The present chapter contains three parts. The first interprets the significance of your scores on the eleven items on Result Form 1 that covers Part I of the Profile(s); there you ranked the degrees of goodness or badness of value items found in religion outside yourself, in the world, in other people, and as you express your spirituality to other people. The second interprets the significance of your scores on the eleven items on Result Form 2 that covers Part II of the Profiles; there you ranked religious value statements according to the degrees to which you agree with them as applied to your own spiritual life. The third "Combined Values" section covers Result Form 3; it measures your spiritual maturity and shows the differences and potential conflicts between your scores on Parts I and II.

Before you begin to interpret your scores, you should first become acquainted with some key concepts. Your scores center around your degrees of development in three spiritual value dimensions, so to understand them you need some familiarity with these three basic dimensions of value.

A. Three Dimensions of Value and Valuation

Three kinds of *value* and *valuation* are represented in the Religious Value Profile (RVP) and the Christian Value Profile (CVP). These Profiles are sensitive both to *what* we value and *how* we value. *What* we value (value objects) we will call "values," and *how* we value will be called "valuations."

(1) Three Kinds of Valuable Things or Value Objects (*What* We Value)

As identified by Robert S. Hartman,[5] the three kinds of valuable things and/or types of values represented in these Profiles are:

(1) *Systemic Values*, (S): conceptual constructs that exist in our minds.

Examples: definitions, ideas, ideals, norms, rules, beliefs, truths, doctrines, musical notations, mathematical and logical systems, and the like.

Religious Examples: The ideas and meanings within books of scripture; religious doctrines or beliefs; rules like the Ten Commandments; ritual forms, *etc.*

(2) *Extrinsic Values*, (E): tangible things, actions, and actual or potential means to ends located and observable in our common world of space and time.

Examples: physical objects and processes, bodies, books, houses, cars, human actions, behaviors, social memberships, roles, conventions, groups, established institutions, *etc.*

Religious examples: Sacred objects like menorahs, Bibles, crosses, temples, holy places; religious groups, religious roles like leader, follower, member, *etc.*

(3) *Intrinsic Values*, (I): things that have value in, of, and for themselves; things that should be valued intrinsically because they are ends in themselves, desirable or valuable for their own sakes.

Examples: unique centers of conscious experience, choice, thought, and valuation such as human persons, non-human animals, angels, and God. (Many philosophers have suggested things like knowledge, pleasure or happiness, freedom, dutifulness, desire fulfillment, etc.; but these only exist within and enrich the lives of those unique conscious individuals who exist *for* themselves).

Religious examples: God, angels, persons made in God's image, *etc.*

(2) Three Kinds of Valuation (*How* We Value)

From the very beginning, people have been attaching value to things or value objects in many different ways. All valuations include cognitive or mental elements—value standards or concepts by which objects of value are measured. Valuations involve judgments by persons about objects of value, judgments that valued objects measure up to or fail to do so to some degree. Valuations also include feelings, affections, emotions, and desires that range on a continuum from minimal (systemic), through ordinary (extrinsic), to maximal (intrinsic) personal involvement.

(1) *Systemic Valuations*, (S): black or white, all or nothing, oversimplifying, and dispassionate or "objective" feelings and judgments.

Examples: "2 + 2 = 4"
"This class will dismiss at 10:35 a.m."
"If you are not with me, you are against me." (Thought in a cold, calculating way)
"Race is all that counts." (Thought in a cold, calculating way)

Religious examples: "Our church has 300 members."
"The scriptures are either totally infallible or totally fallible."
"The only way to find God is my way."

(2) *Extrinsic Valuations*, (S): commonplace roles, practical motives, involvements, activities, and judgments.

Examples: ordinary everyday practical feelings, likes and dislikes, emotions, appetites, needs, interests, actions, vocations, value judgments, classifications, and comparisons.

Religious examples: wanting your religious group to grow; agreeing to take up the offering; writing a check for the offering; managing the everyday business of a religious organization; noting that their congregation increases faster than ours.

(3) *Intrinsic Valuations*, (I): complete self-identification with valued objects; intense personal involvement with, concentration upon, or investment in value objects. This kind of valuation includes all the ways in which conscious individuals like us combine or unite ourselves totally, intensely, and passionately, (either positively or negatively), with objects of valuation, so that distinctions between self and valued other cease to matter or to be noticed, and "the subject/object distinction" is overcome psychologically and valuationally.

Examples: love, empathy, intense delight and joy, conscience, creativity, deep religious devotion, worship, communion, and mystical union.

Religious examples: Loving your neighbor as yourself; praising God wholeheartedly; rejoicing with those who rejoice; suffering with those who suffer; feeling one with all; feeling one with God; profound spiritual devotion and religious experience.

The Religious and Christian Value Profiles focus on the above three dimensions of value and valuation, applied spiritually—on systemic ideas and beliefs, extrinsic things and activities, and intrinsic persons, human and divine—and on how we respond to them valuationally.

Part I: Social or External Religious or Christian Values

1. Social Religious/Christian Values Judgment Capacity, (DIF₁), Result Form 1, Line 1

Your score on Line 1 of Result Form 1 shows your ability to tell the difference between various kinds of religious or Christian values and to understand how they are related. On the Profile(s) you took, the 18 value items or phrases were randomly ordered, and you ordered them according to your own priorities. All these items are combinations of systemic, extrinsic, or intrinsic values or valuations. You were asked to rank them from best to worst according to your judgment of their degree of goodness or badness. Everyone ranks them in a slightly different way. In Part I you ranked the goodness or badness of things of religious significance in your external social religious world. The scores on your Result Forms follow from comparing your ranking of the items on the Profile(s) with standards or norms taken from value theory (axiology). These norms are explained in Chapter Seven. Your actual scores show how closely you conform to or deviate from these norms. If you were very close to the norms, your scores are in the "Excellent" or "Strong" boxes. If you were not very close, your scores were in the "Average," "Fair," or "Weak" boxes. The meanings of these different score ranges are as follows.

Excellent development: An excellent score (between *0 and 22*) indicates a *crystal clear* understanding of the differences between the devotional (intrinsic), practical (extrinsic), and conceptual (systemic) values present in your religious or Christian social world. Score numbers at this level on Result Form 1 mean that you give relatively equal or balanced weight to the Devotional (Dim-I_1) value dimension (Line 2), the Practical (Dim-E_1) value dimension (Line 4), and the Conceptual (Dim-S_1) value dimension (Line 6). Scores at this level do not indicate any problems.

Strong development: A strong score (between *23 and 43*) indicates that you have a *fairly clear* understanding of the differences between the devotional (intrinsic), practical (extrinsic), and conceptual (systemic) religious or Christian values that exist in the social world around you. Dim scores at this level (Lines 2, 4, and 6 on Result Form 1) show that at least one and perhaps two of these spiritual value dimensions is more strongly developed than the other one or two. Scores at this level do not indicate any very serious problems, but the numbers that are slightly out of balance show where you need to apply more energy and effort to achieve more spiritual balance and integration.

Average development: An average score (between *44 and 63*), indicates that you have a *partly clear* understanding of the differences between the devotional (intrinsic), practical (extrinsic), and conceptual (systemic) religious or Christian values that exist in the social world around you. Most religious people, including Christians, score at this level. Most religious people may not be consciously aware of the different nuances of meaning and worth that separate the devotional, practical, and conceptual value items. Understanding your Profile(s) should help you to become more clearly aware of these differences and to develop your spiritual potentials. For improvement, compare your results on Lines 2, 4, and 6 of Result Form 1, and then focus on the weakest ones (the scores that are furthest to the right).

Fair development: A fair score (between *64 and 84*) indicates that you have a *slightly fuzzy* understanding of the differences between the devotional (intrinsic), practical (extrinsic), and conceptual (systemic) religious or Christian values that exist in the social world around you. Your score shows that you tend to experience difficulties in thinking about or emotionally responding to religious devotions, practices, or beliefs; but you have an excellent opportunity to improve and develop your spiritual potentials. Look again at Lines 2, 4, and 6 of Result Form 1, find the highest numbers (indicating the greatest number of deviations), and practice paying more attention to these value dimensions. You may want to discuss them with your spiritual guide(s) counselor(s), or advisor(s).

Weak development: A weak score (of *85 or more*) indicates that you have a *very fuzzy* understanding of the differences between the devotional (intrinsic), practical (extrinsic), and conceptual (systemic) religious or Christian values that exist in the social world around you. Perhaps you did not pay close attention to the value items when you filled out the Profile(s), or perhaps you simply do not understand how these values differ in meaning and worth. Your score suggests that your spiritual potentials are not very well developed, but you have a great opportunity to grow religiously and make spiritual values actual in your life. Go back to Lines 2, 4, and 6 of Result Form 1, find the Dim (dimension) scores with the biggest numbers (the largest deviations). Set one or more goals targeting these areas for improvement—perhaps to pray about these values and to try to become more aware of them in your daily life.

2. Devotional Focus, (Dim-I$_1$), Result Form 1, Line 2

The score on Line 2 *quantitatively* measures your capacity to discern intrinsic religious or Christian values centered on devotional relationships with God and on the loving communion and fellowship of God's people. Line 3, explained on the following page, shows the *quality* of your score on Line 2; it measures the **positive** character of all the differences. Within Part I, the 18 value items in the Religious and/or Christian Value Profiles contain three value items that portray positive devotional relationships and three that portray negative relationships. Your relative ranking of these six values expresses *your judgment* about how high or how low you place these devotional values within the full spectrum of religious or Christian values. Your score numbers summarize your personal ranking of these six values. Find and read the meaning of your development range below.

Excellent development: An excellent score (between *0 and 7*) indicates a *crystal clear* understanding of and appreciation for the religious or Christian devotional values found in your external social world. Scores at this level mean that you ranked these values in such a way that the three positives and the three negatives are right at, or very close to, the mathematical norm, showing a balance among both positive and negative devotional/moral values. Scores at this level do not indicate any problems and suggest a significant degree of spiritual development.

Strong development: A strong level (between *8 and 14*) of devotional values development indicates a *fairly clear* understanding of and appreciation for devotional religious or Christian values in your external social world. Scores at this level indicate that at least one and probably two of either the positive or negative devotional value scores shows stronger development than the other one or two. This does not mean that you have any real problems, but the few items that were ranked a bit out of place show you where you could benefit from applying more energy and effort to achieve a more balanced integration among all six of them.

Average development: An average level of development (between *15 and 21*) indicates a *partly clear* understanding of and appreciation for devotional religious or Christian values manifested in your external social world. The majority of religious people score at this level. Most religious people will not be consciously aware of the nuanced differences in meaning and worth among the three positive and the three negative value dimensions. This profiling process should make these differences clearer to you and help you to develop your spiritual potentials. For improvement, read over and think about the "Devotional Triad" discussion and exercises on devotional values in Chapter Three. Center your time and effort on better understanding and appreciating these devotional values.

Fair development: A fair development score (from *22 to 28*) indicates a *slightly fuzzy* understanding of and appreciation for devotional religious or Christian values in your external social world. A score at this level indicates that you have conceptual, perceptual, or emotional problems with some or most of the six devotional value items. Scores at this level indicate that you have an opportunity to improve the development of your spiritual potentials. Go to the specific "Devotional Triad" items, discussions, and exercises in Chapter Three, and write down a few goals to pursue. Discuss these with your spiritual guide(s), counselor(s), or advisor(s), and practice paying more conscious attention to these values.

Weak development: Scores at his level (*29 or above*) indicate a *very fuzzy* understanding of and appreciation for devotional religious or Christian values in your external social world. Your score may mean that you did not pay close attention to the individual value items when filling out the Profile, or that you simply do not understand the differences in those values. Weak development scores mean that your spiritual potentials are not very well developed, but you have a great opportunity to draw them out and make them actual in your life. Go next to the "Devotional Triad" items, discussions, and exercises in Chapter Three. Try to incorporate devotional values better into your spiritual life—perhaps by embracing devotional values in a deeper way, praying about the devotional value items, and becoming more conscious of them. Then, like an underground stream, they will flow with you, support you, and provide you with a stronger devotional foundation on which you can build.

3. Intrinsic Orientation, (Dim-I$_1$%), Result Form 1, Line 3

Your score on Line 3 expresses how you deviated from the norm in ranking the three positive and three negative devotional items on your Profile(s). It captures the positive or negative biases revealed by your deviations. These biases are usually very deep, non-rational, largely emotional, and heavily programmed or conditioned by other persons or circumstances in your environment, especially while you were very young. Such biases can be very hard to change, no matter whether you are positively biased or negatively biased. A perfect score would be a deviations ranking of zero. The score on Line 3 is also excellent at 50%, when the sum of positive and negative deviations are equal. Ranking these values higher than the others indicates that, in your judgment, these six values contain **more** value than the others. This results in a **positive** intrinsic orientation to a certain degree. (The Result Form accounts for five levels of increasing or decreasing **positivity,** ranging from Excellent to Weak.) Ranking these devotional values lower than the others shows that in your judgment they contain **less** value than the others. This indicates a **negative** intrinsic orientation to a certain degree, which shows up on Result Form 1 as less than 50% positive.

Excellent development: An excellent score (at *50%*) indicates that you have achieved a *crystal clear* qualitative understanding of, appreciation of, and balance among the six intrinsic devotional Christian or religious values in your external social world. This excellent score indicates that you ranked the items in such a way that the six intrinsic devotional values have just as many positive as negative deviations. This shows a mental symmetry in judging devotional values, and it suggests objectivity in evaluating a person's relationship to God and to the loving communion and fellowship of God's people. Scores at this level do not indicate any problems and suggest a high level of spiritual development.

Strong development: A strong level of spiritual development indicates a *fairly clear* orientation toward intrinsic devotional religious or Christian values. The *51% to 60% positive* and *49% to 40% positive* score ranges indicate that at least one and probably two of the six intrinsic devotional values was ranked with a degree of distorting emotional loading. An increased percentage in positive scores indicates that you have a stronger emotional identification with one or two of the devotional value items, and a decrease in positivity indicates that you have some emotional distance or detachment from one or two of the items. Scores at this level do not indicate any real problems, but they still allow room for growth.

Average development: An average development score indicates a *partly clear* orientation toward intrinsic devotional religious or Christian values. Most religious people score at this level. *61% to 70% positive* scores reflect a positive emotional inclination to favor the devotional values above other dimensions, but you may need to gain or regain focus on practical and conceptual values. *39% to 30% positive* scores indicate some emotional distance or detachment from these values. For improvement, go to and reconsider the presentations, discussions, and exercises on the "Devotional Triad" values in Chapter Three.

Fair development: A fair development score indicates a *slightly fuzzy* orientation toward devotional values. This score suggests that you are having conceptual or emotional problems with some or most of the intrinsic devotional value items. *71% to 80% positive* scores indicate that you greatly overvalued three or more of the six intrinsic devotional items. This suggests a strong bias in favor of a personal or mystical relationship to God, to the neglect of the practical and the conceptual or doctrinal aspects of religious or Christian life. *29% to 20% positive* scores indicate a strong emotional distance from the devotional aspects of spiritual life, perhaps in favor of good works or of knowledge and doctrine. Go to the discussion of the "Devotional Triad" values and exercises in Chapter Three. Write down your thoughts about these value items and exercises. Reflect on them, discuss them with your spiritual counselor or guide, work out ways of becoming more aware of them, and try to get them into better balance with values in other dimensions.

Weak development: Scores at this level (*60% or greater*, or *20% or lower*)indicate a *very fuzzy* orientation toward intrinsic devotional values. Your score may mean that you did not pay close attention to the individual value items when filling out the Profile, or that you simply do not understand the differences among those values. *80% positive or greater* scores indicates that your potentials in the intrinsic devotional dimension are far too emotionally charged, without much support from the practical or cognitive dimensions. *20% positive or less* scores indicate a high degree of emotional distance that inhibits your devotional involvement and thereby restricts you from experiencing personal actualization of and fulfillment from devotional values. Go to the discussion of the "Devotional Triad" values and exercises in Chapter Three. Think about them and develop goals targeting intrinsic devotional improvement, for example, praying for guidance in getting your devotional life back into balance with your practical and conceptual or doctrinal values.

4. Practical Focus, (Dim-E$_1$), Result Form 1, Line 4

The score on Line 4 measures your capacity to discern Christian or religious values centered on sacred objects or public spiritual activities and practical values expressing what people do or how they behave within a spiritual social environment. The score in Line 5 shows the *quality* or **positive** character of your score on Line 4. Three positive (desirable) and three negative (undesirable) practical religious value items are included within the 18 values in Part I of the Religious or Christian Value Profiles. Your relative ranking of these six value items represents how high or how low you place these practical values within the full spectrum of Christian or religious values, *as you see them*. This score summarizes your ranking of these six values in mathematical terms as the sum of all deviations from the mathematical norm. Find your score range and its meaning below.

Excellent development: Excellent scores (between *0 and 7*) indicate that you have a *crystal clear* understanding of and appreciation for practical religious or Christian values in your external social world. They also indicates that you ranked the value items in such a way that the practical dimension (Dim-E$_1$) is either in balance with, or favored highest among, the three basic value dimensions (Dim-I$_1$, Dim-E$_1$, and Dim-S$_1$, as found on Lines 2, 4 and 6 on Result Form 1). Scores at this level indicate a very high degree of practical spiritual development and do not indicate any problems.

Strong development: Strong scores (between *8 and 14*) indicate that you have a *fairly clear* understanding of and appreciation for practical religious or Christian values in your external social world. Scores at this level indicate that you give stronger emphasis to at least one and probably two of the six practical (Dim-E) scores than to the other four or five. This does not indicate any serious problems. It means that among the six practical (Dim-E) scores, one or two are a little out of line, and you may need to apply focused energy and effort to restore a balanced integration. Go to the discussion of exercises for practical religious values in the "Practical Triad" exercises in Chapter Three.

Average development: Average scores (between *15 and 21*) indicate a *partly clear* understanding of and appreciation for the practical religious or Christian values in your external social world. The majority of religious people score at this level. Most religious people may not notice the differences that separate practical spiritual values from other kinds of spiritual values. Becoming more aware of these differences will be your first helpful step toward greater development of your spiritual potentials. For improvement, look at the exercises and discussions of practical religious values in the "Practical Triad" exercises in Chapter Three. Give some of your time and effort to better understanding and appreciating these practical values.

Fair development: Fair development scores (between *22 and 28*) indicate a *slightly fuzzy* understanding of and appreciation for practical religious or Christian values in your external social world. Scores at this level mean that you have some conceptual or emotional problems with some or most of the practical value items, and this presents you with an opportunity to improve in this value dimension. Go to Chapter Three, read and study the "Practical Triad" exercises, and write down a few goals for improvement. Discuss these goals and practical value items with your spiritual counselor or guide, practice paying more attention to them, and try to integrate them better with values in the other dimensions.

Weak development: Scores at his level (*20 or higher*) indicate a *very fuzzy* understanding of and appreciation for practical religious or Christian values in your external social world. Your score may mean that you did not pay close attention to the individual value items when filling out the Profile, or that you simply do not understand the differences among those values. Scores in this range indicate that your practical spiritual potentials are not very well developed, but you have a great opportunity to draw out your potentials and make practicing your spirituality actual in your life. Go to Chapter Three, study the "Practical Triad" exercises, and develop goals targeting improvement.

5. Extrinsic Orientation, (Dim-E_1%), Result Form 1, Line 5

Your score on Line 5 expresses how you deviated from the norm in ranking the three positive and three negative practical items on your Profile(s). It captures the positive or negative biases revealed by your deviations. These biases are usually very deep, non-rational, largely emotional, and heavily programmed or conditioned by other persons or circumstances in your environment, especially while you were very young. Such biases can be very hard to change, no matter whether you are positively biased or negatively biased. A perfect score (50%) is an exact ranking where the three positive and negative practical values are neither over- nor undervalued, but are ranked according to the norm. If you ranked these values higher than the norm, these six values contain **more** value for you than the others. This reveals varying degrees of **positive** extrinsic orientation. Result Form 1 reflects five levels of increasing or decreasing positivity, including the "excellent" balanced 50% level. If you rank these practical values lower than the norm, they contain **less** value for you than the others. This reveals varying degrees of **negative** extrinsic orientation, expressed on the Result Form as less than 50% positive. Having a positive orientation toward something means seeing its goodness; having a negative orientation toward something means not being able to see its goodness, or perhaps as seeing it as bad. The meanings of your scores are as follows.

Excellent development: An excellent score at *50%* indicates a *crystal clear* understanding of and orientation toward practical, action- or service-oriented religious or Christian values. Scores at this level show an integrated balance among positive and negative practical values. The *50%* level indicates that you ranked the items in such a way that all six practical values have just as many positive as negative deviations. Scores at this level show a clear mental symmetry in judging action-oriented or practical values, and they suggests objectivity regarding religious or Christian practices. Such scores do not indicate any problems and suggest significant practical spiritual development.

Strong development: Strong scores reflect a *fairly clear* understanding of and orientation toward practical religious or Christian values in your external social world. *51% to 60%* and *49% to 40%* positive scores mean that you ranked one or more of the six practical values with some degree of distorting emotion. An increased positive percentage score indicates a stronger emotional identification with one or more practical value items, and a decreased positive score indicates some degree of emotional distance from one or more of these value items. Scores at this level do not indicate any serious problems.

Average development: An average score indicates a *partly clear* orientation toward socially expressed religious or Christian practical values. Most religious people score at this level. For scores *61% to 70% positive*, your ranking of the 18 items shows a positive emotional inclination to favor practical values above other dimensions, and you could benefit from gaining or regaining integration with devotional and conceptual values. For scores *39% to 30% positive*, your ranking of the 18 items discloses a negative bias, an emotional distance or detachment, that inhibits you from embracing practical values. You should try to focus or refocus on practical spiritual values items, become more aware of them, and grow in the right direction. The "Practical Triad" discussions and exercises on practical religious values in Chapter Three might help.

Fair development: A fair development score indicates a *slightly fuzzy* orientation toward practical religious or Christian values in your external social world. This score indicates that you have some conceptual or emotional problems with one or more of the practical value items. *71% to 80% positive* scores indicate overvaluation of three or more of the six practical items. This suggests a strong bias in favor of participating in Church activities and doing works of service while, to some extent, neglecting the devotional and thinking/believing aspects of religious and Christian life. *29% to 20% positive* scores indicate that you have a strong emotional distance or detachment from the practical aspects of the religious and Christian life, probably in favor of intrinsic devotional or systemic doctrinal dimensions. Go to the "Practical Triad" discussions of practical religious values in Chapter Three, study the discussions and exercises, and write down one or more goals targeting improvement. Discuss these with your spiritual counselor or guide, and practice paying more attention to practical values in order to restore balance with values in the other dimensions.

Weak development: Scores at this level indicate a *very fuzzy* orientation toward practical religious or Christian values. Your score may mean that you did not pay close attention to the individual value items when filling out the Profile, or that you simply do not understand the differences among those values. *80% positive* or greater scores indicate that your spiritual potentials in the practical dimension are far too emotionally charged, too overvalued, without much support from either the devotional or the thinking/believing dimensions. *20% positive* or lower scores reflect a strong emotional distance that more or less inhibits your involvement in religious practice and service, thereby inhibiting your practical, social, religious fulfillment. Go to the "Practical Triad" discussions of practical religious values in Chapter Three, study the discussions and exercises, and develop one or more goals targeting practical improvement. The goals could include praying about these value items, becoming more consciously aware of them in your daily life, and seeking guidance from others in getting these back into balance with your devotional and conceptual values.

6. Conceptual Focus, (Dim-S$_1$), Result Form 1, Line 6

The score on Line 6 measures your capacity to discern mental or conceptual Christian or religious values. These values constitute a religious person's mind set concerning the doctrinal, theological, cognitive, conceptual, believing aspects of the entire sphere of religious or Christian values. The score in Line 7, explained next, shows the *quality* or the **positive** character of the differences summed up in Line 6. The 18 values in Part I of the Religious or Christian Value Profiles contain three positive and three negative doctrinal or theological value items. Your relational ranking of these six values represents how high or how low you place these conceptual values within the full spectrum of Christian or religious values, *as you see them*. This score summarizes the results of your ranking of these six values in mathematical terms as the sum of all deviations from the norm. The meanings of your scores are as follows.

Excellent development: Excellent scores (between *0 and 7*) indicate a *crystal clear* understanding of and appreciation for conceptual or doctrinal Christian or religious values present in your external social world. Scores at this level mean that you ranked the six conceptual items in such a way that the number of deviations for the three positive items are relatively low and are equal to the number of deviations for the three negative items, showing a balanced integration between good and bad conceptual values. Scores at this level do not indicate any problems and suggest a high level of spiritual development.

Strong development: Strong scores (between *8 and 14*) indicate a *fairly clear* understanding of and appreciation for conceptual or doctrinal religious or Christian values existing in your external social environment. Scores at this level indicate that at least one and probably two of the six items making up the systemic dimension (Dim-S) total score shows stronger development than the others. This does not mean that you have any real problems, but the relation among the three dimensions (score numbers on Lines 2, 4, and 6 on Result Form 1) may show you where to apply more of your energy and effort to achieve a better balanced integration. Focus on the score that is the most to the right, which is your weakest score.

Average development: Average scores (between *15 and 21*) indicate a *partly clear* understanding of and appreciation for conceptual or doctrinal religious or Christian values existing in your external social environment. Most religious people will score at this level. Religious people are not always consciously aware of the differences between the six cognitive values included in the 18 items of Part I. This profiling process should help make you more aware of these differences for the sake of greater development of your spiritual potentials. For improvement, go to the "Conceptual Triad" discussions and exercises in Chapter Three, and then focus on improving your understanding of and appreciation for conceptual spiritual values and on getting them into better balance with values in the other dimensions.

Fair development: Fair scores (between *22 and 28*) indicate a *slightly fuzzy* understanding of and appreciation for conceptual or doctrinal religious or Christian values present in your external social world. Fair scores indicate that you are having conceptual or emotional problems with some or most of these value items. Scores at this level present an opportunity to improve and develop your spiritual conceptual potentials. Go to Chapter Three, study the "Conceptual Triad" discussions and exercises on conceptual religious values, and write down one or more goals targeting improvement. Discuss these goals with your spiritual counselor or guide, and practice paying more attention to conceptual spiritual values.

Weak development: Scores at this level (*29 or above*) reflect a *very fuzzy* understanding of and appreciation for the conceptual or doctrinal Christian or religious values present in your external social world. Your score may mean that you did not pay close attention to the individual value items when taking the Profile, or that you simply do not understand the differences between those values. Weak scores indicate that your spiritual potentials are not very well developed, but you have a great opportunity to develop your spiritual mental or conceptual potentials and make them actual in your life. Go to Chapter Three, study the "Conceptual Triad" discussions and exercises on conceptual religious values, and set goals for improvement. These might include praying about these mental religious value items, repeating them several times each day, and focusing more on them in your daily life.

7. Systemic Orientation, (Dim-S$_1$%), Result Form 1, Line 7

Your score on Line 7 expresses how you deviated from the norm in ranking the three positive and three negative conceptual items on your Profile(s). It captures the positive or negative biases revealed by your deviations. These biases are usually very deep, non-rational, largely emotional, and heavily programmed or conditioned by other persons or circumstances in your environment, especially while you were very young. Such biases can be very hard to change, no matter whether you are positively biased or negatively biased. Ranking these values higher than the norm indicates that these six values contain **more** value for you than the others. These scores make a place for varying degrees of **positive** systemic orientation. Result Form 1 reflects five levels of increasing or decreasing positivity, including the balanced 50% "excellent" level. Ranking the systemic values lower than the norm indicates that, in your judgment, these values contain **less** value than the others. This indicates a certain degree of **negative** systemic orientation (expressed in your score as a low positive, that is, as less than 50% positive). Find your development range and study its meaning below.

Excellent development: An excellent score indicates a *crystal clear* orientation toward conceptual or doctrinal religious or Christian values. The *50%* level means that you ranked the items in such a way that all six conceptual or doctrinal values have just as many positive as negative deviations. Such scores show a symmetry in judging conceptual values, and they suggest objectivity concerning your understanding of religion or Christianity. Scores at this level are problem free and indicate that you have achieved a very high degree of conceptual or mental spiritual development.

Strong development: Scores at this level indicate a *fairly clear* orientation toward the conceptual or doctrinal religious or Christian values that you encounter in your external social world. Scores ranging from *51% to 60% positive* and *49% to 40% positive* show that you ranked at least one or more of the six conceptual values with some degree of distorting emotional identification or distance. An increased positive percentage score indicates that you have a slightly stronger emotional identification with one or more items, and a decrease in positivity indicates that you have a slight emotional distance from them. Scores at this level do not indicate any serious problems.

Average development: Average scores indicate a *partly clear* orientation toward conceptual or doctrinal religious or Christian values. Most religious persons, including Christian, score at this level. For scores that are *61% to 70% positive*, your personal ranking suggests a positive emotional inclination to favor conceptual systemic values above other dimensions, and you could benefit from gaining or regaining a more balanced integration of these with devotional and practical spiritual values. Scores that are *39% to 30% positive* indicate that you have a negative bias against certain conceptual spiritual values. As your first step toward improvement, try to focus or refocus on and to become more aware of the cognitive religious value items. Go to Chapter Three and work carefully through the "Conceptual Triad" discussions and exercises.

Fair development: Fair development scores indicate a *slightly fuzzy* orientation toward conceptual or doctrinal religious or Christian values. Fair scores suggest that you have some conceptual or emotional problems with some or most of the conceptual or doctrinal value items. For scores *71% to 80% positive*, you overvalued two or more of the six conceptual/doctrinal items. You may have a strong bias in favor of doctrinal knowledge, while to some extent neglecting the devotional and practical aspects of your spiritual life. If your scores are *29% to 20% positive*, you have developed a strong emotional distance from the doctrinal and structuring aspects of spiritual life, probably in favor of either the intrinsic devotional or the practical dimensions. Go to Chapter Three, read and think about the "Conceptual Triad" discussions and exercises on conceptual religious values, and write down one or more goals targeting improvement. Discuss these with your spiritual guide or counselor, practice paying more attention to them, and try to get them into better balance with spiritual values in the other dimensions.

Weak development: This level indicates a *very fuzzy* orientation toward conceptual or doctrinal religious and/or Christian values. Weak scores may mean that you did not pay close attention to the individual rational value items when filling out the Profile, or that you simply do not understand differences between those values. *80% positive* or greater scores indicate that your spiritual potentials in the cognitive dimension are far too emotionally loaded positively or negatively.

You may overvalue this dimension without having much support from the devotional or practical dimensions. Or you may undervalue conceptual or doctrinal spiritual values. *20% positive* or lower scores reflect a strong emotional distance or detachment that more or less inhibits your cognitive or conceptual involvement and obstructs your finding fulfillment from and in foundational conceptual or doctrinal values. Go to the "Conceptual Triad" exercises in Chapter Three. Work through these cognitive spiritual value items, the discussions, and the exercises. Set one or more goals targeting improvement. The goals could be to practice praying about these value items, to become more conscious of them in your daily life, to work harder at them, and to seek guidance in getting them back into balance with devotional and practical values.

8. Dimensional Harmony, (DIM$_1$), Result Form 1, Line 8

The score on Line 8 measures *quantitatively* your respective valuations of the three major religious or Christian value dimensions: the intrinsic (devotional values), the extrinsic (practical values), and the systemic (conceptual values). Value science assumes that a perfect developmental balance among, and equal emphasis upon, the three value dimensions is the ideal. This assumption correlates with Jesus' expression of the Greatest Commandment: We should love God with **all** our valuational capacities (heart, soul, mind, and strength) as fully as possible. Your relative ranking of the three sets of six values in each dimension shows how high or how low you value these dimensions in comparison to each other. Each dimension consists of six values, three positive and three negative. Most people tend to favor one dimension over the others, and some favor two dimensions over the third. Only rarely does anyone rank them all the same, indicating symmetry, balance, and equal developmental emphasis. This score is a quantitative result of the distance separating your three dimensional or Dim scores. The meanings of your scores are as follows.

Excellent development: An excellent score (between *0 and 3*) indicates a *crystal clear* understanding of, appreciation for, and balance among the three basic Religious or Christian value dimensions operative in your social world. Excellent scores indicate that you see the importance of a relatively equal development of the three basic dimensions; you have achieved a balanced integration of your devotional values, practical values, and conceptual values, the three basic value dimensions (Dim-I_1, Dim-E_1, and Dim-S_1). Scores at this level are problem free and indicate a very high level of spiritual development.

Strong development: Scores at this level (between *4 and 6*) indicate a *fairly clear* understanding of and appreciation for the three basic dimensional differences in the religious or Christian values found in your social world of religious persons. At this level, at least one and possibly two of the dimension or Dim_1 scores shows stronger development than the other one or two. This does not mean that you have any real problems, but the relation among the three Dim_1 scores may show you where to apply more energy and effort to achieve a more balanced integration. See Lines 2, 4, and 6 to locate the ones most to the right, your weakest scores, and give those value dimensions more attention.

Average development: Average scores (between *7 and 11*) indicate that you have only a *partly clear* understanding of and appreciation for the three value dimensions in religious or Christian values. Most religious and Christian people score at this level. Most religious people will not be consciously aware of the differences in meaning and worth between devotional, practical, and conceptual spiritual values. This profiling process should help you become more aware of these differences for the sake of better developing your spiritual potentials. For improvement, look at the relations among the three dimension scores (Dim_1 scores on Lines 2, 4, and 6), and then focus on the weakest ones (the ones most to the right). Devote more time and effort to understanding and appreciating the values that make up your weakest Dim_1 scores. Write down the value items found in

Chapter Three that correlate with those dimension scores. Read and study the discussion and exercises, and set one or more goals for improvement.

Fair development: Fair scores (between *12 and 15*) indicate that you have a *slightly fuzzy* understanding of and appreciation for the three basic religious or Christian value dimensions. Scores at this level indicate that you are having conceptual or emotional problems with some or most of the spiritual value dimensions. They present you with an opportunity for improvement in developing your spiritual potentials. Go back to Result Form 1, find your dimension scores (Dim-I_1, Dim-E_1, or Dim-S_1) and focus on the ones with the highest number (the ones most to the right on Lines 2, 4, and 6). Write down the value items found in Chapter Three that correlate with those dimension scores. Read and study the discussion and exercises, and set one or more goals for improvement. Discuss these values with your spiritual guide or counselor, and practice paying more attention to them.

Weak development: Weak scores (*16 or above*) indicate a *very fuzzy* understanding of and appreciation for the three value dimensions within overall religious or Christian values. Your score may mean that you did not pay close attention to the individual value items when filling out the Profile, or that you simply do not understand the differences among those values. Scores at this level indicate that your spiritual potentials are not very well developed, but you have a great opportunity to draw out your potentials and make spirituality actual in your life. Go to Result Form 1, find the Dim scores with the largest numbers, the ones on Lines 2, 4, and 6 farthest to the right. These are your weakest value dimensions. Then go to the discussion of these value dimensions in Chapter Three. Study and think about the discussions and exercises, and develop one or more goals targeting improvement in harmonizing your religious values. Your goals could include praying about these value items and being more conscious and appreciative of them in your daily life.

9. Stress /Tension
(DIM$_1$%), Result Form 1, Line 9

The score on Line 9 measures the level of anxiety, stress, or tension that you may experience in dealing with religious or Christian values. The score of overall dimensional harmony, DIM$_1$ on Line 8, is derived as a percentage of the total differences score (the DIF$_1$ or total differentiation). We assume a perfect balance among the three value dimensions (Dim-I$_1$, Dim-E$_1$, and Dim-S$_1$ on Lines 2, 4, and 6) as the ideal. A perfect balance score would be reflected in zero stress or tension.[6] This DIM$_1$% measure on Line 9 reveals the degree of your imbalance in the three spiritual value dimensions, which could be extreme. The further your DIM$_1$% is from balance, the less comfort and the more *stress and tension* you will likely experience in your spiritual life. The meanings of your scores are as follows.

Excellent development: An excellent score (from *0 to 10%)* indicates a lack of spiritual stress or tension due to little or no imbalance among the three value dimension (Dim-I$_1$, Dim-E$_1$, and Dim-S$_1$) scores, or it shows that the imbalance is small and not significant as a percentage of the whole. If all three of your Dim$_1$ scores are equally low, this means that you have a *crystal clear* understanding of, appreciation for, and equal emphasis upon the three dimensions of religious or Christian values. If all three of your dimension scores on Lines 2, 4, and 6 are relatively equal, you will feel little or no spiritual stress or tension, but you might still benefit a bit from improving your understanding and clarity regarding each of the three spiritual value dimensions.

Strong development: A strong level of development (from *11% to 20%%)* indicates a *fairly clear* understanding of and appreciation for the three basic dimensions of Christian or religious values. At this level, at least one of the three dimensional or Dim scores shows stronger development than the other one or two. You may occasionally feel a mild degree of tension, but this does not mean that you have any serious problems. The relations among your dimension scores (Dim-I_1, Dim-E_1, and Dim-S_1 on Lines 2, 4, and 6) may indicate where to apply more energy and effort (to the dimension most to the right) in order to restore and maintain a no-stress balanced integration and peace.

Average development: Average scores (between *21% to 30%*) indicate that you have a *partly clear* understanding of and appreciation for the three basic value dimensions within religious or Christian values. Most religious people score at this level. Most religious people are not fully aware of the differences among devotional, practical, and conceptual values. If you are at this level and become more aware of these differences, your increase in awareness itself will be a major step toward greater development of your spiritual potentials. For improvement, look at the relations among your three dimension scores (Dim-I_1, Dim-E_1, or Dim-S_1 on Lines 2, 4, and 6), then focus on the weakest ones, the ones farthest to the right. Commit some of your time and effort to understanding better and appreciating more the values that correspond to your weakest spiritual value dimensions.

Fair development: A fair score (between *30% and 40%*) indicates that you have a *slightly fuzzy* understanding of and appreciation for the three basic value dimensions within religious or Christian values. A fair score indicates that you are having significant religious stress and tension problems. You may be experiencing stress and tension because you are spiritually out of balance, strongly favoring one dimension over the others. Your lack of development and integration of the other one or two value dimensions causes the degree of discomfort or anxiety that you feel. Go to Result Form 1, find your dimension scores (Dim-I_1, Dim-E_1, and Dim-S_1 on Lines 2, 4, and 6), locate the dimension scores most to the right, and review those value dimension in Chapter Three. Write down the value items that correlate with your weakest score and set one or more goals for moving toward more religious comfort and away from your present religious distress. Discuss these value items with your spiritual guide or counselor, pray about them, and practice paying more attention to these spiritual values.

Weak development: This level indicates a *very fuzzy* understanding of and appreciation for the basic dimensions operative within the religious or Christian values realm. Your score may mean that you did not pay very close attention to the individual value items when filling out the Profiles or that you simply do not understand the differences among those values. Scores at this level indicate that your spiritual potentials are not very well developed. You may be very clear about one dimension while blocking out the other two; but you have a great opportunity to expand your spiritual understanding and to create more harmony and balance with less tension and spiritual stress in your life. Go back to the Result Form 1, find the dimension scores (Dim-I_1, Dim-E_1, and Dim-S_1 on Lines 2, 4, and 6), and select the ones most to the right. Then, go to Chapter Three, review the value dimensions corresponding with your lowest Dim scores, and develop one or more goals targeting improvement in your religious comfort and relief from your present religious distress. The goals could include praying about the items in your lowest value dimensions, becoming more conscious of them, and integrating them into your daily life.

10. Spiritual Clarity, (DIS$_1$), Result Form 1, Line 10

The score on Line 10 measures the frequency with which you judge positive religious or Christian values as negative, or negative religious or Christian values as positive. When a positive value is ranked as negative, or a negative value as positive, this results in a **distortion** (DIS$_1$). A distortion involves a confusion of two value items, a confusion of good with bad or of bad with good. There are only nine possible distortion pairs in each 18 item list. When you rank one positive item as a negative, you will then be forced to rank a negative one as positive somewhere in the total ranking process. Your personal ranking of 18 values can have a number of deviations without any distortions at all. In these cases, your spiritual clarity will be excellent, since all positive (desirable) religious or Christian values are judged as positive and all negative (undesirable) religious or Christian values are considered negative. As more and more values are distorted, spiritual clarity decreases. The meanings of your scores are as follows.

Excellent development: An excellent score of *0* on Line 10 indicates a *crystal clear* understanding of and appreciation for religious or Christian values in the sense that positives are seen as positive, negatives as negative, and good and bad are not confused. An excellent score also indicates that you sorted the items in such a way that the deviations are relatively small, and no deviation is large enough to spill over into its opposite, thereby confusing positives with negatives, or vice versa. Scores at this level are problem free, and they suggest a significant level of spiritual development.

Strong development: A strong score on Line 10 indicates a *fairly clear* understanding of and appreciation for both positive and negative religious or Christian values, with a distortion or DIS number of only 2. Due to the forced ranking of the Profile items and the equal number of compositions (good items) and transpositions (bad items), one distortion automatically produces another, for a minimum result of 2. Scores at this level indicate that one distortion (with its forced opposite) may have been overlooked. Perhaps one particular item caught your attention, and you ranked it much higher (or much lower) than it should be ranked. Scores at this level do not mean that you have any serious problems, but you could benefit from being more careful and paying closer attention to seemingly small things.

Average development: An average score of *4* indicates that you have only a *partly clear* under-standing of and appreciation for the positives and negatives within social religious or Christian values. Most religious individuals are likely to score at this level. Most religious people will not notice all the differences in meaning and worth between positive and negative spiritual values and will sometimes confuse good and bad. This profiling process should help you become more aware of these value differences and thus contribute to a greater development of your spiritual potentials. For improvement, look at the total array of Profile items in Part I and find the items you distorted. To do this, find the items that you ranked incorrectly on each part of your Profile(s) by comparing them to the order of correct rankings given in Chapter Seven. Center your time and effort achieving a better understanding and appreciation of how to avoid value distortions: value compositions always add value to each other; only value transpositions subtract or diminish value.

Fair development: A fair score of *6* distortions indicates that you have a *slightly fuzzy* understanding of and appreciation for the differences between positive and negative religious or Christian values. You are somewhat inclined to confuse goodness and badness. A fair score indicates that you are having conceptual problems in coping with your spiritual life. Scores at this level provide you with an opportunity to improve and develop your spiritual potentials by understanding more clearly the differences between good and bad. Go back to items on the Profiles and find the items you distorted. To do this, find the items that you ranked incorrectly on each part of your Profile(s) by comparing them to the order of correct rankings given in Chapter Seven. Discuss any unclear items with your spiritual guide or counselor, and develop a better understanding of and appreciation for why these items were distorted, for why you confused good with bad.

Weak development: This level with *8 or more* distortions indicates that you have a *very fuzzy* understanding of and appreciation for the differences between positive and negative religious or Christian values. Your score may mean that you did not pay very close attention to the individual value items when filling out the Profile, or that you simply do not understand the difference in the goodness or badness of those value items. This level indicates that your spiritual potentials are not very well developed, but you have a great opportunity to draw out your potentials and make them actual in your life by better understanding the differences between goodness and badness. Go back to the value items on your Profile(s), and try to identify the ones that you distorted. To do this, find the items that you ranked incorrectly on each part of your Profile(s) by comparing them to the order of correct rankings given in Chapter Seven. Then, try to improve your ability to recognize, understand, and distinguish between positive and negative or good and bad spiritual values. Your goals could include praying about these value items and becoming more conscious of how and why you distorted them in your personal ranking.

11. Spiritual Balance, (DIF$_1$%), Result Form 1, Line 11

The score on Line 11 measures the overall quality of your religious or Christian values judgment, your general value attitudes toward your religious or Christian world. In both parts of the Profiles, there are 18 values. Nine are positive or desirable *compositions,* and nine are negative or undesirable *transpositions.* Due to the mathematical nature of the forced ranking system, there can not be more positive deviations than negative ones. A balanced score of 50% is ideal, but negative deviations will often take an even larger part of the total DIF$_1$ score. This score represents your total set of negative deviations as a mathematical percentage of your total DIF$_1$ score. This percentage reveals the quality of the entire realm of your religious or Christian values. The more the percentages are negative, the greater is your lack of spiritual openness, adaptability, and versatility. The meanings of your scores are as follows.

Excellent development: An excellent score (from *50% to 54%*) indicates that you have a well developed and *crystal clear* orientation toward the whole realm of religious or Christian values, with only a very small number of deviations. This score also indicates that you ranked the items such that all 18 are relatively close to where they should be. This implies maturity, openness, flexibility, and versatility with regard to all aspects of religious or Christian life. You have the ability to adjust smoothly to changing situations and to demonstrate a high level of responsiveness. Scores at this level do not indicate any problems.

Strong development: A strong score (between *55% and 60%*) indicates that you have only a *fairly clear* orientation toward the whole realm of religious or Christian values. At this level, at least one and probably more than one of the 18 value items shows somewhat weaker development and recognition than the remaining items. This does not mean that you have any serious problems; perhaps a few of the items did not get as much of your attention as the others. A review of these may show you where to apply more effort and pay more attention in order to achieve more balance in all aspects of your religious or Christian life.

Average development: An average score (between *61% and 65%*) indicates that you have only a *partly clear* orientation toward the whole realm of religious or Christian values. Most religious people score at this level. Most religious people will not be consciously aware of all the differences of meaning and worth among the 18 value items. Religious people who become more aware of these differences through this profiling exercise can then take further steps toward developing their spiritual potentials. For improvement, find the items that you ranked incorrectly on each part of your Profile(s) by comparing them to the order of correct rankings given in Chapter Seven. You should allocate some time and effort to understanding and appreciating the correct value rankings provided in Chapter Seven.

Fair development: A fair score (from *66% to 70%*) indicates that you have a *slightly fuzzy and negative* orientation toward religious or Christian values. This score means that you may be having bias problems that result in some degree of religious inflexibility, ranging from fear, indecision, and passive withdrawal from religious values, to strong dogmatism. Scores at this level present you with an opportunity to improve the development of your spiritual potentials.

Find the items that you ranked incorrectly on each part of your Profile(s) by comparing them to the order of correct rankings given in Chapter Seven. Discuss your misplaced value items with your spiritual guide or counselor, pray about them, and practice paying more attention to their relative ranking.

Weak development: This level (*71% or greater*) indicates that you have a *very fuzzy and negative* orientation toward religious or Christian values. Your score may mean that you did not pay close attention to the individual value items when filling out your Profile(s), or that you simply do not understand the differences in those values. Scores at this level mean that your spiritual potentials are not very well developed and that you lack receptivity and responsiveness to values of a spiritual nature. Some event may have happened in your life to cause you to withdraw from, or even to feel and express open hostility toward religious or Christian values. You may experience a high degree of hostile rigidity and negative dogmatism, perhaps anti-religious dogmatism. This score presents you with a great opportunity to improve, to draw out your spiritual potentials and make them actual and positive in your life by opening or reopening yourself to sacredness. Find the items that you ranked incorrectly on each part of your Profile(s) by comparing them to the order of correct rankings given in Chapter Seven. Then, try to develop one or more goals with respect to selected spiritual values. Consider saying these values aloud several times a day, or expressing them purposely in conversations during the course of your day. You may also pray about these value items and work toward becoming more conscious and appreciative of them.

Part II: Personal (Internal) Religious/Christian Values, Result Form 2

The meanings of the scores for Part II of the Religious and the Christian Value Profiles are very similar to those of Part I, but there are some differences. Here, too, you will notice that Lines 2 and 3, Lines 4 and 5, and Lines 6 and 7 are similar. Lines 2, 4, and 6 are numbers expressing absolute differences, while Lines 3, 5, and 7 are *quality* scores expressing the **positive** character of the absolute sums. You ranked the 18 value items in Part I according to your judgment of their degree of goodness or badness. The instructions for Part II directed you to rank the 18 values according to the degree of your agreement or disagreement with how each item applies to or is followed in your own spiritual life. Part II focuses more clearly and immediately on your own personal involvement with religious and Christian values.

For people who are spiritually mature, the scores for both parts will be virtually the same. However, for those who have not yet attained spiritual maturity, the scores may be very different. Having conflicting or disharmonious values is not uncommon, even in religion, where we sometimes pretend in public to be something that we are not in private. The next eleven interpretation items (numbers 1 through 11 on your Result Form 2) will refer more directly to your own personal involvement with spiritual values.

1. Personal Religious/Christian Values Judgment Capacity, (DIF$_2$), Result Form 2, Line 1

The score on Line 1 of Result Form 2 for Part II of your Profile(s) measures your capacity to discern different kinds of personal religious or Christian values and their relations to each other as you experience, apply, and follow them in your own life. The 18 values in Part II are presented in random form, and you were asked to rank them from greatest agreement to least agreement (greatest disagreement). These value items are like pieces of a puzzle, and everyone puts the puzzle together in a slightly different way. Your personal ranking represents religious or Christian values *as you currently use or apply them in your own life*. The summary scores compare your personal ranking of the 18 religious or Christian value items in Part II to a mathematical norm, as explained in Chapter Seven. All your deviations from the norm are contained in your scores. The meanings of your scores are as follows.

Excellent development: An excellent score (between *0 and 22*) indicates *complete* involvement or identification with personal religious or Christian values in your own personal spiritual life. Scores at this level indicate that you ranked the items so that the three basic dimensions receive relatively equal developmental emphasis, indicating a harmonious and balanced integration among the three basic dimensions (DIMs) of spiritual values: intrinsic being/feeling values like your personal devotion to and faith in God; extrinsic Doing/Action-based values like attending church and doing works of religious service; and systemic thinking/believing values like understanding religious doctrines, God's laws, and God's plan for your life (Dim-I$_2$, Dim-E$_2$, and Dim-S$_2$ found in Lines 2, 4, and 6 on Result Form 2). Scores at this level are problem free and indicate a very high level of spiritual understanding and involvement in all dimensions.

Strong development: Strong level scores (between 23 and 43) indicate a *fairly close* personal involvement and identification with intrinsic devotional, extrinsic practical, and systemic doctrinal religious or Christian values in your own life. Scores at this level mean that at least one and perhaps two of your spiritual value dimensions is more strongly development than the other one or two. Scores at this level do not mean that you have any serious problems, but the relation among your three dimension (Dim$_2$) scores may show you where to apply more energy and effort. Compare Lines 2, 4, and 6, select the score most to the right, and give that value dimension some extra attention in order to restore or achieve a more balanced spiritual integration.

Average development: An average score (between *23 and 43*) indicates that you have a *somewhat close* involvement and identification with intrinsic devotional, extrinsic practical, and systemic doctrinal religious or Christian values in your own life. Most religious people score at this level. Many people are not fully aware of the differences among being/feeling, doing/acting, and thinking/believing values. This profiling process should help you become more aware of these differences for the sake of greater clarity and to develop your mental or conceptual spiritual potentials. For improvement, look at the relations among your three Dimension scores (Lines 2, 4, and 6), and then focus on the weakest ones (the ones most to the right). You should concentrate your time and effort on better understanding, appreciating, and getting more personally involved with the values that make up your weakest score.

Fair development: Fair scores (between *64 and 84*) indicate that you have a *slightly distant* involvement or identification with intrinsic devotional, extrinsic practical, and systemic doctrinal religious or Christian values in your personal life. This score indicates that you have some conceptual or emotional problems with some or most of the value items. Scores at this level present you with an opportunity to improve and develop your spiritual potentials in all three value dimensions. On Result Form 2, find the Dimension (Dim$_2$) scores with the highest numbers (the ones most to the right on Lines 2, 4, and 6), and write down the value items correlating with those Dim$_2$ scores. Set one or more goals for improvement. Discuss these spiritual values with your spiritual guide, counselor, or teacher, and pay more attention to them by consciously engaging your weakest spiritual areas on a daily basis.

Weak development: Scores at this level (*85 or greater*) indicate a *very distant* involvement or identification with intrinsic devotional, extrinsic practical, and systemic doctrinal religious or Christian values. Your score may mean that you did not pay close attention to the individual value items when filling out the Profile(s), or that you simply do not understand their differences when judging how these values apply to you. Your spiritual potentials are not very well developed, but you have a great opportunity to draw out your potentials and make them actual in your life. Go to the Result Form 2, find the Dim$_2$ scores (look at lines 2, 4, and 6) with the greatest deviations (the ones most to the right), and set one or more goals targeting how to involve yourself more fully in these areas of spiritual value. Your goals could include praying about these value items and embracing and acting on them in your daily life until they become a part of you.

2. Being/feeling Focus, (Dim-I$_2$), Result Form 2, Line 2

The score on Line 2 *quantitatively* measures your capacity to discern religious or Christian values centered on your intrinsic personal being/feeling relationships to God and on the loving communion and fellowship of God's people. Line 3, explained shortly, expresses the *qualitative* difference in terms of the **positive** character of your absolute difference score on Line 2. Line 2 reflects your personal intrinsic spiritual involvement and identification with conscious individuals, divine and human. The 18 value items in the Religious or Christian Value Profiles, Part II, contain three positive or desirable intrinsic being/feeling value items and three negative or undesirable intrinsic being/feeling value items. Your relative ranking of these six value items represents how high or how low you place them within the full spectrum of religious or Christian values, *as you apply them to your own life.* This score summarizes your personal ranking of these six values. The meanings of your scores are as follows.

Excellent development: An excellent score (between *0 and 7*) indicates a *complete* personal understanding of, appreciation for, and involvement or identification with religious or Christian being/feeling values. Scores at this level indicate that you ranked these values so that the three positives (good items) and the three negatives (bad items) are very close to the mathematical norm, showing a relative balance among both positive and negative being/feeling values. Scores at this level are problem free and represent a very high level of personal spiritual involvement and development.

Strong development: Strong scores (between *8 and 14*) indicate that you have a *fairly close* personal involvement and identification with being/feeling religious or Christian values. Scores at this level mean that one or more value items, either positive (desirable) or negative (undesirable), shows weaker development than the others. Scores at this level do not mean that you have any serious problems, but the few items that you ranked out of place may show you where to apply more energy and effort to achieve a more balanced integration among all of them. Find the items that you ranked incorrectly on each part of your Profile(s) by comparing them to the order of correct rankings given in Chapter Seven. Then set goals for giving your incorrect rankings more effort and attention.

Average development: Average scores (between *15 and 21*) indicate that you have a *somewhat close* personal involvement and identification with intrinsic being/feeling religious or Christian values. Most religious people score at this level. Many people are not fully aware of the differences among positive (desirable) and negative (undesirable) being/feeling values. This profiling process should help you become more aware of these differences in order to achieve greater clarity and to further develop your intrinsic spiritual potentials. For improvement, look at the relations among positive and negative "being/feeling Triad" items in Chapter Four, and read, study, and think about the discussions and exercises. You could benefit from devoting more time and effort to the specific being/feeling values that are most out of place so you can better adjust and harmonize them within your own life.

Fair development: Fair scores (between *22 and 26*) indicate that you have a *slightly distant* personal involvement or identification with intrinsic being/feeling religious or Christian values. Scores at this level mean that you have some conceptual or emotional problems with some or most of the six being/feeling value items. This presents you with an opportunity to improve and develop your intrinsic spiritual potentials. Go to Chapter Four, find the specific being/feeling value items there, and read and study the discussions and exercises. Try to set one or more goals for improving your devotional/moral life. Discuss these intrinsic spiritual values with your spiritual guide, counselor, or teacher, and deliberately pay more attention to them on a daily basis.

Weak development: Weak scores (*29 or above*) indicate that you have a *very distant* personal involvement or identification with intrinsic being/feeling religious or Christian values. Your score may mean that you did not pay close attention to the individual value items when filling out your Profile(s), or that you do not understand those values as they apply to you. Your intrinsic spiritual potentials are not very well developed, but you have a great opportunity to draw them out and make them actual in your life. Go to Chapter Four, and find and study the "Being/feeling Triad" value items, discussions, and exercises. Establish one or more goals to incorporate these better into your spiritual life. Try to embrace these being/feeling value items in a deeper way, and pray about them to become more conscious of them. Then, like an underground stream, they will flow with you and provide you with constant spiritual support.

3. Intrinsic Involvement, (Dim-I$_2$%), Result Form 2, Line 3

Your score on Line 3 expresses how you deviated from the norm in ranking the three positive and three negative devotional items on your Profile(s). It captures the positive or negative biases revealed by your deviations. These biases are usually very deep, non-rational, largely emotional, and heavily programmed or conditioned by other persons or circumstances in your environment, especially while you were very young. Such biases can be very hard to change, no matter whether you are positively biased or negatively biased.

This score is excellent at 50%, where the sum of positive deviations and the sum of negative deviations are equal. Ranking these value items higher than the norm indicates that they contain **more** value for you than the other value items. This indicates a certain degree of **positive** intrinsic personal involvement. Result Form 2 reflects five levels of increasing or decreasing positivity, including the "excellent" balanced level. Ranking being/feeling value items lower than the norm indicates that they contain **less** value for you than the other value items. This indicates varying degrees of **negative** intrinsic personal involvement, expressed on Result Form 2 in scores of less than 50% positive.

Excellent development: An excellent (*50%*) score indicates *complete* personal involvement and identification with the six being/feeling religious or Christian values. Scores at this level mean that you ranked the items so that the six being/feeling values have just as many positive as negative deviations. Excellent scores show symmetry in judging being/feeling values, and suggest objectivity about and harmony within your personal relationships to God and to the loving communion and fellowship of God's people. Scores at this level are problem free and indicate a very high level of spiritual development.

Strong development: Strong scores indicate that you have a *fairly close* personal involvement with being/feeling religious or Christian values. Scores *51% to 60% positive* and *49% to 40% positive* mean that you ranked one or more of the six being/feeling values with some degree of distorting emotion, that you overvalued one or more of these items and undervalued others. An increased positive percentage reflects a stronger emotional identification with one or more of these value items, and a decreased positive percentage indicates some degree of emotional distance from one or more of them. Scores at this level do not mean that you have any serious problems, but they may show you where to focus your effort to restore balance.

Average development: Average scores indicate that you have a *somewhat close* personal involvement or identification with being/ feeling religious or Christian values. Most religious people score at this level. Scores from *61% to 70% positive* mean that your personal ranking reveals an emotional inclination to favor being/feeling values above other dimensions, and you could benefit from restoring balance with doing/acting values and with thinking/believing values. Scores from *39% to 30% positive* mean that some degree of emotional distance separates you from being/feeling values. You should try to focus or refocus on those being/feeling values that you undervalued. Work through the discussions and exercises on "Being/feeling Triad" values in Chapter Four, and practice relating more effectively and objectively to these intrinsic spiritual values.

Fair development: A fair score indicates that you have a *slightly distant* personal involvement or identification with being/feeling religious or Christian values. Fair scores mean that you have some conceptual or emotional problems with some of the being/feeling value items. Scores between *71% to 80% positive* indicate that you greatly overvalued one or more of the six being/feeling items. This suggests that you have a strong inclination to favor your personal relationship to God, while neglecting the doing/acting and thinking/believing aspects of your spiritual life. Scores from *29% to 20% positive* mean that you have developed a strong emotional distance from being/feeling values, probably in favor of doing good works, or of thinking and believing. Go to Chapter Four, study and think about the "Being/feeling Triad" value items, discussions, and exercises; and set one or more goals to help you better internalize values of this kind. Discuss these value items with your spiritual guide or counselor, and pay more attention to them in order to bring them back into balance with the other spiritual value dimensions.

Weak development: Weak scores indicate that you have a *very distant* personal involvement or identification with being/feeling religious or Christian values. Your score may mean that you did not pay close attention to the individual value items when filling out your Profile(s), or that you do not understand how those values apply to you. An *80% positive* or greater score means that your involvement with the being/feeling dimension is far too emotional, without much support from the doing/acting or thinking/believing dimensions. Scores *20% positive* or lower mean that a great emotional distance or detachment hinders your involvement with and finding fulfillment from these being/feeling values. Go to Chapter Four; study and think about the "Being/feeling Triad" value items, discussions, and exercises; and set one or more goals to help you better internalize values of this kind. Your goals could include praying about these value items, becoming more conscious of them in your daily life, and asking your spiritual guide or counselor for guidance in getting these back into balance with doing/acting and thinking/believing spiritual values.

4. Doing/acting Focus, (DIM-E$_2$), Result Form 2, Line 4

The score on Line 4 measures your capacity to attach value to religious or Christian sacred objects, spiritual practices, and good works of service. These values consist mainly in what you actually do or how you act to express your spiritual life. Line 5 below measures the *quality* of the absolute number on line 4, that is, the **positive** character of the number. The 18 values in Part II of the Religious and Christian Value Profiles contain three positive or desirable doing/acting value items and three negative or undesirable ones. Your personal ranking of these six values shows how high or how low you place these personal doing/acting values within the full spectrum of religious or Christian values *in your own life*. This score is a summary of your personal ranking of these six values in relation to the sum of all deviations from the mathematical norm. The meanings of your scores are as follows.

Excellent development: An excellent score (between *0 and 7*) indicates *complete* personal involvement with doing/acting religious or Christian values. Your personal doing/acting Dimension (Dim-E$_2$) is either in balance with, or favored higher than, the other two basic personal spiritual dimensions (Dim-I$_2$ and Dim-S$_2$). You tend to practice what you preach and believe. You understand and engage yourself in worthy spiritual activities, and you take your social and behavioral roles in acting or living religiously very seriously. Scores at this level are problem free and indicate a very high level of spiritual development.

Strong development: Strong scores (between *8 and 14*) indicate that you have a *fairly close* personal involvement with doing/acting religious or Christian values, but you give stronger emphasis to one or more of the six practical (Dim-E$_2$) items than to the others. You may be more focused on doing/acting works of service than on searching for or contemplating religious truths, or on loving God and identifying fully with your fellow human beings. Scores at this level do not mean that you have any serious problems, but you may want to examine your scores that are a little out of line; the corresponding value items may show you where to apply more of your energy and effort in order to restore a more balanced integration.

Average development: Average scores (between *15 and 21*) indicate that you have a *somewhat close* personal involvement with doing/acting religious or Christian values, but you do not consistently practice your faith. Most religious people score at this level. Many people will not be consciously aware of all the differences among the six practical values, or of how they apply to their own lives. This profiling process should help you become more aware of the value of religious practices and activities for the sake of developing your spiritual potentials. For improvement, go to Chapter Four; study the "Doing/acting Triad" value items, discussions, and exercises; and set one or more goals to help you better internalize values of this kind. Perhaps you could benefit from devoting more time and effort to the actual practice of your spiritual values.

Fair development: Fair scores (between *22 and 28*) indicate that your personal involvement with doing/acting religious or Christian values is somewhat distant or detached. Much of the time you are inclined not to act upon your religious convictions. Perhaps you have conceptual or emotional problems with some of the personal doing/ acting spiritual value items. Scores at this level present you with an opportunity to improve by preparing yourself to practicing what you preach and believe. Go to Chapter Four; study and think about the "Doing/acting Triad" value items, discussions, and exercises; and set goals to help you do better at putting your faith into practice. Discuss doing/acting spiritual values with your spiritual guide or counselor, pay more attention to religion-based activities, and try to integrate these better with spiritual values in the other dimensions.

Weak development: A weak score of (*29 or above*) indicates that you have only a *distant or detached* personal involvement with doing/acting religious or Christian values. You seem to avoid or evade religious activities and practices. Your score may mean that you did not pay close attention to the individual value items when filling out your Profile(s), or that you simply do not understand how doing/acting values differ from others, or how they apply to your own life. A weak score means that your practical spiritual potentials are not very well developed, but you have a great opportunity to draw out your potentials and actually live out your convictions in the future. Go to Chapter Four; study and think about the "Doing/acting Triad" value items, discussions, and exercises; and try to internalize values of this kind. Your goals could be to pray about really putting your religion into practice, and to make a conscious effort to become more involved with religion-based activities in your daily life.

5. Extrinsic Involvement, (Dim-E$_2$%), Result Form 2, Line 5

Your score on Line 5 expresses how you deviated from the norm in ranking the three positive and three negative practical or doing/acting items on your Profile(s). It captures the positive or negative biases revealed by your deviations. These biases are usually very deep, non-rational, largely emotional, and heavily programmed or conditioned by other persons or circumstances in your environment, especially while you were very young. Such biases can be very hard to change, no matter whether you are positively biased or negatively biased. Your score reflects the intensity of your personal involvement with doing/acting values within the full spectrum of the 18 Christian value items in Part II. A balanced score (50%) means that you ranked the three positive and the three negative doing/acting values according to norm. If you ranked these value items higher than the norm, you have **more** involvement with them than with the value items in the other value dimensions. This suggest varying degrees of **positive** extrinsic involvement, alongside varying degrees of noninvolvement.

Result Form 2 reflects five levels of both increasing and decreasing positivity, including the balanced "excellent" 50% level. If you ranked the doing/acting value items lower than the norm, you are **less** involved with them than with the others. This indicates varying degrees of **negative** extrinsic involvement, that is, of noninvolvement; and this shows up on the Result Form as a score that is less than 50% positive. The meanings of your scores are as follows.

Excellent development: An excellent score indicates *complete* personal involvement with doing/acting religious or Christian values. Scores at this level reveal an integrated balance among the positive and negative doing/acting values, the six items composing the extrinsic (Dim-E$_2$) dimension. The *50%* level indicates that you ranked the items so that all six personal doing/acting values have just as many positive as negative deviations. This shows a symmetry in your understanding of, appreciation for, and involvement with doing/acting values. It suggests objectivity about doing religious and/or Christian works and about participating in spiritually oriented practices and activities. Most of the time you actually practice what you preach and believe. Scores at this level are problem free and represent a very high level of spiritual development.

Strong development: A strong score indicates that you have a *fairly close* involvement with doing/acting religious or Christian values. Scores that are *51% to 60%* and *49% to 40% positive* indicate that you ranked one or more of the six doing values with a slight degree of distorting emotion. A positive score greater than 50% indicates that you have an overly strong emotional identification with one or more value items, and a score less than 50% positive indicates that you are experiencing some degree of emotional distance or detachment from one or more of them. You hesitate to get involved. Scores at this level do not mean that you have any serious problems, but they show you where to focus your efforts for further growth.

Average development: Average scores indicate that you have a *somewhat close* personal involvement with doing religious or Christian values, counterbalanced by some hesitation or ambivalence. Most religious people score at this level. Scores that are *61% to 70% positive* indicate that you have a positive emotional inclination to favor doing/ acting values above other value dimensions, and you should try to gain or regain better focus on being/feeling and thinking/believing spiritual values. Scores that are 39% to 30% positive suggest that you have a negative personal bias against, or an emotional distance or detachment from, actively putting your religious values into practice. Go to Chapter Four; study and think about the "Doing/acting Triad" value items, discussions, and exercises; and try to internalize and act upon values of this kind.

Fair development: A fair score indicates that you have either a *slightly distant or detached* personal involvement with doing/acting religious or Christian values, or else that you value them *excessively*. Perhaps you have some conceptual or emotional problems with several of the extrinsic value items. On the one hand, you may be overvaluing religion-based activities and practices. Scores that are *71% to 80% positive* mean that you attach too much value to some of the six doing/acting items. Perhaps you have a strong preference for getting things done. You favor participating in organized religious activities and doing religious or Christian good works, while to some extent neglecting the being/feeling and thinking/believing aspects of your spiritual life. On the other hand, scores that are *29% to 20% positive* mean that you have a strong emotional distance from the doing/acting aspects of religious or Christian life, perhaps in favor of the being/ feeling or the thinking/believing dimensions. You really don't want to get involved. Go to Chapter Four; study and think about the "Doing/ acting Triad" value items, discussions, and exercises; and try to internalize and act upon values of this kind. Discuss them with your spiritual guide or counselor, pay more attention to them, and try to get them into better balance with values in other dimensions.

Weak development: Weak scores indicate that you have either a *distant* personal involvement with doing/acting religious or Christian values, or else you have an *excessive* involvement. A weak score may mean that you did not pay close attention to the individual value items when filling out your Profile(s), or that you simply do not understand those values and how they apply to your own life. Scores *80% positive* or greater indicate that your spiritual potentials in the personal doing/ acting dimension are excessively charged emotionally, without much support from the being/feeling or thinking/believing value dimensions. By contrast, scores *20% positive* or less indicate a significant emotional distance or detachment that obstructs your active involvement in religion-based activities and prevents you from achieving fulfillment through putting your convictions into practice. Go to Chapter Four; study and think about the "Doing/acting Triad" value items, discussions, and exercises; and try to internalize and act upon values of this kind. Pray about these value items, become more conscious of them in your daily life, remove the obstacles that block your participation, and seek guidance in getting your active religious life back into a balance with your being/feeling and thinking/believing values.

6. Thinking Focus, (Dim-S$_2$), Result Form 2, Line 6

The score on Line 6 measures your capacity to discern religious or Christian values that involve systemic or systematic thinking and believing such as doctrinal inquiry, contemplation, religious learning, theological study, teaching and reasoning, and verbally or conceptually formulating and expressing what you believe is actually true. Line 7, explained below, measures the *quality* of the absolute number in Line 6. It shows the **positive** character of the number in the Line 6 score. Within the 18 values in Part II of the Religious or Christian Value Profiles are three positive thinking/believing value items and three negative ones. Your relative ranking of these six value items represents your closeness to or distance from them. Thinking/believing values fall within the full spectrum of many other Christian or religious values *as you actually live and relate to them.* This score summarizes your ranking of these six values in relation to the sum of all deviations from the mathematical norm. The meanings of your scores are as follows.

Excellent development: An excellent score (from *0 to 7*) indicates *complete* personal involvement with the doctrinal thinking/believing

Christian or religious values in your own life. This score shows that when you ranked the items your emphasis on the thinking/believing religious dimension was very close to your emphasis on the other two value dimensions. This shows a balance in your involvement with being/feeling, doing/acting, and thinking/believing values (Dim-I$_2$, Dim-E$_2$, and Dim-S$_2$ on Lines 2, 4, and 6). Scores at this level are problem free and indicate a very high level of spiritual development.

Strong development: A strong score (between *8 and 14*) indicates that you have a *fairly close* personal involvement with thinking or conceptual religious or Christian values. Scores at this level mean that one or more of your Dimension (Dim-S$_2$) scores shows a keener personal involvement than the others. You may be more focused on adhering to your religious or Christian convictions or to God's commandments than you are on clarifying or further unfolding God's plan for your life. Scores at this level do not mean that you have any serious problems, but they may show you where to apply more energy and effort to achieve greater balanced development and integration.

Average development: Average scores (between *15 and 21*) indicate that your have a *somewhat close* personal involvement with doctrinal thinking/believing religious or Christian values, but you do not fully identify with them. Most religious people score at this level. Many people will not be consciously aware of the differences of meaning and worth among being/feeling, doing/acting, and thinking/believing spiritual values. This profiling process should help you become more aware of these differences for the sake of better developing your spiritual potentials. For improvement, look carefully at each value item, the discussions, and the exercises in the section on the "Thinking/believing Triad" in Chapter Four. Then devote more of your time and effort to developing your awareness of and appreciation for conceptual spiritual values.

Fair development: A fair score (between *22 and 28*) indicates that you have a *slightly distant* personal involvement with doctrinal thinking/believing religious or Christian values. Perhaps you are having conceptual or emotional problems with some or most of the personal systemic or conceptual value items. Scores at this level present you with an opportunity to improve and to develop your mental spiritual potentials, to understand and love God his creatures with all your mind. For improvement, look carefully at each value item, the discussions, and the exercises in the "Thinking/believing Triad" in Chapter Four. Then devote more time and effort to developing your awareness of and appreciation for conceptual spiritual values. Discuss these values with your spiritual guide or counselor, and pay more conscious attention to them.

Weak development: Weak scores (*29 or above*) indicate that you have a *very distant or detached* personal involvement with doctrinal thinking/believing religious or Christian values. In other words, you do not like to think about religion and its meaning. Perhaps you did not pay close attention to the individual value items when completing your Profile(s), or perhaps you simply do not identify with mental values or understand and appreciate their differences. Weak scores mean that your thinking/believing spiritual potentials are not very well developed, but you have a great opportunity to draw out your potentials, make them actual in your life, and learn to love God and his creatures with all your mind. For improvement, look carefully at each value item, the discussions, and the exercises on the "Thinking/believing Triad" in Chapter Four. Devote more of your time and effort to developing your awareness of and appreciation for conceptual or doctrinal spiritual values. Your goals could include praying about these value items, becoming more conscious of them in your daily life, giving more of your time and effort to them, and seeking help with them.

7. Systemic Involvement, (Dim-S$_2$%), Result Form 2, Line 7

Your score on Line 7 expresses how you deviated from the norm in ranking the three positive and three negative conceptual items on your Profile(s). It captures the positive or negative biases revealed by your deviations. These biases are usually very deep, non-rational, largely emotional, and heavily programmed or conditioned by other persons or circumstances in your environment, especially while you were very young. Such biases can be very hard to change, no matter whether you are positively biased or negatively biased. If you ranked these doctrinal thinking/believing values higher than the other values, you are **more** involved with them than with the others. You thus have a high degree of **positive** systemic involvement. Result Form 2 reflects five levels of both increasing and decreasing positivity, including the balanced "excellent" 50% level. If you ranked these doctrinal thinking/ believing values lower than the others, the results show that you feel **less** personally involved with them than with other kinds of spiritual value. This indicates that you have some degree of distance from or **negative** involvement with doctrinal thinking/believing spiritual values. This shows up on the Result Form 2 as a score of *less* than 50%. The meanings of your scores are as follows.

Excellent development: Excellent scores indicate that you have *complete* personal involvement with thinking/believing doctrinal religious or Christian values. A *50%* score indicates that you ranked the items so that all six personal thinking/believing doctrinal values have just as many positive as negative deviations. Scores at this level disclose a symmetry in your involvement with personal thinking/ believing doctrinal values, and they suggest objectivity about how you apply doctrinal values in your life. Scores at this level are problem free and reveal a very high level of spiritual development.

Strong development: A strong score indicates a *fairly close* personal involvement with thinking/believing religious or Christian values. If your scores are *51% to 60%* and *49% to 40% positive*, you ranked one or more of the six personal systemic values with a slightly inappropriate degree of emotion. A higher positive percentage score indicates a stronger emotional identification with one or more items, and a lower positive percentage score indicates a slight emotional distance from one or more doctrinal value items. Scores at this level do not mean that you have any serious problems, but they may show you where to focus more time and energy to restore balanced integration.

Average development: Average scores indicates that you have either a *somewhat close* personal involvement with thinking/believing religious or Christian values, or else that you are *somewhat distanced* from them. Most religious people score at this level. Scores that are *61% to 70% positive* mean that your personal ranking indicates an inclination to favor thinking/believing values above the other value dimensions, and you could benefit from re-establishing or creating a more balanced integration with being/feeling and doing/acting spiritual values. By contrast, scores from *39% to 30% positive* mean that you have some emotional distance or detachment from thinking/believing doctrinal values. For improvement, look carefully at each value item, the discussions, and the exercises in the "Thinking/believing Triad" in Chapter Four. Devote more of your time and effort to developing your awareness of and appreciation for conceptual or doctrinal spiritual values.

Fair development: A fair score indicates that you have a *slightly distant* personal involvement with doctrinal thinking/believing religious or Christian values. Perhaps you have personal conceptual or emotional problems with one or more of the thinking/believing value items. Scores that are *71% to 80% positive* mean that you overvalued several of the six thinking/believing value items. You may have a strong inclination to favor thinking or doctrinal belief values, while ignoring the being/feeling and doing/acting aspects of your spiritual life. By contrast, scores that are *29% to 20% positive* suggest that you have a strong emotional distance or detachment from the thinking/believing aspects of your personal spiritual life, probably in favor of being/feeling or doing/acting. For improvement, look carefully at each value item, the discussions, and the exercises in the "Thinking/believing Triad" in Chapter Four. Devote more of your time and effort to developing your awareness of and appreciation for conceptual or doctrinal spiritual values. Discuss these with your spiritual guide or counselor, pay more attention to them, and try to get them into better balance with spiritual values in other dimensions.

Weak development: Weak scores indicate that you have a *very distant* personal involvement with religious or Christian thinking/believing values. You tend to neglect and perhaps even to disvalue them. Perhaps you did not pay close attention to the individual thinking/believing value items when you filled out the Profile(s), or perhaps you simply do not understand the meaning and worth of such values for your own life. Scores that are *80% positive* or greater reveal that your spiritual involvement in the thinking/believing dimension is far too emotionally charged, without much support from the intrinsic or extrinsic spiritual value dimensions. By contrast, scores that are *20% positive* or less indicate a strong emotional distance that greatly restricts your personal thinking/believing involvement and inhibits your personal capacity to derive fulfillment from the thinking/believing or doctrinal spiritual perspective. You tend to neglect, perhaps even to disvalue, thinking and believing in religion. Go to the "Thinking/believing Triad" in Chapter Four. For improvement, think carefully about each value item, and work through the discussions and the exercises. Devote more of your time and effort to developing your awareness of and appreciation for conceptual or doctrinal spiritual values. You might pray about these value items, become more conscious of them in your daily life, write them down and reading them over several times a day, and seek guidance to get these back into balance with your being/feeling and personal doing/acting values.

8. Dimensional Harmony, (DIM_2), Result Form 2, Line 8

The score on Line 8 measures quantitatively your relations to the three major personal religious or Christian value dimensions: being/feeling (intrinsic), doing/acting (extrinsic), and thinking/believing (systemic). A balance among or equal development of the three value dimensions is the ideal. This ideal correlates with Jesus' expression of the Greatest Commandment: We should love the Lord with **all** our valuational capacities (heart, soul, mind, and strength). Your personal ranking of the values in Part II shows either equal or unequal personal involvement with these dimensions. Most religious people favor one dimension over the others, and some favor two dimensions over the third. Rarely does anyone rank them with nearly equal emphasis, indicating symmetry and balance among them. This score is a quantitative result of the distance separating your three value Dimension (Dim_2) scores on Lines 2, 4, and 6. The meanings of your scores are as follows.

Excellent development: Excellent scores (between *0 and 3*) indicate that you have a *complete* personal involvement and identification with all three religious or Christian value dimensions. Scores at this level mean that your developmental involvement with the three basic dimensions is relatively equal, that you have achieved a balanced emphasis on being/feeling, doing/acting, and thinking/believing spiritual values ($Dim-I_2$, $Dim-E_2$, and $Dim-S_2$ scores on Lines 2, 4, and 6). Scores at this level are problem free and indicate a very high level of spiritual development.

Strong development: Strong scores (between *4 and 6*) indicate a *fairly close* personal relation with all three dimensions of religious or Christian values. Dim_2 scores at this level also indicate that your relation to at least one or more of the spiritual value dimensions is more developed than to the others. Scores at this level do not mean that you have any serious problems, but they may show you where to apply more energy and effort to achieve a more developed and balanced spiritual integration.

Average development: Average scores (between *7 and 11*) indicate a *somewhat close* personal relation with all three religious or Christian value dimensions. Most religious people score at this level. Many people will not be consciously aware of the differences among the being/feeling, doing/acting, and thinking/believing values. This profiling process should help you to become more aware of these differences in order to further develop your spiritual potentials. For improvement, look at the relations among your three Dim_2 scores (on Lines 2, 4, and 6), and then focus on the weakest ones (the ones most to the right). You should devote more time and effort to understanding and appreciating the values that make up your weakest Dim_2 scores.

Fair development: Fair scores (between *12 and 15*) point to a *slightly distant* personal relation with values in the three basic religious or

Christian value dimensions. Perhaps you have conceptual or emotional problems with some or most of the value dimensions, but this presents you with an opportunity to improve and to develop your spiritual potentials across the board. Find your weakest dimension scores (Dim-I_2, Dim-E_2, or Dim-S_2 on Lines 2, 4, and 6), and then focus on the weakest ones, the ones most to the right. You should devote more time and effort to understanding and appreciating the values that make up your weakest Dim_2 scores.

Weak development: Weak scores (*16 or above*) indicate a *very distant* relation to the three personal religious or Christian value dimensions. Perhaps you did not pay close attention to the individual value items when filling out your Profile(s), or perhaps you simply do not recognize the differences of meaning and worth in those values in your own life. Weak scores mean that your spiritual potentials are not very well developed, but you have a great opportunity to draw out your potentials and make them actual in your life. Review your scores on Result Form 2, Lines 2, 4, and 6, and find the Dimension (Dim_2) scores most to the right, the largest deviations and your weakest scores. Then devote more time and effort to understanding and appreciating the values that make up your weakest Dim_2 scores.

9. Stress/Tension
(DIM_2%), Result Form 2, Line 9

The score on Line 9 measures the level of anxiety, stress, or tension that you experience in your personal involvement with religious or Christian values. A balanced and equal developmental emphasis among your three value dimensions (Dim-I_2, Dim-E_2, and Dim-S_2) is the ideal, and it involves no stress or tension. This score expresses the significance of the DIM_2 score (Line 8) in relation to the overall sum of the differences, DIF_2 (Line 1), and it represents your total personal capacity to differentiate spiritual values. The DIM_2 score is calculated as a percentage of the DIF_2 score; it indicates the degree of your imbalance, which could be extreme. The further removed you are from a balanced involvement with each of your three dimensions, the more *stress and tension* you are likely to experience in your personal spiritual life. The meanings of your scores are as follows.

Excellent development: An excellent score (from 0% to 10%) indicates a clear understanding of and a *balanced* personal involvement with all three dimensions of religious or Christian values. This balanced emphasis indicates the absence of spiritual stress and tension that results from a balanced and equal involvement with all three dimensions, Dim-I$_2$, Dim-E$_2$, and Dim-S$_2$. If all three of your Dim$_2$ scores are equally low (good), this demonstrates your *crystal clear* understanding of, appreciation for, and equal emphasis upon the three dimensions of personal religious or Christian values. If all three of your Dim$_2$ scores are equally high (not very well developed), this also indicates that you feel no stress or spiritual tension because you are somewhat dull in all dimensions. You could benefit by improving your overall understanding of, appreciation for, or clarity regarding all three dimensions. A small imbalance is not particularly significant. A score at this level indicates a significant degree of spiritual development.

Strong development: A strong score (between *11% to 20%*) indicates a *fairly clear* understanding of and balanced emphasis upon the three basic personal religious or Christian value dimensions. At this level, one or more of your Dim$_2$ scores shows stronger development than the other one or two. Occasional spiritual tension may be felt here, but this does not mean that you have any serious problems. The relation among your three Dim$_2$ scores may show you where to apply more energy and effort to maintain a lower-stress, more balanced spiritual integration.

Average development: Average scores (from *21% to 30%*) indicate a *partly clear understanding of* and a nearly balanced emphasis upon the three basic personal religious or Christian value dimensions. Most religious people score at this level. Many religious people are not fully aware of the differences of meaning and worth among being/ feeling, doing/acting, and thinking/believing spiritual values. This profiling process should help you to become more aware of these differences to achieve greater development of your spiritual potentials. For improvement, look at the relations among your three personal Dimension (Dim$_2$) scores on Lines 2, 4, and 6; then focus on the weakest ones, the ones most to the right. Devote more time and effort to understanding and appreciating the values that make up your weakest Dim$_2$ scores. To avoid spiritual stress, try to bring your weakest value dimensions into an integrated development of and balance with the other spiritual dimensions.

Fair development: A fair score, (from 31% to 40%) indicates a lack of clarity about and/or *a degree of detachment* from the three basic personal religious or Christian value dimensions. This score also indicates that you feel some degree of stress and tension in your religious life. The stress and tension arise because you are out of balance, because you strongly favor one spiritual dimension over the others. Your lack of integration with the other one or two personal spiritual value dimensions causes varying degrees of discomfort or internal tension. Find the Dimension scores (Dim-I$_2$, Dim-E$_2$, or Dim-S$_2$ on Lines 2, 4, and 6) with the greatest number of deviations, the ones most to the right. Then devote more time and effort to understanding and appreciating the values that make up your weakest Dim$_2$ scores. Discuss your weakest values with your spiritual guide or counselor, pray about them, and pay more attention to them on a daily basis.

Weak development: Weak scores (*41 and above*) indicate a severe lack of clarity about and *very distant* relations with the three basic personal religious or Christian value dimensions. Perhaps you did not pay close attention to the individual value items when filling out the Profile, or perhaps you simply do not understand the differences in their meaning and worth as applied to your own life. A weak score indicates that your spiritual potentials are not very well developed. You may be very clear about one dimension while blocking out the other two. Yet, you have a great opportunity to expand your spiritual understanding and to create more harmony and balance with less tension and spiritual stress in your life. Find the Dimension scores (Dim-I$_2$, Dim-E$_2$, or Dim-S$_2$ on Lines 2, 4, and 6) with the largest deviations, the ones most to the right. Then devote more time and effort to understanding and appreciating the values that make up your weakest Dim$_2$ scores. Pray about these value items, become more conscious of them, and try to integrate them into your daily life.

10. Spiritual Clarity, (DIS$_2$), Result Form 2, Line 10

The score on Line 10 measures the frequency with which you mistakenly identify positive personal religious or Christian values as negative, or negative personal religious or Christian values as positive. In both parts of the Profile(s), nine of the 18 value items are positive and nine are negative. When you rank a positive or desirable value as negative or undesirable, or a negative or undesirable value as positive or desirable, the result is a **distortion** (DIS$_2$). If you see one positive item as negative, you will automatically have to rank a negative one as a positive, due to the forced ranking structure of the Profile(s). There are only nine possible distortion pairs in each 18 item list. Your personal ranking of the 18 value items can have a significant number of deviations without any distortions at all. In these cases, your personal spiritual clarity will be excellent, since all positive personal religious or Christian values are judged as positive, and all negative values are considered to be negative. The meanings of your scores are as follows.

Excellent development: An excellent score, *0*, indicates a very *clear* understanding of, appreciation for, and involvement with personal religious or Christian values in all three dimensions because all positives are seen as positive, and all negatives are identified as negative. An excellent score means that you ranked the items so that the deviations are relatively small, and no deviation is large enough to spill over into its opposite (positive into negative, or negative into positive). Scores at this level are problem free and indicate a significant level of spiritual clarity and development.

Strong development: Strong scores with a distortion (DIS$_2$) number of only *2* indicate a *fairly clear* understanding of, appreciation for, and involvement with both positive and negative inner religious or Christian values in all three dimensions. A distortion involves the association of two items, so the score is based on pairs. Strong scores indicate that one distorted item (with its forced opposite) may have been overlooked. Perhaps one item caught your attention and you ranked it much higher (or much lower) than you should have. By getting one item out of place, you were then forced to rank another item much lower or higher than you should have. Scores at this level do not indicate any real problems, but you could benefit from being more careful and paying closer attention.

Average development: An average score of only *4* distortions indicates a *somewhat clear* understanding of and involvement with positive and negative personal religious or Christian values in all three dimensions. Many if not most religious persons score at this level because most people are not fully aware of the differences in meaning and worth between positive and negative being/feeling, doing/acting, and thinking/believing values. This profiling process should help you become more aware of these differences for the sake of better developing your spiritual potentials. Go back your Profiles and find the items you distorted. To do this, first find the items that you ranked incorrectly on each part of your Profile(s) by comparing your rankings to the correct order of rankings given in Chapter Seven. Distortions will be single digit items that you ranked as double digit, or double digit items ranked as single digit. Discuss any unclear items with your spiritual guide or counselor, and try to develop a better understanding of and appreciation for why these items were distorted, for why you confused good with bad. Target how to recognize, understand, and distinguish between positive and negative spiritual values, and try to become more conscious of how and why you distorted some value items in your personal ranking.

Fair development: Fair scores of *6* indicate a *slightly fuzzy* understanding of and personal involvement with positive as opposed to negative religious or Christian values in all three dimensions. This score involving 6 distortions indicates that you have conceptual or emotional problems in coping with your spiritual life. Scores at this level present you with an opportunity to improve and to develop your spiritual potentials. Go back your Profile(s) and find the items you distorted. To do this, first find the items that you ranked incorrectly on each part of your Profile(s) by comparing your rankings to the correct order of rankings given in Chapter Seven. Distortions will be single digit items that you ranked as double digit, or double digit items ranked as single digit. Discuss any unclear items with your spiritual guide or counselor, and try to develop a better understanding of and appreciation for why these items were distorted, for why you confused good with bad. Target how to recognize, understand, and distinguish between positive and negative spiritual values, and try to become more conscious of how and why you distorted some value items in your personal ranking.

Weak development: A weak score (of *8 or more*) indicates a *very fuzzy* understanding of and personal involvement with positive as opposed to negative religious or Christian values in all three dimensions. Your 8 or more distortions may mean that you did not pay close attention to the individual value items when you were filling out your Profile(s), or that you simply do not understand the differences in meaning and worth among those values. A weak score indicates that your spiritual potentials are not very well developed, but you still have a great opportunity to draw out your potentials and make them actual in your life. Go back your Profiles and find the items you distorted. To do this, first find the items that you ranked incorrectly on each part of your Profile(s) by comparing your rankings to the correct order of rankings given in Chapter Seven. Distortions will be single digit items that you ranked as double digit, or double digit items ranked as single digit. Discuss any unclear items with your spiritual guide or counselor, and try to develop a better understanding of and appreciation for why these items were distorted, for why you confused good with bad. Target how to recognize, understand, and distinguish between positive and negative spiritual values, and try to become more conscious of how and why you distorted some value items in your personal ranking.

11. Spiritual Balance, (DIF₂%), Result Form 2, Line 11

The score on Line 11 measures the overall quality of your personal religious or Christian values involvement with all three dimensions of spiritual value. This score refers to your general or overall personal spiritual attitude or stance. In both parts of the two Profiles, the 18 items can be separated into nine positive and nine negative values. Due to the mathematical nature of the forced ranking system, there cannot be more positive deviations than negative ones. However, the negative deviations will often make up the largest part of your total Differentiation or DIF_2 score. This score is a mathematical representation of your total set of negative deviations as a percentage of your total DIF_2 score. This percentage reveals the overall quality of your personal religious or Christian values involvement. The greater the percentage of negativity, the greater is your lack of understanding of and participation in spiritual values. This correlates with varying degrees of personal spiritual unhappiness that can range from inflexibility to severe spiritual depression. The meanings of your scores are as follows.

Excellent development: An excellent score (from *50% to 54%*) indicates almost *complete* understanding and personal involvement with all 18 personal religious or Christian values, with very few if any deviations. An excellent score means that you ranked the items so that all 18 are where they should be, or very close to it. This indicates openness, flexibility, and versatility with regard to all aspects of your personal involvement in your spiritual lifestyle. You have strong inner spiritual convictions, controls, and resources; and you have the ability to work in harmony with and feel that you are an integral part of the spiritual world around and inside you. You tend to be a dynamic and flexible person who has developed a spiritual coping style that greatly enhances your life. Scores at this level are problem free and show a very high level of spiritual development.

Strong development: A strong score (from *55% to 60%*) indicates a relatively clear understanding of and *fairly close* personal involvement with religious or Christian values. Scores at this level may indicate that you personally identify more with one or more of the spiritual value items than with the others. Scores at this level do not mean that you have any serious problems, but they may show you where you could intensify your efforts and involvement. Review your greatest deviations by comparing your rankings with the correct rankings given in Chapter Seven. This may show you where to apply more effort in order to achieve a more developed and balanced involvement with all dimensions of spiritual value.

Average development: Average scores (from *61% to 65%*) indicate an average understanding of and a *somewhat close* personal involvement with religious or Christian values. Most religious and Christian believers score at this level. Many religious people are simply not aware of the differences of meaning and worth among the 18 personal spiritual values. This profiling process should help you to become more aware of these differences for the sake of better developing your spiritual potentials. For improvement, go back to your Profile(s) and compare your rankings with the correct rankings given in Chapter Seven. Then, look at your items with the greatest deviations, and focus on those that are most out of line. You should devote time and effort to understanding and better appreciating these values.

Fair development: Fair scores (from *66% to 70%*) indicate some degree of unclarity about, and/or a *slightly distant* personal involvement with (*i.e.* a slight noninvolvement with) religious or Christian values. Fair scores indicate some degree of spiritual inflexibility and distance, ranging from unhappiness with certain aspects of your religious life to severe depression and actual withdrawal from the spiritual community. Scores at this level present you with an opportunity to improve and to develop your spiritual potentials. For improvement, go back to your Profile(s), and compare your rankings with the correct rankings given in Chapter Seven. Then look at your items with the greatest deviations, and focus on those that are most out of line. You should devote more time and effort to understanding and better appreciating these neglected spiritual values. Discuss these values with your spiritual guide or counselor, pray about them, and concentrate more on them on a daily basis.

Weak development: A weak score (*71 % or greater*) indicates a lack of clarity about and/or a *very distant* personal involvement with (*i.e* a noninvolvement with) religious or Christian values. Your score may mean that you did not pay close attention to the individual value items when filling out the Profile, or that you simply do not understand the differences of meaning and worth expressed by those values. Weak scores indicate that your personal spiritual involvement is not very well developed and that you lack receptivity or responsiveness to values of a spiritual nature. You may have experienced an event that caused you to withdraw from, become depressed over, or even to feel and express personal hostility toward spiritual values. Recognizing this presents you with a great opportunity to refocus on your spiritual potentials, to embracing them as actual and positive forces in your life. For improvement, go back to your Profile(s) and compare your rankings with the correct rankings given in Chapter Seven. Then look at your items with the greatest deviations, and focus on those that are most out of line. You should devote more time and effort to understanding and better appreciating these values. You might write them down and read them several times a day or regularly and deliberately express these values in thoughts and sentences. Pray about these value items, and work toward becoming more conscious and appreciative of them. Think about how involving or re-involving yourself in all spiritual value dimensions will add value to your life.

Part III: Combined Values, Result Form 3

The scores for Part III of the Religious and/or the Christian Value Profiles result from comparing your Part I scores to your Part II scores. In almost all cases, scores on Part I will be different from scores on Part II. Result Form 3, Line 1, interprets the general or overall meaning of your Part I scores (DIF_1) when compared to the overall meaning of your Part II scores (DIF$_2$). This comparison measures the degree of your *spiritual maturity and harmony*.

The overall DIF scores break down into their Dim-I, Dim-E, and Dim-S components, so three more interpretive elements are provided to cover the differences in Part I versus Part II scores in each of the three spiritual value dimensions. Discussions below of lines 2, 4, and 6 will help you to understand where your spiritual immaturity may presently be anchored or stuck, where you may be experiencing spiritual tension or irritability, and what you can do to overcome these problems and move toward greater spiritual maturity and harmony.

1. Social/Personal Religious and/or Christian Values, (DIF$_1$ / DIF$_2$), Result Form 3, Line 1

The score on Line 1 measures the harmony or discord of your religious values by comparing how you ranked the religious and/or Christian values in Part I with how you ranked them in Part II. The Part I rankings are according to the degree of goodness or badness (ranging from best to worst) that you judged each of the 18 items to have. The Part II rankings of how the 18 value statements apply to your own life range from most agreement to greatest disagreement. If you ranked the two parts according to different criteria, your scores on one part will be very different from your scores on the other part. Your combined score reveals the absolute difference between the two parts. To obtain this score, we subtract the lowest from the highest Differentiation score (DIF$_1$ and DIF$_2$ on Line 11) on your first two Result Forms. The best score results when both DIFs are the same. A "fair" score involving a difference of 22 or more points indicates that you have a maturity problem in your spiritual development, that you are somewhat unsettled or unsure about some of your spiritual values, and that you are likely experiencing some degree of spiritual irritability, frustration, or tension. The meanings of your scores are as follows.

Excellent development: An excellent score (between *0 and 7*) indicates an almost *complete harmony* between your value judgments about religious or Christian values located outside yourself, and your value judgments about the religious or Christian values operative in your own personal life. Your objective "better or worse" value judgments are in accord with your personal "agree or disagree" value judgments. The best scores indicate an excellent level or degree of spiritual maturity and harmony. Excellent scores mean that you are using most of your spiritual potentials, both on the outside and within yourself, and that you have settled or resolved most if not all of your religious value questions. Scores at this level do not indicate any problems; they show a very balanced level of inner and outer spiritual development. Of course, if both of your DIF scores fall at the average or lower level, even if they are the same or very close to equal, you could benefit from bringing one or more spiritual value dimension into sharper focus, both externally and internally.

Strong development: Strong scores (from *8 to 14*) indicate *fairly close harmony* between the religious or Christian values in your social world and those within your own personal life. Scores at this level indicate that one of the Differentiation (DIF) scores shows somewhat stronger development than the other. This does not mean that you have any serious problems, but the difference reveals that you still have room to improve your understanding of and appreciation for either social (external) or personal (internal) religious or Christian values; it shows you where to target your efforts for spiritual growth.

Average development: Average scores (between *15 and 21*) indicate only a *somewhat harmonious* relation between social (external) and personal (internal) religious or Christian values. Most religious people score at this level. Many people are most familiar with social religious or Christian values and less aware of the internal values that constitute and guide their own spiritual lives. A minority of religious people will have the reverse pattern. This profiling process should help you become more aware of the differences between social and personal religious or Christian values so you can clarify how and what you value and further develop your own spiritual maturity. For improvement, look at the relation between the two Differentiation (DIF) scores (on Line 11 of your first two Result Forms) and then focus on the weakest one, the one most to the right. Try to devote more time and effort to understanding and appreciate the value items that correspond to this weakest DIF score.

Fair development: Fair scores (between *22 and 28*) indicate *disharmonious* or conflicting relations between the Differentiation (DIF) scores of Part I and those of Part II (on Line 11 of your first two Result Forms), that is, between your external and your internal spiritual values. This score discloses that you have some maturity problems, as indicated by the difference between the two DIF scores. Scores at this level present you with an opportunity to improve and develop your own spiritual maturity. Go back to Result Forms 1 and 2, find the Differentiation score (DIF_1 or DIF_2),[7] with the greatest deviation, the one most to the right on Line 11, and study the corresponding value items, resolving to become more familiar with them. Discuss these values with your spiritual guide, counselor, or teacher, and practice paying more attention to them.

Weak development: Weak scores (*29 and above*) indicate *very disharmonious* or conflicting relations between your Differentiation scores (DIF_1 and DIF_2) on Line 11 of your first two Result Forms, that is, between your external and internal spiritual values. Your score may mean that you did not pay close attention to the individual value items when filling out the Profile, or that you simply do not understand how those values differ in meaning and worth. Your spiritual maturity is not very well developed, but you have a great opportunity to draw out your spiritual potentials and make them actual in your life. If your DIF_1 is very good and your DIF_2 is not, you will experience spiritual tension and disharmony because your spiritual concern is centered on values outside yourself rather than on your own life. If your DIF_2 is very good and your DIF_1 is not, you are much more focused on spiritual values in your own personal life, while being less concerned about what goes on around you. Scores at this level indicate a lack of understanding of, or a fear of engagement and involvement with religious or Christian values outside yourself. Remember, Jesus said, "Do not be afraid, I have set before you an open door—come in." Fear of involvement is a common problem, and it will disappear as soon as you consciously and effortfully embrace all dimensions of religious or Christian value. Go back to Result Forms 1 and 2, find the Differentiation score (DIF_1 or DIF_2), with the greatest deviation, the one most to the right on Line 11, and study the corresponding value items. Resolving to become more familiar with them, discuss them with your spiritual guide, counselor, or teacher, and practice paying more attention to them.

2. Intrinsic Harmony
(Dim-I$_1$ / Dim-I$_2$), Result Form 3, Line 2

The score on Line 2 measures the degree of your *intrinsic* spiritual maturity based on the absolute difference between your intrinsic dimension ($Dim-I_1$ and $Dim-I_2$) scores on Parts I and II. It reveals the harmony or discord between your judgments about the devotional values in Part I compared to your agreement and active involvement with the being/feeling values as expressed in Part II. This score is the first of three scores that reflect the degree of your spiritual maturity or immaturity. Immaturity scores indicate that you are experiencing some degree of conflict or frustration. Your spiritual irritability may have several sources, and the difference between social and personal intrinsic spiritual values examined here may be only one of them.

Excellent development: Excellent scores (between *0 and 3*) indicate almost *complete harmony* between your social intrinsic devotional and your personal being/feeling religious or Christian values. This score indicates that you ranked the items in both Parts such that your social devotional values and your internal being/feeling values are relatively equal in number of deviations (between 0 and 3 points of difference). This level shows a symmetry between judging objective devotional values and your personal involvement with being/feeling values. This score suggests objectivity and maturity with regard to your general understanding of and appreciation for anyone else's relationship to God and your own personal relationship with God. Scores at this level are problem free and indicate spiritual maturity with no irritability or conflicts.

Strong development: A strong score (between *4 and 7*) indicates a *fairly harmonious* relation between your social devotional and your internal personal being/feeling religious or Christian values. This score indicates a difference of only 4 to 7 points between your intrinsic dimensions (Dim-I_1 and Dim-I_2) on Parts I and II. One or more of the intrinsic items may be out of line and ranked with an inappropriate degree of emotional loading. This indicates that you identify strongly with one or two items, but to some extent you neglect the remaining intrinsic devotional or being/feeling values. Scores at this level do not mean that you have any serious problems, but they can show you where to concentrate your effort to restore a more balanced integration and to reduce potential intrinsic religious conflict or discord.

Average development: An average score (*8 to 11* points of difference) indicates a *somewhat harmonious* relation between your social devotional and your personal being/feeling religious or Christian intrinsic values. Most religious and Christian people probably will score at this level. According to this score, your personal ranking reveals a positive emotional inclination to favor either the social observer point of view or the personal involvement point of view on intrinsic spiritual values. Try to gain or regain focus on the intrinsic dimension (Dim-I_1 or Dim-I_2) items with the greatest deviations, those most to the right, by examining the specific scores that create this difference. Compare your rankings on your Profiles with the correct rankings given in Chapter Seven. You should focus or refocus on the social devotional or personal being/feeling values that were less valued or devalued in your personal ranking. Discuss these with your spiritual guide or counselor, pay more attention to them, and try to apply them better in your own life in order to get them into better balance.

Fair development: A fair score (between *12 and 15*) indicates disharmonious or conflicting relations between your two intrinsic dimensions (Dim-I_1 and Dim-I_2) of religious or Christian values. This score suggests that you experience some degree of discord or frustration with either the social devotional or the personal being/feeling value items. This score includes a difference range of 12 to 15 points. Go to Result Forms 1 and 2, find the Dim-I_1 or Dim-I_2 scores (Line 2 on both Result Forms) with the greatest deviation, the one most to the right on the page. Compare your rankings on your Profiles with the correct rankings given in Chapter Seven. You should focus or refocus on the social devotional or personal being/feeling values that were less valued or devalued in your personal ranking. Discuss these with your spiritual guide or counselor, pay more attention to them, and apply them better in your own life to get them into better balance.

Weak development: A weak score (*16 or above*) indicates *very disharmonious* or conflicting relations between your social devotional and your personal being/feeling religious or Christian values. Your score may mean that you did not pay close attention to the individual value items when filling out your Profile(s), or that you simply do not understand the differences between social and internal intrinsic values. Scores at this level involve a difference of 16 or more points, an extreme difference. Go to Result Forms 1 and 2, find the Dim-I_1 or Dim-I_2 scores (Line 2 on both Result Forms) with the greatest deviation, the one most to the right on the page. Compare your rankings on your Profiles with the correct rankings given in Chapter Seven. Focus or refocus on the social devotional or personal being/feeling values that were less valued or devalued in your personal rankings. Discuss these with your spiritual guide or counselor, pay more attention to them, and try to apply them better in your own life in order to get them into better balance.

3. Extrinsic Harmony, (Dim-E_1 / Dim-E_2), Result Form 3, Line 3

The score on Line 4 measures the degree of your *extrinsic* spiritual maturity based on the absolute difference between your extrinsic dimension (Dim-E_1 and Dim-E_2) scores on Parts I and II of your

Profile(s). See Line 4 on your two previous Result Forms. It reveals the harmony or disharmony between your evaluation of the practical spiritual values in Part I as compared to your personal involvement with the doing/acting values of Part II.

This score is the second of three scores that reveal the source of your spiritual maturity or immaturity. Immaturity scores indicate that you experience some degree of spiritual conflict and frustration. Your irritation may have several sources, and difference between your two extrinsic perspectives may be only one of them.

Excellent development: Excellent scores (from *0 to 3*) indicate *complete harmony* between your social practical and your personal doing/acting Christian or religious values. This score means that you ranked the items in both parts of your Profile(s) so that the general practical values and the personal doing values are relatively equal in number of deviations, having only 0 to 3 points of difference. This level shows a symmetry between your evaluation of practical spiritual values as an external observer and your personal involvement with doing/acting spiritual values. This score suggests objectivity, maturity, and harmony with respect to your understanding of and appreciation for participation in spiritual activities by other people and your own personal involvement with doing/acting spiritual values. Scores at this level are problem free and indicate extrinsic spiritual maturity with no irritability.

Strong development: Strong scores (between *4 and 7*) indicate a *fairly harmonious* relation between social, practical, and personal doing/acting religious or Christian values. This score involves a difference of from 4 to 7 points between your two extrinsic dimension (Dim-E$_1$ and Dim-E$_2$) rankings. One or more of your extrinsic items was out of line and was ranked with some degree of distorting emotional loading. This difference indicates a stronger identification with, understanding of, and appreciation for one or two items, while to some extent ignoring one or two other practical or doing/acting values. Scores at this level do not mean that you have any serious problems, but they may show you where to concentrate your effort to restore more balanced practical integration and to avoid extrinsic spiritual conflicts and frustrations.

Average development: An average score (between *8 and 11* points of difference) indicates a *somewhat harmonious* relation between social practical and personal doing/acting religious or Christian values. Most religious people score at this level. This score, derived from your personal rankings, discloses a positive emotional inclination to favor either the external social observer perspective on practical spiritual values, or personal involvement with doing/acting spiritual values. Try to gain or regain focus on the extrinsic dimension (Dim-E$_1$ or Dim-E$_2$) with the largest deviation, the one most to the right, that creates this difference. Then focus or refocus on the social practical or the personal doing/acting values that are out of line in your ranking.

Fair development: A fair score (between *12 and 15*) identifies a *disharmonious* relation between the extrinsic (Dim-E$_1$ and Dim-E$_2$) religious or Christian values on Parts I and II of your Profile(s). This score indicates that you experience some irritability or frustration with either the social practical or the personal doing/acting value items. This score involves a difference of from 12 to 15 points. Go to Result Forms 1 and 2, find the Dim-E$_1$ or Dim-E$_2$ scores (Line 4 on both Result Forms) with the greatest deviation, the one most to the right of the page. Compare your rankings on your Profiles with the correct rankings given in Chapter Seven. Focus or refocus on the social practical or the personal doing/acting values that were less valued or devalued in your personal rankings. Discuss these with your spiritual guide or counselor, pay more attention to them, and try to apply them better in your own life in order to get them into better balance.

Weak development: A weak score (*16* or above) indicates a *very disharmonious* relation between the practical and the personal doing/acting religious or Christian values on the two parts of your Profile(s). Your score may mean that you did not pay close attention to the individual value items when filling out the Profile(s), or that you simply do not understand the differences between internal personal and external social extrinsic values. Scores at this level involve a difference of 16 or more points, an extreme difference. Go to previous Result Forms 1 and 2, find the Dim-E_1 or Dim-E_2 score (Line 4 on both Result Forms) with the greatest deviation, the one most to the right on the page. Compare your rankings on your Profiles with the correct rankings given in Chapter Seven. Focus or refocus on the social practical or the personal doing/acting values that were less valued or devalued in your personal rankings. Discuss these with your spiritual guide or counselor, pay more attention to them, and try to apply them better in your own life in order to get them into better balance and reduce the extrinsic spiritual disharmony that you are experiencing.

4. Systemic Harmony, (Dim-S_1 / Dim-S_2), Result Form 3, Line 4

The score on Line 6 measures the harmony or discord indicated by comparing your evaluation of social conceptual values in Part I with your personal involvement with thinking/believing values in Part II. This score measures the degree of your *systemic* spiritual maturity based on the absolute difference between your two systemic dimension (Dim-S_1 and Dim-S_2) scores. This score is the third of three scores that reflect the source of your spiritual maturity or immaturity. Immaturity scores indicate that you are experiencing some degree of spiritual frustration and conflict. Your spiritual irritations may have several sources, and the systemic source examined here may be only one of them.

Excellent development: An excellent score (between 0 and 3) indicates *complete harmony* between your social conceptual/doctrinal and your personal thinking/believing Christian or religious values. This score means that you ranked the items in both parts so that your social conceptual values and the personal thinking/believing values have a relatively equal number of deviations, with only 0 to 3 points of difference. This indicates a symmetry between your evaluation of social conceptual values and your own personal involvement with thinking/believing values. This score suggests objectivity and maturity with regard to your understanding of and appreciation for the doctrines, quests, and beliefs of other religious persons and your own personal involvement with theology and doctrines. Scores at this level are problem free and indicate spiritual maturity with no disharmony.

Strong development: Strong scores (between *4 and 7*) indicate a *fairly harmonious* relation between your social conceptual and your personal thinking/believing religious or Christian values. This score involves a difference of only 7 to 14 points between your two systemic dimension (Dim-S$_1$ and Dim-S$_2$) scores. One or more of the systemic or doctrinal items may be out of line and ranked with an inappropriate degree of emotional loading, indicating a stronger identification with one or two items, while to some extent ignoring or discounting one or two other social conceptual or personal thinking/believing values. Scores at this level do not mean that you have any serious problems, but they may show you where to concentrate your effort to achieve or restore an even more balanced integration.

Average development: An average score (*8 to 11* points of difference) indicates a *somewhat harmonious* relation between your social conceptual and your personal thinking/believing religious or Christian values. Most religious people score at this level. This score means that your ranking involved a positive emotional inclination to favor either social observer evaluation of conceptual spiritual values or your own personal involvement with thinking/believing spiritual values. Try to gain or regain focus on the systemic dimension (Dim-S$_1$ or Dim-S$_2$) items with the greatest deviation, the one most to the right; and compare your ranking of the individual items with their correct rankings given in Chapter Seven. Then focus or refocus on the social conceptual or the personal thinking/believing value items that are being devalued in your personal ranking. Greater awareness is the best first step toward improvement.

Fair development: A fair score (between 12 and 15) indicates *disharmonious* or conflicting relations between your systemic dimension (Dim-S$_1$ and Dim-S$_2$) religious or Christian value scores on the two parts of your Profile(s). This score suggests that you experience some frustrations with or conflicts between your social conceptual and your personal thinking/believing spiritual value items. This score involves a difference of from 12 to 15 points. Go back to Result Forms 1 and 2, find the Dim-S$_1$ or Dim-S$_2$ score on Line 6 with the greatest deviation, the one most to the right; and then compare your ranking of the individual items with their correct rankings as given in Chapter Seven. Then focus or refocus on the social conceptual or the personal thinking/believing value items that were devalued in your personal ranking. Try to develop a deeper understanding of and appreciation for them, and seek guidance about how to utilize them better in your personal life. This should help you to get the Dim-S$_1$ and the Dim-S$_2$ back into balance with each other and reduce the systemic spiritual discords or conflicts that you are now experiencing.

Weak development: A weak score indicates *very disharmonious* relations between your social conceptual and your personal thinking/believing religious or Christian values. Your score may mean that you did not pay close attention to the individual value items when filling out the Profile, or that you simply do not understand the differences in these systemic conceptual values. Scores at this level involve a difference of 16 or more points, an extreme difference. Go back to Result Forms 1 and 2, find the Dim-S$_1$ or Dim-S$_2$ score on Line 6 with the greatest deviation, the one most to the right; and then compare your ranking of the individual items with their correct rankings given in Chapter Seven. Then focus or refocus on the social conceptual or the personal thinking/believing value items that were devalued in your personal ranking. Try to develop a deeper understanding of and appreciation for them, and seek guidance about how to utilize them better in your personal life. This should help you to get the Dim-S$_1$ and the Dim-S$_2$ back into balance with each other and reduce the systemic spiritual discords or conflicts that you are now experiencing.

CHAPTER THREE

For Your Further Spiritual Growth and Development, Part I

In addition to developing a sense of spiritual responsibility, we actually need to be spiritually responsible. This means putting our religious principles into practice. This chapter provides specific exercises and recommendations for further spiritual development in all dimensions: conceptually, by increasing and improving your knowledge and understanding; practically, by putting your spiritual understanding into positive action; and intrinsically, by developing a closer and more intimate personal relationship with God, and more love and compassion for our fellow human beings. Individuals who have developed a firm faith, grounded in understanding, and rooted in daily practice, are generally healthier and much better at coping with adversity than those who have not. Implementing the teachings of your own religion in your daily life is most important, and this means more than merely attending churches or visiting temples, shrines, and holy places. Also, religious teachings are of little value if they remain at the intellectual level and do not enter the heart.

Our sincere efforts to transform ourselves spiritually make us genuine religious practitioners. Conversion alone will not make us better persons; it does not automatically make us more disciplined, compassionate, or warm-hearted. We must concentrate on transforming ourselves spiritually through the practice of restraint, virtue, and compassion, while remaining firmly committed to our faith. Ultimately, our religion should facilitate and enhance our love, compassion, forgiveness, patience, and other moral and spiritual gifts.

If we neglect these, religion will be of no real help to us. Until we put our own spiritual teachings into practice, we will never be taken seriously, and this entails setting a good example.

Time passes quickly, and we cannot turn the clock back and start over. All we can do is use the present well. Then, when our final day on earth comes, we should be able to look back and see that we have lived full, productive, and meaningful lives. We appeal to our readers to make the rest of their lives as meaningful as possible. Do this by engaging in spiritual practices sincerely and with persistence. The saints are those who persevere in righteous and Godly living. If you persevere, then, gradually, with God's help, your habits of and attitudes toward inner peace, godliness, happiness, and kindness will be reordered and strengthened.

This chapter tries to help you understand better and internalize *positive* religious and Christian values. Possible consequences of overvaluing or undervaluing positive spiritual values are also explored. Through emphasizing positive values, you can make great strides in developing your spiritual potentials and make them real and actual in your daily life.

This chapter and the next offer a number of spiritual exercises for strengthening your religious and/or Christian values. Only one or two of the exercises may be beneficial for you, but we hope that more will be. We diligently try to cover a broad spectrum, so you should have a good chance of finding exercises that can really help you to develop your spiritual potentials further. Most if not all of these exercises may be beneficial to you if used as daily devotionals or meditations.

In addition to the exercises, references from both the *Old* and the *New Testaments* of the Bible are provided. Value-laden biblical references are listed to help you deepen your understanding, and you are encouraged to look them up and reflect upon them as you continue your study. Jews recognize the *Old Testament* as scriptural; Christians accept both the *Old* and the *New Testaments*; and Islam's *Koran* recognizes many *Old* and *New Testament* figures as authentic messengers from God. But what was their message? What religious values did they sponsor?

This book is not intended to cover all spiritual topics. It is dedicated to helping people better understand and apply spiritual values through the formal system of axiology, the science of value and valuation. The insights you get from this material should help you in your overall quest to develop more of your spiritual potentials, to grow your own spiritual branches higher and your roots deeper.

In many ways, children are taught something about right and wrong. They first discover that if they do what is right and develop good habits, they are praised and rewarded; and if they do what is wrong and develop bad habits, they are likely to be punished. This process also applies to religious and spiritual learning and teaching. Early in life, children are also taught the religious beliefs and practices of their parents by their by words and examples, and most children accept these parental words and deeds as their spiritual foundations. In addition, their religious community significantly influences their religious beliefs and moral attitudes and behaviors. Children may attend religious or church schools and regular worship services where they learn about the scriptures and their religious and ethical teachings and practices, and they are usually provided with religious literature written for their level of understanding. In a broader religious community, they they learn more about God and are introduced to religious guides about how to act like the Ten Commandments and the Sermon on the Mount. Eventually, they refine, select, and internalize what they have been taught and what they have been empowered to think about and discover for themselves. Against this background, please consider the following features of *systemic, extrinsic, and intrinsic* values and valuations as applied to religion and spirituality.

The *systemic* value dimensions of any religion, including your own, are its mental or conceptual structures and meanings. This is the value realm of ordered religious understanding, reflecting, knowing, contemplating, critical thinking, teaching, and believing. It includes an understanding of God's laws, religious truths, moral guidelines, God's commands and instructions, knowledge or information about God and divine things, the history of our particular religion, its ritual or sacramental patterns, respect for spiritual authority, and the established disciplines, guidelines, rules, policies, and procedures of our faith. It is the mental foundation of and for our spiritual being, acting, and growing. It challenges us to study, learn, and achieve deeper spiritual wisdom and understanding.

The *extrinsic* value dimensions of religion are its physical and behavioral components. Among other things, this realm of value includes religious books, buildings, shrines, ornaments, and accessories, as well as acting on religious and moral convictions about such things as justice and the well being of others. Its doing/acting focus centers around participating in religious activities, services, rituals, programs, practices, and projects. This includes going to religious services, taking part in religious ceremonies and practices, actually reading and studying the scriptures, doing the works of justice, love, mercy, and devotion, developing good habits, and using our physical and social skills and initiatives to serve God and bring others to God. It encompasses acting out our understanding of our place and our proper roles in our society, especially in our religious community, as well as being a good steward all the time of our God-given talents, time, and possessions.

The *intrinsic* value dimensions of religion include the inner devotional and emotional or feeling aspects of spiritual life such as reaching out to others in love, hope, compassion, forgiveness, and reconciliation. To this value level belong our recognition of and keen sense of God's presence everywhere all the time, and our loving God and all of God's creation with our whole being. It involves being attuned to the still small voice of God within us, the voice of universal conscience, which is an integral part of our being. It involves being attuned to the inner promptings that are unique to our own individuality. At this value level, we recognize all others, not just a chosen few, and not just ourselves, as children of God; and we act accordingly with empathy, compassion, kindness, forgiveness, mercy, faith, hope, and love. In the intrinsic dimension, we profoundly live out our lives before and in the presence of God so that our life becomes a prayer, and thus we pray without ceasing. We live constantly in communion with God and keenly experience God's presence with us.

Use the following exercises in connection with Part I of the Religious and Christian Value Profiles.

I. Exercises for Part I, Compositions

1. Devotional Triad

The three positive intrinsic devotional value items in Part I of the RVP and the CVP are:

CVP
Jesus, our Redeemer
Rejoicing in Christlike living
Loving scriptural truths

RVP
God's love for us
The glory of God in creation or nature
Total devotion to religious truths

Spiritual Development Opportunity: Devotional values are *intrinsic* values or valuations that express intimate relations between God and us, our sense of the presence of God everywhere and always, as well as in special times and places, and the loving communion and fellowship of God's people (all people). If you ranked the above items close to the top, your scores are problem free. If you ranked other items so far ahead of these that your score is fair or weak, you could benefit from bringing this dimension into better perspective and balance with the other value dimensions. The two kinds of ranking errors that might arise are: overvaluation and undervaluation. If you overvalued or undervalued any items on your Profile, you may have some but not all of the following problems, and then only to a degree. Or you may not have these problems at all if you misunderstood the item(s) or the ranking process itself.

Overvaluation
Overvaluing the devotional aspects of the intrinsic realm means that you attach too much worth to intrinsic devotional values. In the absolute sense, this is not possible, for nothing is higher than the intrinsic. But

in relation to other dimensions of value, this is possible, because you can be so focused on the intrinsic realm that you seriously neglect extrinsic and systemic moral and religious values. From an absolute perspective, intrinsic value items cannot be ranked higher than 1, 2 and 3, although 2 can be ranked as 1, and 3 can be ranked as 1 or 2. Over- or under valuation and development in any dimension is not possible without over- or under valuation and development in some other dimension. If you overvalued the intrinsic, then to some extent, depending on your degree of deviation, you may have some or all of the following moral and spiritual problems, though this is by no means an exhaustive list:

- You tend to think that the primary focus of religion is or should be on God's redeeming love, and you are so conscious of the reflection of God within yourself and in your surroundings that you maintain a constant state of devotional awe and reverence, mainly in a personal or feeling sense, rather than focusing on religious principles or knowledge or participating in your religious community by sharing and doing practical works of service to others. Your religion may not get translated into everyday learning, doing, and living.

- Your own approach to spirituality and morality may be primarily feeling-based, romantic, or sentimental.

- You may believe that having religious faith primarily involves feeling good inside.

- You tend to believe that the best religious and ethical approach is emotional and feeling-based, as opposed to being highly structured and disciplined, or clearly defined or refined by thinking.

Undervaluation
Undervaluation or negative evaluation of positive intrinsic devotional value items means that you do not see the value in them that they

deserve. If you disvalue or undervalue positive intrinsic items, this means that to some extent, depending on your degree of deviation, you might have some or all of the following problems, though this list is by no means exhaustive:

- You may lack clear knowledge of and appreciation for some, perhaps all, of the areas identified above that belong to the devotional, intrinsic dimension because you think the primary focus of religion should be action-based or founded on religious principles and knowledge, rather than devotionally based.

- To some degree, it may be difficult for you to establish and maintain close, intimate, and loving personal relationships with God and with other people.

- You may have difficulty focusing on devotional values like quiet reverent awe or gratefulness for God's redeeming love, because you are overly focused on religious activities or on increasing your religious knowledge.

- You may be in some stage of despair, depression, or anxiety, which could make it difficult for you to maintain strong faith and hope, or trust God for help, or feel that you are safely in his hands, or experience God's peace and joy within you.

Can you think of other problems that might arise from over- or undervaluing intrinsic spiritual values? If you have any of the above problems, what steps do you think you could take to correct them? Ministers, religious counselors, or guides may be of help. You may be able to improve your appreciation and internalization of devotional values by engaging in one or all of the following exercises.

General Religious Exercises:

1. Imagine your consciousness as an arrow, and focus all attention on its point. The past is dead; the future is not yet; there is only this moment. Then point this arrow to your spiritual feelings of

awe, reverence, adoration, trust, love, commitment, and faithfulness to God. Practice this several times a day. Practice being quiet in solitude; consider that solitude is not loneliness; it is alone-ness. It isn't negative, but positive. It is not the experience that others are not with me, but that "I Am" is present. Let everything else fade from your mind, and feel your own presence before the living God. Feel the sheer joy of breathing, of being, of participating in existence, of existing as a part of God's creation, of living out your life before God. Just to be is a miracle; and existing with, in, and before God is a fantastic blessing. Prayer and meditation are all about the art and practice of changing loneliness into aloneness and solitariness into blissful communion. Also practice reflecting on the higher values that religious people embrace: joy, peace, love, forgiveness, mercy, justice, honesty, humility, truth, goodness, and beauty. What is the secret of the beautiful lilies in the field? The answer is simple: they live in this moment; this moment is everything; nothing is behind or ahead. Relish this moment in God's presence with your total being. Be still, and know that God is God. If you desire inner peace, happiness, and serenity, don't postpone your life until tomorrow. Live now, as well as in the past and in the future; but don't live only in the past or only for the future. No merely quantitative change can really transform your life. You need a new birth as a new being, a qualitative transformation of your existence. Your life can become full of goodness and light. You can have inner richness if you practice squeezing all the juice out of each moment.

2. Try to develop more empathy for and understanding of the devotional values of other religious people. This requires "feeling-your-way" into their devotional values and practices. This cannot be done with the mind alone; use the feelings of your heart also. Read over the above devotional value items again, put your mind in neutral, then try to discern and experience intense reverence and adoration as a person of a different faith might experience them. Try to develop a spirituality that embraces others; and pray that your concern for and acceptance of your fellow human beings, regardless of race, nationality, culture, or creed, may lead to deeper

understanding, mutual respect, and peace on earth. Be secure enough in your own religious values so that you can rejoice in the religious values of others and not feel threatened by them. You can be much happier and more fulfilled in God's world by appreciating and being more tolerant of the views and opinions of others. God works everywhere in many mysterious ways. Focus on valuing the fullness of creation and of life, your own and that of others, not just on valuing beliefs alone. When you walk in nature, taste her purity, observe her beauty, experience her strength, and know that you are a part of it all. Practice seeing yourself and others as "part of" or "one with" instead of as "outside of," "separate from," or "other than." You belong to this universe and this planet, and what you do affects the value experiences of other lives. Your respect for yourself should come with a respect for environment, property, other people, different cultures, the world of nature, and God. Ask God to help you value the richness and diversity of value or goodness in others and in the world. If you can develop a spiritual unity and bond with all of creation, you can celebrate differences as well as similarities, and you can accept and embrace others more easily. Let your religion be more than just believing certain doctrines; let be a total way of life. Then, perhaps to your surprise, your own life will be much richer and more abundant.

3. Think of God as the sun—always present, always available to you. The sun rises each morning, its light shines, and buds open and become flowers. The light helps flower buds to open, but the flowering and fragrance come from within the buds themselves. God, the Creator, is like the sun and its light; and we are like the buds of flowers. God's presence makes us aware of the moral, religious, and personal potentials that are within us, and God helps to fulfill them. Think of yourself as a sunflower, and think of God as the sun; wherever the sun moves, the sunflower moves that way. Like the sun, the sunflower is also a symbol, a metaphor, for the disciple who is sensitive and responsive to God. See the light, and open yourself to living, flowering, caring, and sharing. Other people and the birds are blessed by the sunflower and its

seeds as well as by the sun itself. Think about the religious significance of this analogy: It is much easier for us to look directly at the sunflower than at the sun.

4. Try reflecting on the totality of space, which, like God, is everywhere and contains all; but nothing (except God) contains all of space. Space penetrates and constitutes everything, but it never interferes. It penetrates without trespassing. It is non-violent, non-intrusive, and accepts all, the sinner and the saint, the good and the bad, the beautiful and the ugly, the sunshine and the rain. It is open and available to all, whether or not they know it or consciously want to partake. It protects but never patronizes. It surrounds and permeates you and everything else within and without. These are also qualities of God, who is unobtrusively present everywhere. Black and white clouds come and go, but space endures and makes a place for them. Space is ancient, yet as fresh as dewdrops. When you have time, lie down on the ground, and look toward the sky and all around. Let all of space be the object of your contemplation, whether you are praying or meditating. Sometimes open your eyes, sometimes close them, and realize that space itself is as vast within as it is without. You are standing on the threshold of, and are a part of, all of spacetime, and there are two ways to dissolve into the rest of it. If you dissolve into external space, this is devotional prayer, adoration, and communion; if you dissolve into inner space, this is mystical union and meditation, which can become complete identification with God. You are the dividing line; and when you disappear or dissolve, the two spaces become one, and God radiates through you.

5. If God loves you, what does that mean? It means first that God knows who you are, everything that you are, and all that you experience and do. From God, none of your secrets, joys, or sorrows are hidden. It also means that God not only knows you but is empathetically one with you. God takes your total being into his being and identifies with everything that you are going through. God is with you, in you, and for you, no matter what. In return, God also wants you to respond to him, to love him and

all that he loves as he loves you, to unite with him with all your heart, soul, mind, and strength, and to be loyal to and loving toward all his other loved ones, even if they are very different. God desires mutual union with all his loved ones, including you. God wants all obstacles to this union removed, including your past sins, and even your bent toward sinning. God forgives as he loves, but he expects you to repent, ask for forgiveness, and change your errant ways. God wills your well-being, both here and hereafter. God is compassionate and suffers with you and for you when obstacles prevail within you and against you. God works with you and others to bring as much goodness out of evil as possible. He wants you to have the best life you can possibly have here and now, as well as in eternity, a life that is as rich in value as you and he, working together, can make it. Now is an integral part of eternity. God wants the unique individual that you are to be happy and fulfilled, not only in your general humanity, but also in your own distinctive personal way. God rejoices and delights in your very existence as a unique individual, in your happiness and prosperity, in your freedom to choose, and in your mental, moral, and spiritual growth. God knows everything about you, not to condemn you, but to save and love you for what you are and for what you can become. "God loves me" means all these things, and so much more; and everyone can truthfully say "God loves me."

6. Practice looking for God everywhere, and eventually you will be able to find God everywhere (except, of course, in evil!). Where do you think God is? Is he in Heaven? Is he merely in Heaven? Do you believe, with the prophet Jeremiah, that God fills heaven and earth? (Jeremiah 23:23) Can you, with the Psalmist, find the glory of God in the heavens, and in the vastness, intricacy, and beauty of our universe? (Psalms 19) Do you think that there is any place you can go to escape or hide from God? (Psalms 139:7-10) Do you really believe that your own body is a temple of God, and do you act accordingly? Can you find God in small things near at hand, in all things bright and beautiful? Is your mind trained to love God? Can you see God's creativity and closeness

in all things great and small? Can you sense or feel God's presence to some degree in everything that has being? Have you awakened to a keen personal relationship with God? If to some degree many non-human animals can love, think, make conscious choices, act sacrificially, and be devoted parents, do they also exist in the image of God? Does everything that exists reflect God in some way and to some degree? How so, or not so? Does God love all human beings, even sinners while they are yet sinners? Does God love all his creatures, all living things, all non-living things, not just human beings? If so, shouldn't we? Would our lives be richer or poorer in value if we do as God does? Even if you are not a Christian, is God, for you, as for St. Paul, the all-inclusive reality who is not far from us (or from anything) because in him we live, and move, and have our being (Acts 17:28)? Try to experience every place as a holy place, and try to make every day a holy day. Meditate on these things day and night, and be joyful that you are in God and God is in you.

You may deepen your understanding of the following intrinsic devotional values and practices by looking up, reading, and reflecting on the following *Old Testament* references:

"God's love for us," Exodus 34: 6; I. Kings 8:23; Psalms 36:5-10; 86:15; Jeremiah 31:3; Hosea 2:18-20; 11:1-4; 14:4; Psalms 36:7; Jeremiah 33:11 (In the *New Testament*, compare I. John 4:7 and 16)

"The glory of God in creation or nature," Genesis 1; Numbers 14:21; Deuteronomy 4:39; Psalms 19; 24:1-2; 104; 139:1-18; 148; Proverbs 8:1, 22-31; Isaiah 6:3; Jeremiah 23:24

"Total devotion to religious truths," Joshua 1:8; Psalms 1:1-2; 19:7-14; 119

Christian Exercises:

1. Experience for yourself the true meaning of "the communion of the saints" by associating with a loving and supportive church

group or Christian community, especially if you have not done so already. Try to find and identify yourself with a group of Christians who are actually and deeply engaged in a fellowship of love and who are striving to grow in grace and in the knowledge and love of God. No such group is perfect, but where else can you do better? With all their faults, where else can you turn to find a more caring, supportive, sincere, and devoted group of people? If you can find this elsewhere, go there! God can use us even before we have achieved perfection; otherwise, God would never be able to use any of us! Read and meditate upon the following biblical passages that deal with the loving communion of God's people: Leviticus 19:15-18; Matthew 5: 43; 22:39; Mark 12: 31; Galatians 5:24; James 2.8; I. John 4:7-21. Repeat often to yourself that you belong to and with other dedicated and like-minded people who hold and practice deep and Christlike moral and spiritual values. Romans 15:5 says, "Now the God of patience and consolation grant you to be like-minded one toward another according to Christ Jesus." A compassionate and merciful lifestyle is a sign of Christlikeness (Luke 6:36). Seek for and practice likeness to the mind of Christ as well as to the heart, soul, and life of Christ.

2. We can achieve unity in diversity by becoming more Christlike, but unity is not the same thing as uniformity. We are all different members of the one body of Christ, having unique gifts, talents, responsibilities, and personalities. Celebrating and appreciating our differences, while sharing the common goal of loving and serving God and one another, is true Christian unity. St. Paul said in Galatians 3:28 that there is no Jew or Gentile, slave or free, male or female, for we are all one in Christ Jesus. Unity, as a shared sense of history, purpose, and devotion, is very important for living meaningfully. How wonderful it is, how pleasant, when brothers and sisters live together in harmony (Psalms 133:1). Cooperation is far better than competition. By respecting and cherishing our differences as well as our similarities, we can all live fulfilled lives and dwell in peace and harmony with one another. Being a Christian means that we love our neighbors, *all*

others, all of God's children everywhere, all of our brothers and sisters under and before God. If you envy, resent, or hate others, you deeply harm yourself, for all of these are miserable emotions or states of mind; they are immense barriers to your own moral and spiritual growth as well as to the realization of the Kingdom of God on earth as it is in heaven. Hating is proof that you still live in darkness (I. John 2:9). Indifference can be as devastating as hatred. Help to make your own religious community a more disciplined, challenging, thinking, loving, caring, accepting, forgiving, comforting, compassionate, and understanding fellowship, for these are Christlike qualities. Think of some specific things that you might to do or say to help yourself and others live in imitation of Christ.

3. Practice praying for insight into devotional and spiritual values. Do not pray in the request or petitionary mode, but pray with praise and adoration. Open yourself to the presence of God in Jesus, and nurture the devotional practices through which Christians relate successfully to him. Think about God's majestic glorious splendor and all that God has done for you (Psalms 145:5). Praise God with your time (I. Chronicles 23:30). Cultivate an attitude of gratitude by giving thanks regularly, morning and evening, every time you think about God, others, and God's world. By living prayerfully with a sense of God's presence, you can pray without ceasing. Your prayers should always include thanks and praise to God for his goodness to us (Psalms 9:1-2). Prayer is an act of humble worship in which we seek God with all our hearts. Meditation involves waiting quietly and patiently before God, putting hope in God, sensing God's presence, and listening to God's wisdom (Psalms 62:1, 5); this is how to experience an intimate relationship with God. You can improve your ability to listen to God by praying regularly and waiting expectantly (Psalms 17:6; 5:3). God doesn't ask us to understand always, but he asks us to trust. Proverbs 3:5-6 reminds us, "Trust in the Lord with all thine heart and lean not unto thine own understanding. In all thy ways acknowledge him, and he shall direct thy paths." This counsel should be balanced against those scriptures that admonish us to

love God with all our minds, as well as with all our hearts, souls, and strengths.

4. Practice loving each and every individual person as another child of God, and refrain from thinking of others in the abstract as mere generic instances of "humanity," or "rationality," or "the moral law," or as only "Americans," "Whites," "Christians," or "Moslems." How should you live among your non-Christian neighbors? The whole law can be summed up in this one command: "Thou shalt love thy neighbor as thyself" (Galatians 5:14). You may ask, "Who is my neighbor?" Your neighbor is anyone who needs God's strength, mercy, forgiveness, compassion, and friendship. Luke 10:36-37 provides the answer. The person who shows mercy to the man who had fallen among thieves is the true neighbor; and Jesus says to us, as he said to his listeners, "Go, and do likewise." We should love our non-Christian neighbors, live honorably and graciously with and before them, do business with them, not shun them, be an example of godliness to them, share God's ways with them, and refuse to judge or condemn them. Judging others should be left to God, who is the ultimate instance of and model for accepting others. Romans 12: 14-18 tells us, "Bless them which persecute you; bless and curse them not. Rejoice with them that do rejoice; weep with them that weep. Be of the same mind one toward another. Mind not high things, but condescend to men of low estate. Be not wise in your own conceits. Recompense to no man evil for evil. Provide things honest in the sight of all men." Do we Christians support national policies that accord with such directives? On a personal level, do we practice what we preach? Is this The Way?

5. Growing morally and spiritually usually means changing your values, rearranging your priorities, learning to put God's Kingdom of love first in your life instead of the things of the world and/or high social standing and power over others within the world. Spiritual changes can happen in very sudden and dramatic conversion or enlightenment experiences, or they may occur more slowly in gradual, incremental, and progressive experiences of growth. Either way you are converted, you are changed into a

new person, re-centered on new values, born again as a new, more loving, and more devoted individual. Your former idolatries are "dethroned" and their power over you diminishes. New, vibrant, and deeply fulfilling meanings satiate, inspire, and sustain your soul, your mind, your heart, your strength; your life is intensely purposeful, and meaningless existence becomes a ghost of the past. You are now disposed to love God and everyone, not just your own kindred and kind. Your loves become more inclusive and universal, like God's. Your being consents to all being. Your loving is no longer limited by prejudice, hatred, selfishness, and ignorance. You achieve new ways, new levels of thinking, imagining, feeling, choosing, and acting. Your priorities now coincide with God's priorities, your values with God's values. You live in faith, hope, and love and are no longer faithless, hopeless, and loveless. You live in peace, and you study war no more. You live joyfully, even when there is sorrow. You become a new person in God through Christ. When Christlikeness becomes your total way of life, you have abundant life here and now. In Jesus, God showed us how to be fully developed spiritually and morally.

6. St. Paul said that we should be imitators of Christ (Ephesians 11:1) and of God (Ephesians 4:23; 5:1), and that Jesus left us an example that we should walk in his steps (I. Peter 2:21). Of course, we can't take these words too literally. None of us will ever be responsible for the entire universe, like God; and none of us will ever know, or love, or influence everything, as God does. Most of us wouldn't want to be poor, or homeless, or jobless, or celibate, or childless, or literally crucified, like Jesus; and we couldn't be the incarnate Son of God even if we tried! In deciding whether to marry, to take a good job, or to buy a new car, "What would Jesus do?" won't work for us if we think that we have to be *exactly* like him. Yet, we as Christians have to take this question seriously. In our own unique modern circumstances, in our own time and place, we have to discern how to be Godlike without being God, how to be Christlike without being Christ, how to bear our own

metaphorical crosses. Godliness was and is never easy to understand, much less to imitate; yet this is our challenge, your challenge. How do you think that *you* should be Christlike while still being the unique 21st Century person that you are today and that you hope to become tomorrow? "What would Jesus do?," not if you were he, but if he were you? Think hard about how you might have to change, both to be more like Christ, and to be joyful in it.

7. The *New Testament* constantly challenges us to bear our own crosses, metaphorically speaking, as Jesus literally bore his, but how far are we willing to go to be a Christlike cross-bearer? Jesus constantly bore metaphorical crosses and "died daily," to borrow some words from St. Paul, even before he faced his final literal cross and death. Lifting up the meek and lowly did not win Jesus any friends in high places because being "superior" means that others have to be "low down." Jesus loved and tried to change people with wealth, power, and high social status; but usually they did not love him. Daily he bore the cross of their disapproval and animosity long before they literally crucified him. He wept for Jerusalem. He was exquisitely sensitive to and hurt by the wickedness of the people of Jerusalem, who did not know how to make peace (Luke 19:41). Is such overwhelming sensitivity to and being hurt by evil and sinfulness the way that Jesus takes our wickedness upon himself and bears our sins? Is this the way that he shows us the very nature of God? Is God still suffering today for Jerusalem because its people do not know how to make peace? Do all of us today wound him in our sinfulness? Could Christlike sensitivity heal us? Should we too be exquisitely sensitive to and hurt by internal human wrongfulness and external wrongdoing wherever we find it? Being compassionate is suffering with those who suffer, feeling their pains of soul and body. Acting compassionately is doing something about it. In his own compassionate being and doing, Jesus showed us that and how God is compassionate and that we should grow to exist in his image. Can we rejoice as we carry our own crosses with Christlike sensitivity?

You may deepen your understanding of the following intrinsic devotional values and practices by looking up, reading, and reflecting on the following *New Testament* references.

"Jesus, our Redeemer," John 3:16-18; Galatians 3:13; Luke 21:28; Ephesians 1:7; Colossians 1:14; Hebrews 9:12

"Rejoicing in Christlike living," Matthew 16:24-28; 20:25-28; Luke 1:47; 10:20; John 13:15; Acts 5: 41 Romans 12; I. Corinthians 11:1; Ephesians 5:1-5; Philippians 4: 4-9; I. Peter 2:21

"Loving scriptural truths," Luke 24: 27, John 5:39; 8:31-32; 10:35; Acts 17:11; I. Corinthians 14:20; I. Timothy 4:13; II. Timothy 3:16; Titus 1:1; I. Peter 1:13

2. Practical Triad

Please consider the following positive extrinsic practical value items from Part I of the RVP and the CVP:

CVP
Personal salvation expressed by good works
Participating in church activities
Witnessing about the Gospel

RVP
Helping needy people
Attending a house of worship
Living according to God's laws

Spiritual Development Opportunity: Practical religious and Christian values are *extrinsic* values or valuations that have thing—or action-oriented spiritual significance. They involve participating in religious activities, ceremonies, sacraments, rituals, and doing works of reverent service. If you ranked these items close to the middle of the scale, your scores are problem free. If you ranked other items so far ahead of these that your extrinsic score is fair or weak, you could benefit from bringing this dimension into better perspective and into balance with the other value dimensions. The two kinds of ranking errors that might arise are: overvaluation and undervaluation.

Overvaluation

Overvaluing the above religious value items may mean only that you are a very effective religious worker or leader, but overvaluation of extrinsic value items *in all of life* as well as in the religious domain can indicate serious moral and spiritual problems. Overvaluation in the extrinsic practical realm involves attaching more worth to extrinsic value objects than they really have, usually to the detriment of intrinsic value items. Most of the following problems arise from overvaluing extrinsic value objects in everyday living, not just in the expressly religious parts of life, but they nevertheless have profound moral and religious significance. Think of some everyday extrinsic value objects, not just the religious ones above. If you consistently overvalue the "*things* of the world," then to some degree, depending on your degree of deviation, you may have some or all of the following spiritual problems:

- You may be so focused on *doing* good works and *participating* in various religious activities that you tend to neglect systemic religious principles and beliefs as well as devotional values like quiet reverent awe, joyous praise, or gratefulness for God's redeeming love.

- You may believe that active expressions of religion are much more important than other spiritual values because your consciousness tends to be focused on or absorbed in your immediate social and sensory worlds.

- You may personalize things and social roles, especially your own, and you may attach too much significance to social status and/or material prosperity.

- You may be too competitive, which could cause you to dismiss or overlook opportunities for cooperation.

- You may be somewhat prideful regarding your religious activities and try to use religion to impose your will or beliefs and practices upon others. This could cause you to be a religious exclusivist rather than a religious inclusivist.

- You may understand religious language and symbolism too literally.

Undervaluation

Undervaluing or negative evaluation of positive, practical, extrinsic value items means that you see less value in them than they really have. If you disvalue or undervalue positive extrinsic items, this means that to some extent, depending on your degree of deviation, you may have some or all of the following problems, though the list is not exhaustive:

- You may lack a clear understanding of and appreciation for some, perhaps all, of the good things identified above that belong to the practical extrinsic dimension. Your strongest focus may be either on systemic religious principles and beliefs or on devotional values.

- You may find it difficult to express your faith in works and active religious participation.

- You may choose to worship God privately and study the scriptures alone and only for personal growth instead of worshiping and sharing with others.

- You may not put "love your neighbor," "have faith," and "be hopeful" into daily practice, so you could benefit from developing the practical and social skills required for *doing* the works of love.

- You may not live according to God's laws on a daily basis, and you may not understand how to put your faith into daily practice.

- You may be confused about your place or role in religious groups and perhaps in other social groups as well.

Can you think of other problems that might arise from over—or undervaluing extrinsic spiritual values? If you have any of the above problems, what steps do you think you could take to correct them? Ministers or religious counselors or guides may be of help. You may improve your understanding and appreciation of practical religious values by studying and applying one or all of the following exercises.

General Religious Exercises:

1. Inward and spiritual graces stand in need of outer and bodily expression. Think about what religious people actually do and have done to express and celebrate their spiritual convictions socially or publicly. Good examples are: participating in religious ceremonies, rites, and rituals; providing aid and comfort to the sick, downtrodden, poor, and needy; teaching and learning about God and God's relations with all creation, sharing the joy of this knowledge and faith with others, forgiving and helping to restore the fallen to positions of social grace and acceptance, praying regularly both in private and in public, working in innumerable ways to make the world better, and abiding constantly and lovingly by God's laws. In which of these activities are you personally involved? Think of these activities as social or public expressions of a religious person's true convictions. Do you so express your convictions publicly? Genuine convictions are expressed most clearly in what people do, but not always in what they say. Actions usually speak louder than words.

2. Prayer with words and meditation with openness and receptivity are common to all religions; each both creates and results from religious joy or happiness. They are like medicine for those who are ill. Religious people who want to be happy do not need to

think much about praying; it just happens to them almost instinctively, like a second nature; wherever they go and whatever they do, their life IS prayer, even without words. So, decide to be joyful in, open to, and responsive to God, and prayer will happen almost of its own accord. Gandhi said, "Prayer is not asking. It is the language of the soul." Most of us are taught that prayer is talking to God, or asking God for something that we want, but prayer is much more than this. It is cultivating a personal relationship with God, a two-way street where you can talk to and experience God, and God can talk to and experience you. You must listen quietly and prayerfully to God's still small voice within you. To cultivate and develop any personal relationship that works and grows, including your relationship with God, you have to spend a lot of time at it and exert a lot effort. You really have to work at it! Practice makes perfect! Sooner or later, God-awareness and God-likeness become second nature.

3. Faith without works is dead. Practice doing good works on a daily basis, but remember that service should not be just a "duty," something externally imposed, encouraged, and practiced. This ends up being hypocrisy. Your ego should not be involved in doing the works of love; you should not ask for anything in return. Don't try to serve God for merely selfish reasons. Don't try to earn something that cannot be earned because it is a gift from God. Let your service be an expression of your unselfish love and devotion, not just a way of getting your own back scratched by scratching others or of trying to earn favor and credits with God. Service is something you do for others out of love, compassion, empathy, and gratitude, but without greed. Ask God to fill you with love like his. When love is overflowing in you, only then can it be shared. You will feel grateful that others do not reject your unselfish love, that they accept and welcome it. Service is a joy in itself, its value is enormous, and it can be an abounding expression of your spiritual joy. At its best, service involves feeling and being one with a greater whole, one with other(s); and consciousness of the difference between "I and thou"

disappears or ceases to matter. Focus on serving for the right reason; do it for the well being of all, thereby doing the will of God, and thereby finding unexpected joy in it.

4. Do you think that some people do good works, attend religious services, give of their money and time, and obey God's laws for the wrong reasons, or at least not always for the best reasons? Carefully and thoughtfully consider the following reasons for doing such things, and determine how they apply to yourself. Rank them. Which reasons are best? Which are less than best? Which, if any, should have no place at all? Why?

I do what my religion requires:

because attending religious services is good for business;
because religious rules should be followed for their own sake;
because resting one day a week enables me to work harder and
    earn more the following week;
because I want to express my love and gratitude to God;
because religious people always prosper and succeed;
because God said so;
because I will be healthier if I do;
because my heart is filled with concern and compassion for those
    I meet and can help;
because God knows and commands what is best for everyone;
because I want to find and unite with God through doing God's
    will;
because the Bible tells me so;
because this is the only way I can go to heaven.

You may deepen your understanding of the following extrinsic or practical spiritual values and practices by looking up, reading, and reflecting on the following *Old Testament* references:

"Helping needy people," Exodus 23:10-11; Deuteronomy 15:7-11; Psalms 41:1-3; Proverbs 14:31; Isaiah 58:6-7; Micah 6:8

"Attending a house of worship," Psalms 27:4, 55:14; 84:1 and 10; 122:1; Isaiah 2:3; Micah 4:2; Habakkuk 2:20

"Living according to God's laws," Exodus 20:1-17; Deuteronomy 5:6-21; I. Kings 8:57-61; Ecclesiastes 12:13-24; Psalms 19:7-14; 119

Christian Exercises:

1. Think about the purpose of the church and its ministry. The church is a gathering place for those who are saved by faith in and love to God in Christ. Jesus promises to be with us when we meet together as a loving religious community (Matthew 18:20). St. Paul explained that the church is like a body, Christ's body, in which all the parts work and grow together in love as each part does its distinctive work (Romans 12, I. Corinthians 12, Ephesians 4). The church exists in part to equip God's people to do God's work and to instruct and encourage them in their faith and moral resolve. One of the church's purposes is to show God's holiness to its members and to the world. The church exists to help increase both the knowledge and love of God and neighbor and the acts that flow from these. The human body has many parts, but the many parts make up only one body. So it is with the body of Christ. Though we are many, we are baptized into Christ's body in and by one spirit (I. Corinthians 12:12-13). In Christ's spirit, the church demonstrates unity and reconciliation between people who are different and imperfect. It is inclusive, yet very diverse. Meeting together with other religious people is a good thing. It provides enjoyable fellowship or companionship, sympathetic listeners, informed teachers, guides, and counselors, like-minded friends, experienced travelers, new and different perspectives, and constructive critics. It extends forgiveness, restoration, and renewal when we have stumbled. Can you think of other ways in which belonging to a religious group can be helpful? Since God gave each of us unique personal gifts, we must find the best ways to invest those gifts for him that will benefit our church, our community, and God's world (I. Corinthians 14:12).

2. You can keep your life focused on things of genuine worth by doing God's will and telling others about God and his self-disclosure to us in Christ. Acts 20:24 suggests that our lives are worth nothing unless we use them for doing the work assigned us by Jesus, especially the work of telling others the good news about God's wonderful kindness, grace, and love. If we want Christ to acknowledge us as his redeemed, we must acknowledge him as our personal Redeemer, as one through whom we are best enabled to love God and our fellow human beings. He will claim us before God as we claim him before our fellow human beings (Matthew 10:32). Witnessing isn't just preaching on a street corner or in a pulpit; it is talking to others in our own small way and at an appropriate time about the gospel of Christ, the good news that God's love is manifested in Christ. To communicate this gospel to others is the last "Great Commission" that Jesus gave to his followers (Mark 16: 15). Even if circumstances or the attitudes of others are not favorable, we should speak out anyway, each of us in her or his own way. We never know how God will use our words to affect someone's life (Ezekiel 2:5-7). We can overcome our fear of witnessing if we nurture and reflect God's image and then trust God to speak to and through us. Luke 21:15 promises that God will give us wisdom and the right words so that our opponents will be overcome. Remember to use gentle words in teaching others, especially un-religious or other-religious people. II. Timothy 2:24-25 reminds us that the Lord's servants must not quarrel but should be kind to everyone. We must be patient with difficult people. We should gently and lovingly teach those who oppose the truth as we see it. Perhaps they will change their minds and hearts and acknowledge God's truth; perhaps they will change our minds and hearts and show us a better way.

3. A life of humble service is a necessary part of being like Christ. In John 13:14-15 Jesus reportedly said, "If I, then, your Lord and Master have washed your feet; ye also ought to wash one another's feet. For I have given you an example, that ye should do as I have done to you." This can either be taken literally, as do the Primitive Baptists, or as a metaphor for a life of humility and service. God

is pleased even by our simple acts of kindness toward others, as when we cheerfully offer to others the basics of hospitality, a place to stay, and a good meal (I. Peter 4:9). Romans 12:13 tells us to share with God's people who are in need. Jesus did this with publicans and sinners! Luke 6:35 admonishes us to love even our enemies and to do good to them. You can bring great joy and consolation to others by expressing your love through kindness (Philemon 1:7). As reported in Luke 14:12-14, Jesus said that we should not invite those who already have ample resources to our dinners; instead, we should invite those who could never repay us, like "the poor, the maimed, the lame, and the blind;" then God will repay us "at the resurrection of the just." Try to be like Jesus, who said that he came to serve, not to be served (Mark 10:45). Do you live as if you came to be served, not to serve? God shows his care for us by protecting, providing for, and preserving us (Psalms 121:7-8); and as God shows his care and concern for us, so we can show his care and concern to and for others. In Matthew 25:36-37, Jesus tells us how to show others we care, "For I was hungry and ye gave me meat: I was thirsty, and ye gave me drink: I was a stranger, and ye took me in: Naked, and ye clothed me: I was sick, and ye visited me: I was in prison, and ye came unto me." A good way to expose your love for God is by showing your love to needy people. God loves everyone, especially "low down" people, "the least of these," as the world measures greatness; and we should learn to love everyone that God loves. In Matthew 10:42, Jesus promised to reward those who give a cup of cold water to one of the world's lowliest, but we should not do it just to be rewarded ourselves. Do it "for the least of these."

4. God has given you many special talents and your own unprecedented place in and perspective on the universe, including other people. No other "you" has ever occurred before in the entire history of creation, and no other "you" will ever occur again within this created natural order. Physically, working through natural processes, God gave you absolutely unique fingerprints, eye patterns, and a distinctive set of genes and cells.

Spiritually, God gave you not only common humanity but also a qualitatively distinct and unique human soul or self; and God regards it, or you in your totality, as worth saving and developing, even if and when you don't. Socially, God has given you your own particular station in life, its many special projects and duties that no one else in the world could execute or fulfill. You have innumerable unique specific relationships with your own family, friends, co-workers, fellow church members, and fellow citizens of the universe. Jesus and Paul used many metaphors from the human body because they valued extrinsic embodiment; and Jesus was the Word made flesh. No member of the body of Christ, the church, has all the functions of or total responsibility for the whole body. You can't do everything, but you can do a lot. You may be a good hand, but not a very good head; you may be a good heart, but not a very good hand. You can and should grow in all the ways in which you are now less than adequately developed, but you will always have your own special gifts and talents, and you will still excel in some ways but not in others. As St. Paul indicated, no matter how gifted and developed we are, we should still "earnestly desire the higher gifts" (I. Corinthians 12:31). Learn to value intrinsically not just the common embodied humanity that you share with all other people but also your unique differences, your total holistic individuality, along with the individuality of others. Try to find your own special niche, your own special place to be and to serve within the body of Christ. Know yourself, and then try to discover how God can best use you right where you are, even with all your imperfections. You don't really know yourself unless you know *your world* and how to express *yourself* within it for the glory of God.

If you are a Christian, you may deepen your understanding of the following extrinsic or practical values and practices by looking up, reading, and reflecting on the following *New Testament* references.

"Personal salvation expressed by good works," Acts 9:36; 20:28-35; I. Timothy 5:10; James 1:22-25; 2:14-20

"Participating in church activities," I. Corinthians 12:4-31; Acts 2:36-47; 4:31-37; 5:1-11

"Witnessing about the Gospel," Mark 13:10; 16:15; Romans 10:14-17; I. Corinthians 1:17; 9:16-18; II. Timothy 3:16; 4:2

3. Conceptual Triad

Please consider the following positive conceptual or systemic value items from Part I of the RVP and the CVP.

CVP
Learning about Jesus
Actions guided by Christian principles
Christian beliefs that support one another

RVP
The principle of forgiving others
Health and healing resulting from religious beliefs
Knowing God's commandments

Spiritual Development Opportunity: In religion, concepts, ideas, and beliefs are *systemic* values or valuations expressed in doctrinal convictions, theological knowledge, spiritual truths, ritual forms, and religious laws and principles. If you ranked the systemic items just above the middle of the 18 point scoring range, your scores are problem free. If you ranked other items so far ahead of these that your score on religious knowing and believing is only fair or weak, you could benefit from bringing this dimension into better perspective and into balance with the other value dimensions. The two kinds of ranking errors that might arise are: overvaluation and undervaluation.

Overvaluation
Overvaluation in the systemic conceptual realm means that you attach more worth to cognitive religious values than they really have. If you overvalue principles, beliefs, rules, rituals, doctrines, and the like,

then to some extent, depending on your degree of deviation, you may have some or all of the following moral and spiritual problems, though this list is by no means exhaustive:

- You may tend to think that faith consists mainly of knowing and accepting or affirming religious beliefs or propositions, and your approach to morality and spirituality may be primarily intellectual or doctrinal.

- You may allow believing certain doctrines to become a form of "works righteousness" through which you try to earn your salvation.

- You may personalize ideas and ideals, especially those having religious significance.

- You may be inclined to judge beliefs, practices, and other people in black-or-white, all-or-none categories, and you may have difficulty seeing shades of gray.

- You may tend to be religiously and morally ideological, dogmatic, authoritarian, or even fanatical.

- You may be perfectionistic, utopian, and inflexible, as well as prejudiced and biased rather than open and fair-minded. This could result in your valuing or loving others only to the extent that they accept your religious beliefs and practices.

- You may identify intrinsically with words about God but not with God himself.

Undervaluation

Undervaluing or negative evaluation of positive systemic value items means that you assign less worth to them than they really have. If you disvalue, neglect, or undervalue beliefs, principles, rules, rituals, doctrines, and the like, then to some extent, depending on the degree of your deviation, you may have some or all of the following problems, though the list is not exhaustive:

- You may lack a clear understanding of and appreciation for some, perhaps all, of the areas or items identified above that belong to the conceptual or systemic dimension.

- Your religious faith may be fuzzy, poorly defined, and not mentally well developed, organized, or mature.

- You may rely on your feelings alone without having a solid conceptual foundation on which to base your beliefs.

- Your moral and religious thinking may be unclear and unstructured, which could cause you to be frustrated, confused, hesitant, doubtful, or skeptical.

- You may find it difficult to discover meaning and order in established religion, social orders, nature, creation, and God. If you are confused or unable to make much sense out of what exists and what happens, you may tend toward depression or despair because you find it difficult to hope and trust in God.

- You may be easily dominated or victimized by strong, dogmatic and charismatic religious leaders.

Can you think of other problems that might arise from over- or undervaluing systemic spiritual values? If you have any of the above problems, what steps do you think you could take to correct them? Ministers or religious guides or counselors may be of help. You may improve your understanding and appreciation of conceptual religious values by studying and applying one or all of the following exercises.

General Religious Exercises:
1. Try to understand better the doctrines and essential truths of your religion. Resolve to read and study the scriptures of your faith on

a regular basis, and seek out qualified publications, commentaries, and teachers to explain and help you to understand essential spiritual doctrines. What you are searching for is already there; the truth, the bliss, the love, and God are all there. You simply have to work to discover and uncover what is already there. Finding religious truth is like digging a well or a gold mine; the water or the gold is already there. You only have to remove the layers of dirt, stones, and rocks; but that could take a lot of hard work! What you seek is buried in a mine, and you have to dig for it! God made it so! The moment you remove enough of the barriers, the water or gold becomes visible and available. If you regularly read, study, and think intensely about the scriptures, you will grow in wisdom and in the knowledge and love of God. The scriptures will become living words that you make your own and apply to your life on a daily basis; they will become the waters of life that constantly provide you with greater and greater moral and spiritual nourishment and strength; they will be of more value to you than gold.

2. Seek help and guidance from a recognized religious leader, teacher, or writer, perhaps more than one. Someone who has traveled the road before can be immensely helpful. The word "discipline" comes from the same root as the word "disciple." Learning can be disciplined, ordered, effortful; and "learning" can be a verb as well as a noun. Active learning isn't knowledge; it is the process of acquiring it. Knowledge is the end result, the destination; learning is the conscious process, the road to be traveled, wonderful for the journey itself as well as for its final destination. Learning is like a river, always moving from the known to the unknown, always ready and open. Knowledge stops, but learning never ends, and mysteries never cease. The more we learn, the less we seem to know! Be open to new insights from many sources. Stay in a prayerful learning stage, but don't adopt an "I know the whole truth and nothing but the truth" attitude. If you think that you already know all the answers, then you presume that you have "arrived," and learning ceases. You become "brain dead" spiritually! To avoid this, remain a seeker and learner. Continue

to study the scriptures and the writings of great moral and religious thinkers and teachers.

3. Being free means being capable of choosing and doing either right or wrong. Freedom means that you can choose either to fall down with the devils or to rise up with the angels. Freedom is a ladder; the down way separates you from God, perhaps forever; the way up reaches the very realm of God, perhaps forever. It is the same ladder; and the choice is yours. Throughout the Bible, men and women were confronted with choices; some of them chose goodness, others evil. All too often, wrong is easier to do than right. Doing wrong is a downhill roll, and doing right is an uphill climb. Going uphill can be difficult and arduous. The higher you go the harder it may become in some respects, but it may get easier in other ways as you become a more experienced and skillful traveler. It will be easier if you travel with a road map and go with knowledgeable guides and companions who can direct, support, and encourage you along the way. Tumbling downhill is very easy and requires very little knowledge; gravity does almost everything for you. If you take the easy way and roll like a rock from the hilltop, soon you will reach the very bottom, and you will not like what you find there. Strive instead to *rise* spiritually and reach the very highest and most glorious peaks of justice, beauty, truth, goodness, love, and bliss. The uphill climb may be wearisome at times, but it will be much less so if you stop to smell the roses along the way. Your life's journey won't be trouble-free; but it can be a great adventure, especially if you learn to enjoy the trip itself. The trip, as well as the destination, can be with God, who gave you life and liberty at the same time.

4. Health has two aspects: one is the physical, the other is the spiritual. Your body is both your temple and God's temple; don't neglect it; respect it! Health is not merely a physical phenomenon; that is only one of its dimensions. The most valuable kind of health exists somewhere inside of you, in your consciousness. The words "healing," "health," and "holy" all come from the same root. To be healed means to be "joined with the whole." To be ill means to

be "disconnected from the whole." A sick person has blocks between him or herself and the whole; something is disconnected. The function of a healer is to re-connect. The greatest healer and doer is God, the utmost Whole. Let God occupy the same space, mind, and spirit that you occupy, and thus expand your soul. Ask God to help you become more aware of him as your healing source and to re-connect your parts with God. When you become quietly aware of the supreme source of all healing and all else, healing can then be experienced as belief, as prayer, as God, as love, and as being part of and connected to the Whole. Love is the most healing force in the world. Nothing goes deeper than love; it heals not only the body and the mind, but also the soul; and we become whole. To be whole spiritually is to be holy. By comparison with spiritual health, physical health is relatively superficial; it can happen through medicine or science; but the innermost core of our being can be healed only through love and spiritual growth. Those who know the secret of God's love know the greatest secret of life. Yes, the body will become old and die, but love reveals the truth that you are not merely a body; you are also consciousness; and to live in full consciousness and thoughtfulness is to live in tune with God. Bliss and health are byproducts of living harmoniously with God—physically, socially, mentally, and spiritually.

5. Being right with God and with your fellow human beings involves forgiving and being forgiven, not just in the abstract, but in the real world in which we live. None of us are without fault; all of us have broken the rules; all of us have hurt others; we all need forgiveness; we all need to ask for forgiveness. All of us also need to forgive. It has been said that revenge is sweet, but forgiveness is so much better. When we have been hurt or wronged, the passion for revenge is one of our most powerful elemental natural urges. In practice, it usually prevails over our inclination to forgive, but almost always with disastrous results in the long run. The passion for revenge always hurts us, usually much more than it hurts our "offenders." Vengefulness is itself a miserable

state of mind; and while we are the mood for revenge, our body goes into a self-destruct mode, as many medical tests can show. Also, the vicious cycle of doing evil for evil, of seeking an eye for an eye, is endless. That's why even the Bible could not stand it! Think about the miserable places in the world today where vengeance is being exacted. We must overcome evil with good and learn to "turn the other cheek." Wouldn't the world be so much better if all the lives, energy, time, and money spent on revenge were spent instead on reconciliation and reconstruction? Did someone hurt you today? If so, did you respond vindictively, or did you forgive and reach out for reconciliation? Did you or will you forgive, even if they don't ask for it? Did you hurt someone today? If so, are you too proud or too fearful to ask for forgiveness? Forgiveness heals and lets everyone involved move on to better things; but the cycle of revenge goes on forever. Forgiveness should be more than a principle; make it a practice.

6. Have you ever heard of "tough love"? Real love is often confused with something else like giving in to every demand of those we love. Real love aims at and acts to help achieve the well being of loved ones, but this means that it does not give in to their self-destructive or other-destructive desires, deeds, and dispositions. Real love does not coddle the bad habits of loved ones. The Prodigal Son returned home only once, and after that he straightened himself up; but many of our sons, daughters, friends, and loved ones are Super-prodigal. They err and pretend to repent repeatedly and relentlessly! What if our Super-prodigal children drag themselves home after every weekend begging for money to pay off their drinking, drug, and gambling debts? What if they are addicted to drinking, drugs, gambling, or innumerable other vices? What if they pretend to repent after ever binge, yet you know from bitter past experience that it isn't so and won't last? True love is not blind. Tough forgiveness is an expression of tough love. We should forgive "seventy times seven times," i.e., endlessly; but forgiveness should not be confused with co-dependency or complicity. Meaningful relationships with our errant loved ones

should not depend on our perpetuating or cooperating with their weaknesses and errant ways; that isn't forgiveness; it is moral weakness. Forgiveness comes out of moral strength, not out of moral frailty. Super-prodigal loved ones may be adults in years, but they are not so in moral and spiritual development. Like good parents, by our teachings and our examples we should show our immature loved ones positive and constructive ways to live and to grow morally and spiritually; but we should also set limits and say "no" to activities that are incompatible with their becoming mature, responsible, self-respecting, and other-respecting adults. We should do no less for ourselves. Turning the other cheek must also be compatible with tough love toward those we love, as well as with loving ourselves. Turning the other cheek puts an end to the cycle of revenge, but it does not put an end to all moral weakness and vices, especially those of your Super-prodigal children who would constantly violate you and your rights. Self-sacrifice should have a noble purpose; it should not just perpetuate evil. You as well as your "beloved enemies" are equally children of God. Through tough love, kindness, and understanding, enemies and Super-prodigal children can be changed into friends. They can also be changed internally. Abraham Lincoln was right: we can eliminate our enemies by turning them into friends!

You may deepen your understanding of the following systemic conceptual values and practices by looking up, reading, and reflecting on the following *Old Testament* references:

"The principle of forgiving others," Genesis 49:17-21; 1 Kings 8:36; Psalms 32:1; 86:5

"Health and healing resulting from religious beliefs," Exodus 15:26; Numbers 12:13; 2 Chronicles 7:14; Psalms 103:3; Jeremiah 17:14; 33:6

"Knowing God's commandments," Exodus 20; Deuteronomy 5; Joshua 1:8; Psalms 1:2; 19:7-14; 119

Christian Exercises:

1. Think of yourself as fully capable of understanding Christian teachings, and continue to read and study until you learn the most essential Christian beliefs, principle, ideals, and guidelines for living. Psalms 119:105 tells us, "Thy word is a lamp unto my feet and a light unto my path." The Bible is filled with God's instructions and promises. It gives comfort, guidance, and encouragement in this life as well as confident assurance of everlasting peace and security with God. The Ten Commandments show us how to live with God and with one another in reverence, respect, peace, and harmony. The Sermon on the Mount as well as the parables and other teachings of Jesus spell out the ideal of going beyond the minimal requirements of the law in order to achieve an even deeper moral and spiritual life. Religious ideals can come to us in many ways. Jesus instructed us not only with words but also with his example of saintly, holy, godly living, suffering, and dying. St. Paul admonished us to, "Be ye kind to one another, tenderhearted, forgiving one another, even as God for Christ's sake has forgiven you" (Ephesians 4:32). Christlikeness, imitating Christ, following in Christ's footsteps, is one of the most powerful Christian ethical and religious ideals. I. Peter 2:21 says that Christ suffered for us, leaving us an example, that we "should follow in his steps." Verse 23 says that he did not retaliate when he was insulted, and when he suffered, he did not threaten or try to get even. He also taught us to turn the other cheek, to pray for our persecutors, and to love our enemies instead of hating them (Matthew 5:38-44). He lived up to and died by his own ideals. Can we do any less?

2. Pray regularly for disclosure of the truth, and open your mind to the loveliness of God, especially in his powerful self-disclosure in Jesus. Obedience to God's laws is an essential element of a meaningful relationship with him, not to earn our salvation, but as a result of it. Good works will not earn our salvation, will not be the cause of it; but they are definitely the effects of it. Even if, as most Christians believe, we are saved by grace alone, not by

good works, we must still express our salvation, faith, and gratitude through obedience, through humbly doing the works of ideal justice and mercy. That is what the Lord requires of us (Micah 6:8). Devotedly doing the works of love, as Jesus did, fulfills not every letter of the law, but what is really essential in it, the spirit of it. When Jesus was asked to prioritize the Sabbath law versus people, he ranked people first (Mark 2:27). Jesus forgave the adulteress (John 8:3-11) instead of condemning her to death as the law required (Leviticus 20:10, Deuteronomy 22:22). Jesus repudiated (Matthew 5: 38-39) the law of "An eye for an eye" (Exodus 21:23-25); but he did follow and endorse the Ten Commandments. So did St. Paul. People who love actually honor their parents; they do not murder; they do not steal, they do not commit adultery; they do not even envy or covet; they treat others the way they would like to be treated themselves; they forgive those who have offended them. People who love avoid the seven harmful and deadly sins—pride, covetousness, lust, anger, gluttony, envy, and sloth. Like Jesus and Paul, Christians must hold love and law in delicate balance. Loving people need explicit guidance about how love actually manifests itself in real life, while allowing room for honest disagreements and uncertainties. Being told to "Act lovingly," or "Love others, then do as you please" doesn't give us much direction, especially if we are told nothing more. More specific instructions are required, hence "the law." Love can't be total lawlessness, but neither can it be rigid moralism or legalism. Sometimes it finds a more excellent way, a more loving way, than following the letter of the law. St. Peter and St. Paul suspended scriptural laws on circumcision and diet in order to take the gospel of love to the Gentiles (Acts 15:1-11; Romans 14:14-23; I. Timothy 4:4). Being selective for the sake of love about which scriptures to emphasize is very scriptural!

3. When interpreting the scriptures, don't be too literal-minded. If you are, you will often be confused and could miss many important things. The disciples misunderstood Jesus when they took him too literally (John11:11-13). When the Psalmist called God his

"rock," "fortress," and "redeemer," (Psalms 18:2) do you really want to interpret all of those words literally? When Jesus called himself "the bread" (John 6:35) and "the vine" (John 15:5), do you take those words literally? The scriptures serve many diverse religious purposes and contain many different levels and kinds of meaning and language. Sometimes the scriptures just communicate information—factual, ethical, or theological. Very often their purpose is to stimulate us to think more broadly and deeply and to "reason together" with God. The scriptures often use metaphors, allegories, images, stories, myths, symbols, analogies, songs, poetry, paradoxes, parables, prophecy, and prescriptions to help us understand, serve, care, worship, and love more deeply. Metaphorical language is the language of poetry and love. It is not to be taken literally, but it helps us to expand our awareness and our horizons, to take the point of view of others, to empathize with, affirm, and identify with those who are like ourselves and with others who are very different from ourselves—with strangers, with our enemies, with God. Learn to read the scriptures with discernment and understanding, and train yourself to identify and appreciate the many kinds of religious language within them. Try to find honest, truthful, faithful, meaningful, moral, and relevant interpretations of spiritual beliefs, even if they are not absolutely literal.

4. Let your religious beliefs support one another; let them be clear, consistent, coherent, comprehensive, and faithful to experience; but also let them support Christian values that are even more significant than mere concepts, symbols, or beliefs. Believing plus doing what you believe is more valuable than merely believing. Believing plus doing what you believe in love is even better. For yourself as a Christian, which is more important, believing or loving? If you had to downplay the importance of beliefs or doctrines in order to be more loving to those who believe differently, would you do it? Should you do it? St. Paul did not hesitate to rank the importance of believing versus loving. He said that if we believe so intensely that we can move mountains but don't have love, we are nothing (I. Corinthians 13:2); and

when he ranked faith (believing?), hope, and love, he found that the greatest of these is loving, not believing (I. Corinthians 13:13). Having religious faith is often equated systemically with affirming or believing certain religious doctrines, though it may be more appropriate to equate faith intrinsically with profoundly trusting and identifying ourselves fully with something ultimate that exists beyond our doctrines, beliefs, and thoughts, something to which our concepts of God or Ultimate Reality point inadequately. Signs point to something beyond themselves, and so do most words. With the very best of our theological words, we see only dimly, not face to face. Christian faith is about the Holy One to whom our symbols point. Intrinsic faith involves us completely as whole persons, our whole being, not just our cognitive minds; and its object is not beliefs as such but that Ultimate Reality, that Holy One signified by our beliefs. Believing should not become another form of "works righteousness" through which we try to earn our salvation.

5. To experience the joy of living fully, you must be active mentally, physical, and socially at work, at home, in your church, and in all your other roles. You must be willing to experiment, to try new thoughts and things, and not to get bogged down in any one particular activity or way of thinking. Water that is not flowing and moving gets stagnant and begins to dry up. Think of yourself as being like a river, always moving, flowing over obstacles and around bends, gaining strength, clarity, and power. A "flowing" approach to life evolves from an inner sensitivity to and knowledge of the natural rhythm of things, from knowing and working in harmony with God's plans and life's circumstances. Our lives unfold according to our own plans and expectations; they don't just "happen" to us; we can envision new futures for ourselves and change directions if we wish. We can engage in life more fully both on the outside and on the inside. Life is not made up of static endings and beginnings; it is a dynamic continuum. Listen to the guidance of God and your inner voice, and then set new goals that you really want to achieve, that you find energizing. You may have to let go of aspects of yourself that no longer fit

who you want to become. Learn about God's special plan for you by applying the scriptures to yourself and by listening to the many ways that God speaks to you.

6. Read or re-read exercises 5 and 6 in the preceding "General Religious Exercises."

If you are a Christian, you may deepen your understanding of the following systemic conceptual values and practices by looking up, reading, and reflecting on the following *New Testament* references:

"Learning about Jesus," the whole gospel of Matthew; Mark 8:27-38, 12:28-34; Luke 2:52; II. Corinthians 4:1-6; Colossians 2:2-4; Hebrews 5:12-14; II. Peter 3:18

"Actions guided by Christian principles," Matthew 19:16-22; 28:20; John 5:23-24; 10:27; 14:15; Romans 13:8-10; Galatians 5:14; I. John 2: 3-6; II. John 1:6; James 1:25

"Religious beliefs that support one another," Titus 1:9-11; 2:1; Hebrews 13:9; II. Timothy 2:22-26; 3:8-9; 4:1-4; II. John 1:7-12

CHAPTER FOUR

For Your Further Spiritual Growth and Development, Part II

Please use this Chapter in connection with Part II, the personal dimension of the Religious and /or Christian Value Profiles.

Exercises for Part II, Compositions

1. Being/Feeling Triad

Please consider the following positive intrinsic being/feeling religious value items from Part II of the RVP and the CVP:

CVP

I love Christ with my whole heart, soul, mind, and strength.
Christ's love is expressed in everything I do.
My life is centered around Christian principles.

RVP

I am fully devoted to God.
I love doing the Lord's work.
I love the words of God.

Spiritual Development Opportunity: The above devotional being/ feeling religious values are *personal intrinsic* values that affirm your own relationship with God and God's whole creation, especially with other religious people. These values express your personal commitment to internalizing spiritual values in all segments of your life, to let your religion or spirituality become a total way of life. If you ranked these items close to the top, your scores are problem free. If you ranked other items so far ahead of these that your score is fair or weak, you could benefit from bringing this dimension into better perspective, and into balance with the other value dimensions. The two kinds of ranking errors that might arise are: overvaluation and undervaluation. Note that over- or undervaluing a value dimension in Part I suggests many of the same vulnerabilities as over- or undervaluing the same dimension in Part II. If you overvalued or undervalued any items on your Profile, you may have some but not all of the following problems, and then only to a degree. Or you may not have these problems at all if you misunderstood the item(s) or the ranking process itself.

Overvaluation

Overvaluation in the intrinsic being/feeling dimension means that you attach too much value to personal intrinsic religious values. In the absolute sense, this is not possible, for, according to the axiological system used here, nothing is higher than the intrinsic. But in relation to other dimensions of value, this is possible, because you can be so completely involved in the intrinsic realm that you seriously neglect extrinsic and systemic religious involvement. Absolutely, intrinsic value phrases cannot be ranked higher than 1, 2 and 3, although 2 can be ranked as 1, and 3 can be ranked as 1 or 2. If you overvalued the intrinsic, then to some extent, depending on your degree of deviation, you may have some or all of the following moral and spiritual problems, though the list is by no means exhaustive:

- You may be so focused on feeling devoted to God that you get overly involved in meditation, prayer, or personal devotions rather than concentrating on increasing your spiritual knowledge through daily learning, or following God's plan for your life, or putting your love for God into positive action by supporting and attending your religious group or church regularly.

- You may think that having faith mainly involves only your own personal, private, intimate relationship with God and your feelings about God and/or his word.

- Your approach to spirituality may be primarily emotion or feeling-based and may not get translated into daily doing and learning. This may be because your faith is not clearly defined or refined by knowledge and thinking or because it not be reflected in your daily actions.

Undervaluation

Undervaluing or negative evaluation of the above personal positive intrinsic being/feeling value phrases means that you do not see the value in them that they deserve. If you disvalue or undervalue the personal positive intrinsic items, this means that to some extent, depending on the degree of your deviation, you are likely to have some or all of the following problems. This list is by no means exhaustive.

- You may lack a clear understanding of and appreciation for some, perhaps all, of the above items in the being/feeling intrinsic spiritual dimension. This may be because you place more importance on your religious knowledge and/or your religious roles and activities.

- If you lack faith, hope, and love to any degree, it will be difficult for you to develop and maintain close, intimate and loving personal relationships with God and with other people.

- You may have difficulty seeing yourself and others as having intrinsic worth, as being children of God.

- You may feel personally insufficient and lack self confidence, and your religion does not help you to overcome these difficulties.

- You may not know or possess salvation from despair, depression, guilt and/or other overwhelming emotional burdens; you may not hope and trust in God or experience God's peace and joy within you.

Can you think of other problems that might arise from over- or undervaluing personal intrinsic spiritual values? If you have any of the above problems, what steps do you think you could take to correct them? Ministers or religious guides or counselors may be of help. You may improve your appreciation for and involvement with religious being/feeling values by understanding and practicing one or all of the following exercises.

General Religious Exercises:

1. Try to remember and meditate upon the times and places when you personally have experienced devotional feelings of tremendous and fascinating mystery, majestic holiness, awe, reverence, adoration, love, and personal commitment to and communion with God. If such religious experiences are not familiar to you, try to place yourself in circumstances in which others typically have them. Practice doing so as often as possible. Become an astronaut of inner space. To show your full devotion to God, give some of your time and energy to silent moments because in such moments are you likely to experience a sense of God's presence and achieve inner peace and joy. People who have tasted God's peace are immensely rich in soul because they have begun to know the inner kingdom of God. Quietness is the door to the inner kingdom of God. Silence helps us to know peace, and peace can lead us into God. Be still and know that God is God. Relax deeply and feel peaceful as many times a day as possible. The more often you do so, the better. This is a good way to begin each day. After a few days of conscious effort, you will begin to feel that peace has been established. It will become a part of you, but there are many levels of peace. You can produce one level of mental peace around and within yourself just by feeling it, by suggesting to yourself that you are peaceful. Like self-hypnosis,

it is something you create. Another layer comes out of the first but goes beyond it. Something beyond your own mind and control fills you with peace; it does not come out of your efforts; this peace is divine, the work of God's Spirit within you. In this kind of peace, all mental processes are absent; no thoughts are racing, no desires are pressing, no imagination is working. Yet, this peace is positive; it is not just an abstraction of the mind; it is not an absence but a presence, a well being, a song ready to burst forth; it is alive, pulsating, life-affirming, creative, and active. It is life abundant, full of light, but not *of* the world. It is full of divine light, love, joy, and hope. It is union with God.

2. If you truly love the words of God as they are written in the scriptures, in the "book of nature," on our consciences, and in our minds and hearts, you will never stop learning or teaching. Teaching is sharing with others what you have learned. Preparing yourself to teach something to others is really the best way to learn it yourself! Those who keep learning and teaching stay young and fresh in spirit. Your spiritual life can and will be so much richer and more exciting if you open up your awareness. Let everything you think you understand have a new "ring." Words, ideas, relationships, and your awareness of God should be constantly growing, expanding, and producing fresh insights and greater enlightenment. The full richness of God's reality can never be fully captured or represented by our thoughts; but we should do the best we can. Ask God to help you seek and to share insights that go beyond what you presently believe and understand. You must understand before you can share or teach; you must listen before you give advice. By associating with and identifying yourself with spiritual "winners" you too can "win," but not as the world measures "winning." With God's grace and help, you can win your soul, but you must do your part just as God does his!

3. Real seekers always feel grateful to parents, to teachers, to anyone who has helped them. When you become enlightened and reborn spiritually, you will realize and appreciate how much all of them helped. Everything that ever happened to you has brought you to

this point in your life. This includes all the valleys as well as the high points. We need to rejoice and be happy in and with the peak experiences of life, but we also need to be restless and continually motivated until we rest finally in God. Thank God for restlessness as well as for joy! Can we rejoice as we carry our own crosses? Are we patient and joyful even in tribulation? Beautiful dawns and mornings follow many dark nights. Gratitude to God and to others who help us along life's way is a fundamental religious virtue. Gratitude can be kind of prayer through which you can become aware of the presence of God. In gratitude we acknowledge what we owe to someone else, that someone else has helped us along life's way. So what do you owe to God? How has God helped you along life's way? Be thankful that God is with you when your life is at its best; be even more thankful that God is present with you, suffers with you, and fully understands when your life seems at its worst. We can never feel grateful enough often enough. We can express our thankfulness to God through prayer, praise, singing, service, spiritual growth, and living as we should (Psalms 119:7). Remember to thank God for being wise and good, and for his faithfulness and love for you. Don't forget to express thanks to other people who have meant a lot to you. Do these things while you still have a chance!

4. Concentrate on your heartfelt religious emotions or devotional feelings of awe, reverence, adoration, love, and personal commitment to and communion or union with God. Let your devotional heart be an open door to the living presence of God, and invite God to come in and dwell within you. God is already there, but you may not have felt or experienced it yet. Sleepers, awake! Think of your devotional heart as a flame, the fire of God, that radiates warmth and light through your soul and into your surroundings through the way you speak and act. Try to stay focused on your heart as a flame, the spark of divinity within you, no matter what else you may be doing, whether walking down the street, working, eating with your family, or going to sleep. No detail of your existence is too trivial to be beyond God's concern. Let the Spirit of God dwell constantly within you

and transform your soul. Let your mind be the mind of God, your body be the body of God, your soul be the soul of God. Be Godlike in your whole being in the fullness of your time. Before very long, other people will notice a great change in you. You will even notice it yourself. Your whole outlook on life will be transformed. You will be reborn spiritually. Your actions and behaviors will become kinder and more loving, encouraging, and supportive. Your thoughts will become truthful. Your dealings will be fair and just. You will become a light to the world.

5. This exercise will help you begin to please and help others in a way that includes pleasing yourself. There is an old story of a man watching his son try to lift a fallen tree from his bicycle. The boy struggled until the father asked, "Why can't you lift it, son?" The boy replied, "I'm using all my strength, but it won't move." His father then said wisely, "Son, you're not using all your strength. You haven't asked me to help." Remember! Our strength lies not only within us but also within all of those we care about and who care about us. Others can make us stronger! Draw upon the strength of others and you will multiply your own strength. Your personal religion needs a religious community. Neither merely giving nor merely receiving is best; both giving and receiving are best. When you heart is full of love for yourself and for all, you live in abiding joy right where you are. You have found heaven on earth, so you can go anywhere and carry heaven with you. You will find yourself naturally getting involved in religious activities that add to the quality of your life and the lives of others. As you engage with others and help them solve their problems, your own will fade away when you are thinking of ways to give. Then, you will become a beneficial force in life, a positive force that never dies.

6. "Devotion" is an important word that has a special place in religion. Devotion is profound involvement, concern, and commitment; it is lived worship, or worshipful living. It involves your heart, your mind, your strength, your total being. It concentrates your soul; it is your soul concentrated on what you take most seriously in life. The differences between *knowing* about devotional

practices, rituals, and ceremonies, or just "going through the motions," and really *worshiping* God, are of utmost importance. A devoted person has to be devoted to something. To what are you devoted? Are you really devoted to God? Do you really love God for himself, or are you merely trying to use or manipulate God for your own personal gains? Is it God that you love with your whole being, or is it worldly resources, prosperity, and affluence? Is it God, or is it worldly prestige, with all the powers and privileges thereof? Is it God, or is it high social standing or status, with all the power that this gives you over others? Is it God, or is it doctrines, ideas, beliefs, books? Is it God, or is it your work or career? Is your devotion mere idiolatry? Do you worship things that are not ultimate? What is your treasure? Where is your heart? To what does it, to what do you, really belong? About what are you ultimately concerned?

You may deepen your understanding of the following intrinsic religious values and practices by looking up, reading, and reflecting on the following *Old Testament* references.

"I am fully devoted to God." Deuteronomy 6:4-5; 10:12; Joshua 23:11; Psalms 18:1-2; Proverbs 8:17

"I love doing the Lord's work." Leviticus 19:18, 34; Deuteronomy 10:12; 11:13; Joshua 22:5; I. Samuel 12:24, Jeremiah 9:23-24

"I love the words of God." Deuteronomy 11:18-19; 13:3; 32:46; Psalms 1:2; 119:97, 113

Christian Exercises:

1. The more we reflect God and godliness, the more we radiate his beauty and goodness. What does God consider beautiful? His whole creation, but especially the beauty that comes from within, the unfading beauty of a gentle, quiet, humble, grateful, and loving spirit, a godly character. Beautiful conduct is the fruit of a godly character and thoughts. Jesus said, "Where your treasure is, there will your heart be also" (Luke 12:34). The scales on

which we rank our values register our priorities. Our highest priorities are those for which we are willing to make great sacrifices, if necessary, and perhaps even to sacrifice our lives. They are the valued objects in relation to which everything else takes a secondary place. They are the centers of value around which everything else is organized and to which everything else is subordinated. How do you weigh your love for God? Is it first in your life, last, or somewhere in between? Remember, we focus or concentrate most on what or whom we love the most. Jesus told us what our highest priority should be: "Thou shalt love the Lord thy God with all thy heart, with all thy soul, with all thy mind, and with all thy strength" (Mark 12:29-30). You can put God first in your life by letting him fill and direct your thoughts, your choices, your feelings, and your actions. Do not concentrate only or primarily on things here on earth, but center your whole being on divine things (Colossians 3:2), and bring them down to earth.

2. Practice praying with praise and adoration, and open your soul to the presence of God in Jesus and to his influence over your life. Let your prayers be acts of humble worship in which you turn to God and away from evil ways (II. Chronicles 7:14). Jesus taught that prayer is an intimate reverent relationship with the Father that recognizes our dependency for daily needs, makes a commitment to obedience, and asks for forgiveness of sins (Matthew 6:9-13). There are many kinds of prayer. When you pray, try to include all of the following:

prayers of adoration and worship in which we praise and glorify God for being who and as he is,

prayers of thanksgiving in which we express our gratitude to God for innumerable blessings,

prayers of petition and intercession in which we ask God to meet our needs, the needs of people who are special to us, and everyone's needs,

prayers of dedication and obedience in which we commit ourselves to doing God's will, prayers of confession in which we "come clean" with God about our wicked ways,

prayers of repentance in which we ask for God's forgiveness, reconciliation, rehabilitation, and restoration,

prayers for help, strength, insight, and direction from God in which we acknowledge our dependence on him for guidance and in innumerable other ways,

prayers of communion in which we seek, find, and rejoice in God's presence and influence,

prayers of openness in which we are quiet and receptive to and before God,

prayers of contemplation in which we are thoughtful before God and attentive to God's communications.

3. You can experience an intimate relationship with God by staying close to him and purifying your heart daily and consistently (James 4:8). God desires us to have pure hearts; so pray to God as Psalms 86:11 directs, "Teach me thy way, O Lord; I will walk in thy truth: unite my heart to fear thy name." Psalms 51:6,10 tells us that God wants us to have "truth in the inward parts" and asks God to "Create in me a clean heart . . . and renew a right spirit within me." Proverbs 11:20 says that the Lord delights in those who are upright in their ways. You can please God by honoring him, obeying him, responding to his love, seeking his forgiveness, and walking with him daily. One-on-one time with God is essential for an intimate relationship with him. This includes private scripture reading, meditation, prayer, and wholehearted participation in public or communal worship services. You must set aside special times to be with God, to talk with him, and to let him teach you. "Thy word is a lamp to my feet, and a light unto my path" (Psalms 119:105). You should not love God half-heartedly, says the greatest commandment (Matthew 22:37-38). God requires an "undivided heart" (Psalms 86:11), as well as an undivided mind. "Purity of heart," someone has said, "is to will one thing." With a pure heart, your values are no longer confused, and your loyalties are no longer divided. You are one with your supreme good. Purity of

heart is also to love one thing, but when that one is God, it is to love everything. When you're in love with God, everything else falls into place. "To be spiritually minded is life and peace" (Romans 8:6).

4. The Bible tells us to "Love your neighbor as yourself." How often we focus on the neighbor but forget the self, despite our selfishness! The Bible does not go into great detail about how to love yourself, but it does provide some pointers. All love begins with God's love and with self-love. Before others can drink from your cup, it must first be filled. When your cup runs dry, God, working with you, can best replenish it. Loving yourself includes giving your body the food, exercise, and rest that it needs. It means listening to your feelings and asking others for help without feeling guilty about it. Stop your self-criticism and self-judgment and accept yourself the way you are, as God does. Loving yourself means taking care of your own needs to maintain your wholeness. As you take care of yourself, you will be better able to meet the needs of your friends and loved ones. Once you begin to give to yourself without selfishness, giving to and sharing with others will become natural. As you learn to love and accept yourself, your inner light will shine outwardly to bless your fellow human beings. Set some time aside each day to focus on and practice loving and caring about yourself for *who you are*, without so much emphasis on *what you can do or achieve*. This will help you get in touch with your innermost center, your deepest self, the energy source of your creativity. To love yourself more, practice saying and experiencing the following affirmations:

I am a child of God, and God loves me.
I love and accept myself just the way I am.
I love myself unconditionally.
God's universal love surrounds and fills every cell in my being.
The more I love myself, the more I am able to love others.
My life overflows with the bounties of love.
Your own affirmations: _____

5. Some people know and value themselves somewhat, but they do not know and value themselves sufficiently because of some crisis in their life. Are you such a person? If you are, what stands between you and self-knowledge, self-respect, and faith in yourself? Is it guilt over what you are or have done, unrealistic self-expectations, conflicts at work, disapproval by significant others, doubts about beliefs that you can no longer honestly hold, or conflicting messages from authorities that you respect? Do you find it impossible to forgive yourself? Are you grieving over a profound loss, afflicted by a serious illness, impaired by aging, or afraid of your own death? Has someone you deeply respected and trusted taken unfair advantage of you? Is the turmoil in the world too much for your to bear? Do you sometimes have a sense of impending doom, or feelings of inadequacy anxiety, depression, despair, loss of hope? Do you lack self-confidence and feel like a failure because you have been divorced or "downsized" or because you have been defeated by some project or task for which you are not really talented? If your own beliefs, feelings, and attitudes stand between you and self-love, are they realistic? Do you think that no one could love you, not even God? If any of this is true about you, seek help!

In times of crisis, do your religious outlook and faith, and does your religious community, give you the companionship, meaning, purpose, courage, strength, forgiveness, guidance, assurance, and emotional support you need to overcome your self-destructive thoughts? Jesus said that you should love others as you love yourself, but this presupposes that you really do know, respect, and love yourself, that you cherish yourself intrinsically, that you have a keen sense of self-worth, that you think that you are worth saving and worth giving away. If you do not, then you cannot love others as you should, for you think (mistakenly) that you have and are nothing of value to give. Jesus said that you should love God with all your own heart, soul, mind, and strength; but this is quite impossible unless you both understand and positively esteem your heart, your soul, your mind, and your strength. Where do you fit into this picture? You need to know, respect, forgive, value, and love yourself. This you must do for the sake of God, for the sake of others, for your own sake, and for God's own image within you.

6. During his ministry, Jesus constantly challenged the conventional wisdom of the world, the mind-set of worldliness, which tells us to gain the extrinsic values of the world above all else. The world values successful people with wealth, health, material resources, and social power over others who have less; but Jesus associated and dined with the poor and oppressed and ministered to their needs. The world wants unhealthy people to be out of sight and out of mind as much as possible, but Jesus kept them in sight and in mind as much as possible. The world makes sharp social distinctions between superiors and inferiors: insiders and outsiders, rich and poor, clean and unclean, touchable and untouchable, Jew and Greek, Christian and non-Christian, our race and theirs, males and females, winners and losers, top dogs and underdogs; but Jesus usually sided with and befriended "the least of these." Jesus associated with "low down people" as the world ranks them, and he taught that God loves the meek and lowly just as much as he loves the high and the mighty. Jesus loved "the least of these" just as much as he loved conceited people who think too highly of themselves. He loved everyone, high and low. He constantly questioned and challenged existing "powers and principalities," the social institutions and arrangements that stand in the way of God's love. St. Paul thought that in Christ there are no divisive social rankings into superiors and inferiors. All people have equal intrinsic worth in the eyes of God.

The radical message of the *New Testament* is that in God's kingdom of love, no social distinctions are valid that exalt some people and degrade or diminish others. How close are we to that today? What social and material distinctions, rankings, and values entrap us today, keep us from being Christlike, and prevent us from seeing everyone as an equal before God? Do we follow Jesus in challenging the "good common sense of the world" that says, "Seek ye first splendid things and exalted social standing?" Or do we seek first the kingdom of God and his righteousness? Are we good stewards of our own wealth? Do we ever return evil for evil, ever avenge ourselves? Do we try to overcome evil with another evil or with goodness? Do we really treat everyone as an equal in the sight of God? By our words and examples, what do we teach our children about such things ? Do we support social policies that conform to the world, or do we support Christlike social policies?

7. The writers of the *New Testament* believed that Jesus was Isaiah's "Suffering Servant," a man of sorrows, acquainted with grief (Isaiah 53). At least twice in the *New Testament* we are told that Jesus grieved and even wept for Jerusalem (Luke 13:34, 19:41). Perhaps Jerusalem, the holiest city on earth, represented the whole world that God so loved; in it was colossal sinfulness and monumental undeserved suffering and loss. Jesus also wept over the untimely and undeserved death of his friend Lazarus (John 11:32-35). Jesus responded to human suffering, loss, and sinfulness with overwhelming passion and intensity; he carried metaphorical crosses long before he carried his final literal cross. At a level perhaps unimaginable to us, Jesus intrinsically identified himself with us in our suffering, loss, and sinfulness. He responded to evils with every relevant human and divine "pain of soul," with sorrow, disappointment, regret, frustration, anxiety, despair, depression, grief, horror, alienation, mourning, hopelessness, helplessness, forlornness, indignation, and compassion. What else? Even before his crucifixion, with empathy he experienced every human physical or bodily pain; and with immediacy he suffered them on the cross. On the cross he was taunted to work miracles to deliver himself from human suffering and death, but he worked no such miracles. He did not suffer and die because God had some debt to pay to the devil or because God could not otherwise forgive us. Instead, throughout his life, and to the bitter end, he showed us how God himself responds to our suffering, loss, and sinfulness. God takes them upon himself, as did Jesus. Throughout

his life Jesus bore our griefs, carried our sorrows, and was wounded for our transgressions. Upon him was laid "the iniquity of us all," not just at Calvary, but constantly.

8. Yes, Jesus wept, but he did not merely languish in pain and tears during his ministry. Using St. Paul's metaphors, we can say that Jesus "died daily," but he was also "resurrected daily." While suffering constantly with and for us, he also offered healing, help, salvation. On the cross, he still offered forgiveness in the depths of his own physical and psychic agony. Salvation is now as well as forever. Today is a part of eternity. Amid pervasive sinfulness, suffering, and loss, Jesus redeems us now by mediating God's gifts of spiritual renewal despite our spiritlessness. In place of our indifference and faithlessness he offers faithfulness, care, reconciliation with others, restoration to society, release from sin and guilt, and forgiveness for wrongdoing. He both shows us and enables us for intrinsic goodness, mercy, justice, compassion, joy, faith, hope, and love in and from God. Jesus saves here and now by bringing us ecstatic sensitivity to and union with God and to God's presence with and in us, in everyone, and in everything. Should we, could we, regularly be Christlike in so bearing one another's burdens and in helping to bring a divine "new birth" of goodness, unity in diversity, and abundant life to whosoever will?

9. Read or re-read exercise 6 in the preceding "General Religious Exercises."

   If you are a Christian, you may deepen your understanding of the following intrinsic values by looking up, reading, and reflecting on the following *New Testament* references.

"I love Christ with my whole heart, soul, mind, and strength." Matthew 10:37; 25: 33-40; John 13:34; 21:15-17

"Christ's love is expressed in everything I do." John 13:35; 14:21; 15:9-14; I. Corinthians 13; 16:14; II. Corinthians 4:11; Galatians 5:19-23; Ephesians 3:14-19; Philippians 1:8-11; I. John 4:19; 5:2-3

"My life is centered around Christian principles." Matthew 16:24-26; Mark 12:29-31; John 14:17; I. Peter 1:22; 4:8; I. John 3:11-18, 4:7-7; Romans 12:9-21; 13:8-10

2. Doing/Acting Triad

Please consider the following positive extrinsic value items from Part II of the RVP and the CVP.

CVP
To me, the heavens declare the glory of God.
I support and attend my church regularly.
I practice what I preach.

RVP
My love for others is enhanced by my religious group.
I actively help my religious group to grow.
My actions reflect and support my religious beliefs.

Spiritual development opportunity: Practical religious values are *personal extrinsic* values such as sacred objects, ceremonies and practices, moral actions and behavior, participation in religious and church activities, and active communal roles grounded in religion and/or Christianity. If you ranked the above items close to the middle of the scale, your scores are problem free. If you ranked other phrases so far ahead of these that your score is fair, average, or weak, you could benefit from bringing this dimension into better perspective and into balance with the other value dimensions. The two kinds of ranking errors that might arise are: overvaluation and undervaluation.

Overvaluation
Overvaluation in the personal extrinsic realm means that you attach more worth to extrinsic values than they really have. This may be generally reflected in overactive social-religious involvement to the detriment of other spiritual values. Most of the following problems

arise from overvaluing extrinsic or social involvement in everyday living, not just in the expressly religious part of your life, but they nevertheless have profound moral and religious significance. Think of some everyday extrinsic value objects and activities, not just the religious ones above. If you consistently overvalue the "*things* of the world*" as well as your active religious and extra-religious social involvement, then to some extent, depending on your degree of deviation, you may have some or all of the following spiritual problems. This is by no means an exhaustive list:

- You may be so deeply involved in various religious activities and with actively supporting your church or religious group that you neglect God's commandments and his plan for your life. You may also neglect being/feeling values like taking time out to show your love and full devotion to God quietly and privately, not just publicly.

- You may believe that active involvement with your religious group and community is the most important element of your faith. This can result in personalizing your religious role(s) and in devaluing others who don't believe and practice as you do. This could make you a religious exclusivist rather than an inclusivist; perhaps, for you, only your own "in group" is "in with God."

- You may believe that active expressions of your faith are much more important than other spiritual values because your consciousness is focused on or absorbed in activities and things in your immediate social and sensory world and you lack awareness of other dimensions of reality.

- You may subscribe to a self-serving form of religion. This means that you may try to use morality and religion to sustain and enhance your own worldly or religious status and to impose your will and beliefs upon others.

- You may be too competitive and dismiss or overlook opportunities for cooperation.

- You may understand religious language and symbolism much too literally and be unaware of or disvalue their metaphorical nature and power.

Undervaluation

Undervaluing or negative evaluation of the above positive extrinsic value phrases means that you see less value in them than they really have. If you disvalue or undervalue your religious roles and your active involvement in your religious community, this means that to some extent, depending on your degree of deviation, you may have some or all of the following problems, though the list is not exhaustive:

- You may lack a clear understanding of and appreciation for some, perhaps all, of the good things listed above that belong to the practical or extrinsic spiritual value dimension.

- You may find it difficult to express your faith in good works and in active religious participation.

- You may choose to worship God privately and study the scriptures only for personal growth instead of worshiping and sharing with others.

- You may not put "love your neighbor," "have faith," and "be hopeful" into daily practice, so you could benefit from developing the practical and social skills required for *doing* the works of love.

- You may be confused about your place or role in religious groups and perhaps in other groups as well.

- You may expect religion and religious authority figures to solve all of your problems magically, even those you ought to be actively solving for yourself.

Can you think of other problems that might arise from over- or undervaluing extrinsic spiritual values? If you have any of the above problems, what steps do you think you could take to correct them? Ministers or religious guides or counselors may be of help. You may improve your understanding and appreciation of practical doing/acting religious values by studying and applying one or all of the following exercises.

General Religious Exercises:

1. No one can make you do anything for very long unless you are personally convinced that it is the right thing to do. What do you think God wants you to do? Whatever this is, you need to generate the will and motivation to do it. You have to decide for yourself what you should actually do. Pray for guidance. When you decide, just do it! Get more involved morally and spiritually because a small involvement can lead to a greater involvement, and don't be afraid to involve yourself. Involvement is life, and the deeper you become involved, the more you will know the taste of abundant life. Self-enrichment happens through self-investment. You grow through commitment and by following through on it, by persevering. You develop enduring virtuous and holy traits of character by repeatedly practicing what you preach and believe. Thereby you help to create enduring spirituality within yourself. If you don't get involved, you will not enjoy and enrich your life or the lives of others. Spirituality is a creative and positive energy that always seeks new ways to improve and express itself. It is never satisfied with mediocrity. God is alive in writers, singers, teachers, nurses, farmers, laborers, and in all creative and helpful people. God's hands are our hands, for God works through us as well as in his own mysterious way. In whatever you do, strive for excellence. Demonstrate God's productive energy in your life. Don't get lazy in your comfort zone. Don't let religious peace degenerate into complacency. Always strive to be and to do better!

2. Practice sharing your spiritual experiences with others. Witness to others, help them to understand how your religious beliefs have made life better for you, and invite them to try spirituality for themselves. Listen also to how their own religious beliefs and

practices have made life better for them, and be open to learning from them. Spirituality is rooted in a respect for self that demands an equal respect for others, including their religious outlook. You can expect to be treated kindly and with dignity if you treat others that way. Then they will be attracted to you and be much more receptive to what you say. Always treat other people, no matter who they are, the way you would like to be treated yourself if you were in their shoes. This applies just as much to religion as to anything else. You will find that the more you give to others, the more you will receive—without expecting or asking for it. Giving results in serendipity! Invite the spirit of generosity to fill your heart so you may always reflect the gratitude that also gives. Spiritual abundance rests in giving and sharing, never in hoarding. Paradoxically, you can find yourself only by giving yourself away!

3. Remember that actions speak louder than words, so practice being a living example to others. Acting responsibly is one of life's great privileges and achievements. Your capacity for responsibility is an important gift from God, but you must learn to use that gift. Your sense of responsibility reflects your insight into and your involvement with God's will for his creation. The choices you make, enabled by God's gift of freedom, can both express and create greatness. We human beings are more than puppets on a string or robots. We are co-creative creatures of God who carry the burdens and the joys of responsibility; these are key elements in our universal human dignity. Being responsible means creatively initiating and doing what we do, knowing what we ought to do, choosing and doing the right thing when we could do otherwise, and being accountable to others and to God for our bad choices as well as our good ones. We pass through this world only once, but the choices we make exist forever in God, who never forgets the decisions we make, the help we give to others, or the harm we do to others. If you can show any kindness or do any good thing, do it now. Help somebody today! Don't put it off or neglect it because you may not have the opportunity again. Think of how others showed justice and kindness to you; and when the chance comes, be just, kind, and helpful to others gladly

and from your heart. Commit yourself to using kind words; this will create confidence in you and make communication with you much easier. A soft answer turns away wrath! Try to be kind and receptive in your thinking, for this will help you develop keener insight and understanding. Kindly giving creates and expresses love. It costs you nothing to say hello, smile, listen to another's pain, or show your respect for other people in numerous small ways every day. Your seemingly small responses can make tremendous differences to others.

4. Members of religious groups should encourage and support each other in countless ways. They should reenforce one another's beliefs where those beliefs are sound, and they should question and challenge one another's problematic or troublesome beliefs. They should help one another to grow in insight, wisdom, and knowledge, as well as in grace, or as a part of grace. They should not be afraid of the truth, not even scientific truth, for it will set them free. They should also help one another to feel welcome and accepted, especially those who do not love and respect themselves. Does your congregation minister effectively to those who are filled with guilt or devastated by failure? Can unforgiven people go to your religious group to find forgiveness and be restored to God's community and kingdom? Can unlovable people go to your religious group to be loved? Can poor people, people of another race, people of another religion, find respect and fellowship with you? Do you identify, treat, and shun some people as "outsiders" who are unworthy of your concern? Are you inclusive or exclusive? Is God's love inclusive or exclusive? Religious groups should provide emotional and devotional expression and support for their members while recognizing that different styles of worship appeal to different individuals. Religious communities can't literally be everything to everyone, but they can mean much to many. In your own religious group, do you and your fellow members help one another to find enduring satisfaction, insight, joy, comfort, and peace? Do you find adequate role models for graceful, reverent, and humble but capable leadership? Is doing God's will as important in your group

as knowing it or talking about it? Does your religious group support just causes, policies, and institutions? Is your religious group worthy of being called "God's people"? Where your group falls short, what can you do to help make it better?

You may deepen your understanding of the following extrinsic religious values and practices by looking up, reading, and reflecting on the following *Old Testament* references.

"My love for others is enhanced by my religious group." Leviticus 19:1-2, 17, 34; Numbers 15:15-16

"I actively help my religious group to grow," I. Chronicles 13:2-9; Psalms 22:22, 27-28; Psalms 40: 9-10

"My actions reflect and support my religious beliefs," Deuteronomy 13:4; Psalms 40: 8; Isaiah 1:16-17; Jeremiah 7: 23

Christian Exercises:

1. Develop a desire to devote more of your time to church activities. Resolve to help your congregation meet its goals through your direct participation. Join in an effort initiated by an outreach group in your church. Do all you can to spread the Gospel of love and to help those in need, and don't neglect seemingly small things. Be a friend to someone who is shy, socially awkward, or lonely. Provide rides to church for those who need them; bring food and other needed items to shut-ins; donate extra blankets or clothing; become a "big brother" or "big sister" to a child in distress. Do whatever you can whenever you can to relieve suffering and poverty, and assist others in need. Don't neglect the large things either. Don't pollute; pay your employees a living wage; provide them with medical insurance; initiate a profit sharing plan; give them a stake in the system. You will be pleasantly surprised by the results! In social policy matters, whether in business or in politics or government, be truthful, generous, and just. Treat your employees and your political constituency as ends in themselves and never merely as means, *i.e.*, never as having

merely extrinsic worth. Remember that to God your employees, your customers, and your constituency have just as much intrinsic worth as you have. Rich harvests cannot come from being lazy. You will reap what you sow (Galatians 6:7); and if you don't sow, you won't reap. If you want to bear good fruit in any part of your life, you must get busy now. Of course, there are dangers in busyness. Never confuse mere activity with accomplishment. Busyness without God can come up empty-handed. You can develop the heart of a servant by doing what God asks you to do. God has prepared a spiritual feast for you that starts long before you get to heaven. He wants Jesus to be the bread of your life right now; he wants to be your living water, your way, your truth, and your life today. Eternal life starts today! It is a way of living abundantly that includes today. Don't be content just to know *about* God in Jesus. Seek and pursue a personal relationship with him, and express what you have found with all your resources. "Draw nigh to God and he will draw nigh to you" (James 4:8). A few days after Jesus was crucified, his disciples and followers began to have a keen awareness of his ongoing presence with them. We can have this very same resurrection experiences today. Do you have them?

2. To live your life as a shining example, you must become more like Christ. You can do this by studying how he lived and loved; then invite him to work his powerful love through you. As a young man, Jesus grew not only in stature but also in knowledge, wisdom, and the love of God and of humankind, and so should you. Jesus said that to follow him, we must put aside our selfish ambitions (Luke 9:23). True humility is not thinking too highly of yourself; it is willing to be last instead of first; it is giving up power over others, superiority, pretense, and pretentiousness (Psalms138:6). Like a child, cultivate simple faith and humility before the Lord and act accordingly. Matthew 18:3-4 says that those who are as humble as a little child are the greatest in the Kingdom of Heaven. Many people think that they exist to be served, not to serve; but Jesus said that he came to serve, not to be served. Which is the Christlike way? Which is your way? God

shows his compassion by being merciful and gracious; he is slow to anger and full of unfailing love (Psalms 103:8). If, like Jesus and God, we were all humble and compassionate, war and violence would fade away. Real compassion is not about "I am doing something great" or "duty for the sake of duty." It combines selfless love with empathy and compassion; it suffers with those who suffer and rejoices with those who rejoice. Life's most positive and Godlike emotions are the fruits of God's Spirit in our lives: love, joy, peace, patience, kindness, goodness, gentleness, and self-control (Galatians 5:22-23). By these fruits, the depths of our spirituality are known.

3. One of the best ways to set boundaries for yourself is by studying the scriptures, which clearly state many helpful rules to guide you. We are instructed to avoid many things that may cause others to stumble (I. Corinthians 10:33). Abraham was able to obey God because he trusted God to help him. As your own faith grows, you will find an increasing desire to be obedient and to do the things you know you should do (Hebrews 11:8). You can pursue and practice righteousness by following what you know to be right and good; and the more you do it, the easier it becomes. Knowing what God wants you to do, actually doing it, and having the will power and motivation to do it, are very different, but you need them all. Pursue a godly life full of faith, perseverance, love, and gentleness (Proverbs 21:21). Be patient and forgiving with yourself, because lasting positive change usually takes time. Most people, even with the best of intentions, have at least one, and ordinarily more than one, bad habit. We are all like St. Paul, who confessed in Romans 7:17-19 that he didn't understand himself at all: he really wanted to do what is right, but he didn't do it. Instead, he did the very things he hated. Recognize that with God's help, you can make progress every day, but the road of ethical and spiritual growth is a very long road. After conversion comes sanctification, the process of becoming holy, and that is a lifelong project.

4. Practice looking for God everywhere, and eventually you will be able to find him everywhere. Where do you think God is? Is he in Heaven? Is he merely in Heaven? Do you believe with the

prophet Jeremiah that God fills heaven and earth? (Jeremiah 23:23) Can you with the Psalmist find the glory of God in the heavens, in the vastness, intricacy, and beauty of our universe? (Psalms 19) Do you think that there is any place you can go to escape or hide from God? (Psalms 139:7-10) Do you really believe that your own body is a temple of God, and do you act accordingly? Can you find God in small things near at hand, in all things bright and beautiful? Can you see God's creativity and closeness in all things great and small? Can you sense God's presence to some degree in everything that has being? If to some degree many animals can love, think, make conscious choices, act sacrificially, and be devoted parents, do they also exist in the image of God? Does everything that exists reflect God in some way and to some degree? How so, or not so? Does God love all human beings, even sinners? Does God love all his creatures, all living things, all non-living things, and not just human beings? If so, shouldn't we? Would our lives be richer or poorer in value if we did? Is God for you as for St. Paul the all-inclusive reality who is not far from us (or from anything) because in him we live, and move, and have our being (Acts 17:28)? Try to experience every place as a holy place, and try to make every day a holy day. Meditate on these things day and night, and be joyful that you are in God and God is in you.

If you are a Christian, you may deepen your understanding of the following extrinsic religious values and practices by looking up, reading, and reflecting on the following *New Testament* references.

"To me, the heavens declare the glory of God." Acts 17:24-28; John 1:3, 10, Romans 8:22; Hebrews 1:10; 11:3. (In the *Old Testament*, see: Genesis 1; Numbers 14:21; Psalms 19; 24:1-2; 104; 148; Proverbs 8:1, 22-31;Isaiah 6:3; Jeremiah 23:23).

"I support and attend my church regularly." Romans 12:4-8; I. Corinthians 12:27-31; I. Timothy 3:14-16; Hebrews 10:19-25; I. Peter 3:8

"I practice what I preach." II. Thessalonians 3:13; I. Timothy 4: 12; Titus 2:7; James 2:14-17; II. Peter 1:5-9; I. John 3:10, 16-18;

3. Thinking/Believing Triad

Please consider the following positive systemic thinking/believing religious value items from Part II of the RVP and the CVP.

CVP
My Christian beliefs help me to understand myself and others.
In religion, I put my money where my mouth is.
I understand God's covenant.

RVP
My religious beliefs strengthen my soul.
I try to live by God's commands.
My mind is in harmony with God's plan.

Spiritual Development Opportunity: The above systemic thinking/ believing value items illustrate your own personal understanding of and involvement with doctrinal truth, knowledge about God, religious laws, principles, and ritual forms. If you ranked these items just above the middle of the total 18 item range, your scores are problem free. If you ranked other phrases so far ahead of these that your score is only fair or weak, you could benefit from bringing this dimension into better perspective and into better balance with the other value dimensions. The two kinds of ranking errors that might arise are: overvaluation and undervaluation.

Overvaluation

Overvaluing in the thinking/believing realm means that you attach more worth to cognitive or systemic religious values than they really have. If you overvalue your own religious knowledge, understanding, principles, beliefs, doctrines, rituals, and obedience to God's commands, then to some extent, depending on your degree of deviation, you may have some or all of the following moral and spiritual problems. The list is by no means exhaustive:

- You tend to personalize ideas and ideals, especially those having religious significance for you.

- You may only love yourself to the degree that you conform to your ideal self-image, and you may have difficulty accepting or forgiving yourself and others because you forget that all humans are imperfect.

- You may intrinsically identify with words about God but not with God himself.

- You may tend to think that faith is primarily knowledge about and acceptance of religious beliefs and propositions, and your approach to religion and morality may be primarily intellectual or doctrinal. This can cause you to be morally and religiously ideological, dogmatic, authoritarian, and even fanatical.

- You may be inclined to judge beliefs, practices, and other people in black-or-white, all-or-nothing categories and have difficulty seeing shades of gray.

- You may be perfectionistic, utopian, and inflexible, as well as prejudiced and biased rather than open and fair-minded. This could cause you to value or love others only to the extent that they accept your beliefs and practices and see things your way.

Undervaluation

Undervaluing or negative evaluation of positive systemic value phrases means that you assign less worth to thinking/believing values than they really have. If you disvalue, neglect, or undervalue your personal religious involvement with beliefs, principles, rules, ritual forms, doctrines, and the like, this means that to some extent, depending on your degree of deviation, you may have some or all of the following problems, though the list is not exhaustive:

- You may lack a clear understanding of and appreciation for some, perhaps all, of the good things identified above that belong to the systemic or conceptual dimension.

- Your religious faith may not be well-defined or mature because you rely too much on your feelings and actions rather than on your religious knowledge and understanding.

- Your religious faith may not be mentally well developed or organized, and you may lack a solid conceptual foundation on which to base your beliefs. Unclear and unstructured religious thinking can leave you frustrated, confused, hesitant, or doubtful.

- You may find it difficult to discover meaning and order in established religion, society, nature, creation, and God. If you are confused and unable to make much sense out of what exists and what happens, you may tend toward depression or despair and find it difficult to hope and trust in God or anything else.

- Perhaps you don't try very hard to expand your personal understanding of God's words and commands so can live according to them on a daily basis.

- You may be easily dominated or even victimized by strong, dogmatic, and charismatic religious leaders or authorities.

Can you think of other problems that might arise from over- or undervaluing cognitive systemic spiritual values? If you have any of the above problems, what steps do you think you could take to correct them? Ministers or religious guides or counselors may be of help. You may improve your understanding and appreciation of religious thinking/believing values by studying and applying the following exercises.

General Religious Exercises:

1. Whatever they are, the rules and guidelines you have adopted to live by are deeply religious in nature. They are of deep concern to you. "Religion" means "re-binding" of all the parts. The rules and principles you and others live by are the cords that make binding and re-binding possible. They make social living possible; without it, none of us could exist. Most religious people take their laws and principles from their scriptures and from the priests, teachers, Rabbis, and writings that interpret them. You need to choose rules and guidelines to live by very consciously, deliberately, and thoughtfully. Make sure that your principles are in harmony with the best that the scriptures have to offer, with the still small voice of conscience within you, and with what is best and most fulfilling for everyone. Would your rules or maxims require you to do unto others as you would have them do unto you? Are they the best available way to express justice, mercy, and love? Review, identify, understand, clarify, and apply the rules you would live by and the ones for which you would die. Are you trying to earn your salvation by following God's rules, or does your obedience express your salvation? Try to understand how sincere religious people can honestly disagree among themselves about some religion-based guidelines; acknowledge that grey areas and genuine uncertainties exist. Then, allow your most deeply considered judgments to become the voice of your conscience. Let its inner light guide you down the right path and keep you from wrongdoing. Give God's moral laws unto yourself so that they also become your laws, but remember that the deep spirit of the law can be more important than the details.

2. Think about how you fill your time with meaning. Consider your profession or work; a great deal of your time is spent preparing for and doing your job. Consider also the amount of time you devote each day to prayer or worship. A good practice is to get up

in the morning before dawn and seek God's presence. Fifteen minutes before the sun rises, when the sky is becoming a little lighter, just wait and watch, as if expecting a beloved one: so tense, so deeply awaiting, so hopeful and excited, yet silent. Let the sun rise, and go on watching and waiting. You will get the feeling that something inside of you is also rising. Think of yourself as being a part of God's harmonious plan. Allow your body to sway with the wind. Listen to the birds sing. Be alert, listen, and become an integral part of God's creation. If you do this at least one day per week, there will be a significant change in you. Many days a week would be even better! Your whole day and week will go much better. As you get more in tune with God's harmony and embrace his plan for your life, typical day-to-day problems will disturb you less and less. You will develop more of your godly or divine nature and find yourself giving more of your time and worldly goods to God's service.

3. You have many minds that change often; you are multi-psychic. One moment your mind can be full of belief and in the next full of doubt. Within you conflicts abound, including conflicts between good and evil, right and wrong. The mind often works to segment and divide, and it is great at creating. It can create cures or illnesses, beauty or ugliness, success or failure, righteousness or unrighteousness. Every deliberate action starts with thought. Minds can reflect on pain and pleasure, birth and death—on everything. Once you realize this, the conjurer disappears, and what is left is the truth that liberates; so get a handle on your mind, your thoughts, your beliefs. Whether you feel happy or miserable depends largely on the "scripts" that you allow to run constantly through your consciousness, and you can control these if you try. Repeating and internalizing the following mantra should help you gain better control of your thoughts:

> Watch your thoughts, for they become your words.
> Watch your words, for they become your deeds.
> Watch your deeds, for they become your habits.
> Watch your habits, for they become your character.
> Watch your character, for it becomes your destiny.

5. Your mind is like a huge shipyard; like ships, your thoughts are coming and going all the time, and so are your sense-impressions, desires, memories, and expectations, many of which are very unpleasant and fearful. With God's help, you must take on the job of ticket inspector. Right now, all your negative thoughts are riding for free. Anger, fear, jealousy, and greed are excess baggage; they have nothing to do with your real identity. They are sinking your boat. It is time to throw them overboard! And when they come back, learn to stop them at the dock; instead, let in justice, kindness, compassion, and forgiveness—the real ticket holders. The best way to clear your mind of unwanted baggage is through the kind of meditation that slows down the rush of your thoughts until they finally come to rest. For most of us, this is difficult because our minds do not like to be still and meditate; they want to wander. Yet, when our concentration is complete, even for a few minutes, the rushing turbulent process we call "mind" almost comes to a healing halt. In those few moments all kinds of changes can take place throughout our minds and bodies. Our breathing rhythm may fall drastically—down to 2 to 4 times a minute instead of 16. Other biological processes are also slowed down without our even being aware of it. When we meditate, we may reach such a deeply restful state of spiritual renewal that we will want it again and will do everything we can to make our next period of meditation or communion with God even deeper.

Once the mind is slowed down, then gradually we can discover new ways of thinking, speaking, and behaving. We can choose for ourselves how to respond because we can, with God's help, choose to change ourselves. Meditation or devotion cannot be practiced in fits and starts merely when we happen to think of it, or feel like it, or have nothing else to do. Putting meditation or private devotional time first and making it a regular part of our daily schedules can save us from many doubts, difficulties, and indecisions. Meditation or prayer can get our day off to a good start, and when we go out into the world, we will have a good reserve of spiritual energy and security on which to draw. This will help us to be patient instead of angry, empathetic instead of selfish, and loving instead of resentful. Prayer or meditation is a matter of untying spiritual and mental knots, not of reading books. A dog tied up for a long time takes off like a rocket when released, and we will feel a release of tremendous energy as each psychological knot is undone.

5. Being committed to and reflecting often upon certain religious convictions about you and God will help to strengthen your soul, but which ones? Try to decide for yourself, write your own credo, but consider the following example:

God exists, and God has disclosed to us in many ways that he created us and loves us. God is altogether worthy of our complete devotion, for no better or more worshipful reality can be conceived. God wills communion and fellowship with us, and he wants us to give them to him freely, without coercion from existing powers and principalities. God wants to be loved and served freely, or not at all. God created this universe and chose it for us to live in, but God is not the only creative decision-maker who exists. God has the power to share his creative powers with his creatures, the freedom to make us free. He made us in his image to be co-creators with himself, so we are free and responsible for the choices that we make and the things that we do. God loves us all individually in our uniqueness and concreteness. The goodness that we experience and achieve in our lives does not perish forever with the passing of time; it endures everlastingly in God, who will always cherish us and all that we were and are. Our lives are living sacrifices to God, they are also be living gifts to God, for all the goodness that we create in our own lives and for others is ultimately contributed to God. God will never forget us.

The evils and losses that we inflict on any living being are ultimately inflicted on God who forever suffers with and for those we have harmed. God will never forget our evildoing either, though he will forgive if we repent, seek his forgiveness, and do our best to change our wicked ways. God is the supreme evaluator and conservator of our value and of all else that is dear to us. Because we are all valued infinitely and equally by a loving God, then we are all of infinite and equal value—precisely and only because of God's valuing and loving relationships with us. God's love gives each of us an equal and inexhaustible worth that we would not otherwise have. His love is worth just that much to you and to everyone else.

Let this credo strengthen your soul, and improve it where you can.

You may deepen your understanding of the following systemic religious values and practices by looking up, reading, and reflecting on the following *Old Testament* references.

"My religious beliefs strengthen my soul." II. Chronicles 20:20-21; Psalms 1; 18:1-2; 27:1; 78:1-8; Jeremiah 17:7-8

"I try to live by God's commands." Genesis 18:19; Deuteronomy 11; 28:1-6; 30:9-20; Psalms 119; Proverbs 4

"My mind is in harmony with God's plan." Joshua 1:8; I. Kings 19:11-13; Psalms 1:2; 48:9, 14; Isaiah 25:1; 26:3; Micah 4:1-5; 6:8

Christian Exercises:

1. A biblically balanced Christian has both a full head and a full heart. Burning hearts should not be kindled by brainless heads; we must not have zeal without knowledge, for that is mindless fanaticism. God wants to be loved with our minds as well as with our hearts and souls. Wisdom is a God-like virtue. Like Jesus, we must be intentional learners, as he was at age 12, sitting among the teachers, ". . . hearing them and asking them questions. And all that heard him were astonished at his understanding and answers" (Luke 2:46-47). Jesus continued to increase "in wisdom and stature, and in favor with God and man" (Luke 2:52); and in his ministry he taught others what he had learned, and he also gave us so much more—himself. The Bible clearly values learning, teaching, knowledge, and wisdom. We read in Proverbs 9:9, "Give instruction to a wise man and he will yet be wiser; teach a just

man and he will increase in learning." Proverbs 10:14 tells us that "Wise men lay up knowledge." No matter how much you already know about God, Christ, the Bible, or the Christian life, you still need to make a serious effort to learn because you have not learned it all. Learning is a lifelong spiritual discipline that characterizes wise and devout persons. St. Paul wrote, "And be not conformed to this world: but be ye *transformed* by the renewing of your mind, that ye may prove what is that good, and acceptable, and perfect, will of God" (Romans 12:2). The Bible insists that learning is essential for becoming more Christlike and Godlike. Age and experience alone will not increase your spiritual maturity. Godliness, as I. Timothy 4:7-8 suggests, requires deliberate effort. Discipline yourself to become a lifelong intentional learner. Above all, remember that one important goal of learning is Christlikeness. Jesus said, ". . . learn from me . . ." (Matthew 11:28). Godly learning can lead to Godly valuing and living.

2. Godliness is the result of a disciplined spiritual life, and at the heart of it is how we use our time. A classic scriptural alert is, "Now is the accepted time; behold, now is the day of salvation" (II. Corinthians 6:2). The time to prepare for eternity is right now; right now is a part of eternity. The more scarce something is, the more valuable it tends to be. Time is a scarce commodity. James 4:14 reminds us that we do not know what will happen tomorrow, and our time is very short and uncertain. Time lost cannot be regained. Of his own brief life, Jesus said, "I must work the works of him that sent me, while it is day: the night cometh, when no man can work" (John 9:4). Romans 14:12 reminds us, "Every one of us will give an account of himself to God." We will be held accountable for our earthly use of time. According to Jesus, we are accountable to our Lord for all the talents we have received and for how we use them (Matthew 25:14-30). This should not mean that we try to earn our salvation by knowing and acting upon and abiding by God's laws; doing so is the result, not the cause, of our salvation. Money cannot buy time, and the best way to have no regrets when your time

runs out is to use your time for the glory of God, for growth in God's wisdom and grace, and for doing God's will. Study the scriptures, pray, worship, spread the good news, serve where opportunities present themselves. Start today! A godly life is an abundant life!

3.   You can serve God through a disciplined use of your money and possessions. Ultimately, God owns everything (Job 41:11). The earth is not yours or mine. The earth is the Lord's, and the fulness thereof (Psalms 24:1). This means that we are only managers or stewards of everything that God has given to us. Giving should be much more than a duty or an obligation; let it be an act of worship. Your giving is a tangible indication of how much faith you have that God will provide for your needs (Mark 12:41-44). Giving reflects your spiritual trustworthiness (Luke 16:10-13). If you love Christ with all your heart and are willing to obey him in every area of your life, your giving will reflect that. Giving should be sacrificial and generous, as St. Paul indicates in II. Corinthians 8:1-5. You can receive great joy and fulfillment by giving something away that you cannot keep forever anyway. Generous giving results in many unexpected blessings. Jesus said, "Give, and it shall be given unto you . . . with the same measure that ye mete withal it shall be measured to you again" (Luke 6:38). So, give willingly, thankfully, and cheerfully. The promise of God in II. Corinthians 9:6-8 is that if we sow sparingly will also reap sparingly, but if we sow generously we will also reap generously. This does not necessarily mean that we will reap in kind; physical sowing may or may not result only in spiritual reaping. Each of us should give what we have decided in our hearts to give, but we should not give reluctantly or under compulsion, for "God loveth a cheerful giver."

4.   God's covenant with us is not simply that he will give us his laws through external authorities, even though this has happened, but that he will write his commandments on our minds and hearts (Jeremiah 31:31-34; Hebrews 8:10; Romans 2:13-16). We all go through stages in life when moral authority is vested in persons

and authorities other than ourselves—in the teachings and examples of our parents, in the views and practices of our peers, in the opinions and examples of other church members, in our ministers or priests, or in the holy scriptures. Immediately after birth, we go through a long period of time when we have not yet "eaten of the tree of good and evil," when we don't actually know the difference between right and wrong, good and evil, even if this knowledge lies deeply but unconsciously within us. Human infants really do not know anything, including the difference between good and evil! As we grow and mature morally and spiritually, we do learn, with the help of others, to know the difference; and if "the fall" is learning the difference between right and wrong, good and evil, it is a "fall upward," as someone has said. An early church father said that disobeying God, not gaining knowledge, was Adam's sin. In the Genesis story, God knows what Satan knows—that human beings would be more Godlike if they come to know the difference between good and evil (Genesis 3:5). Eventually, as we mature, we put away childish things; we come to be responsible to and within ourselves for our own values, choices, and actions; we learn to be true to ourselves and to choose ourselves from all the alternatives before us. When mature, we find "the law" within ourselves, where God has written it on our hearts, and thus we give the law to ourselves. When adequately informed and developed, our own consciences, our own minds and hearts, tell us what to value and what to disvalue; and God's covenant with us is kept (Hebrews 8:11).

5. Consider or reconsider exercise 5 above under "General Religious Exercises."

If you are a Christian, you may deepen your understanding of the following systemic religious values by looking up, reading, and reflecting on the following *New Testament* references.

"My Christian beliefs help me to understand myself and others." Matthew 5, 6, 7; Mark 8:34-38; Romans 12; I. Corinthians 13; Galatians 5; Ephesians 2;

"In religion, I put my money where my mouth is." Matthew 5:40-42; 7:9-12; 25:31-40; Luke 16:10-13; Acts 20:35; II. Corinthians 9:6-8; I. Timothy 6:6-10

"I understand God's covenant." Mark 14:17-25; Acts 3:24-26; Romans 12:2; Hebrews 7, 8, 9. (In the *Old Testament*, see: Genesis 9:8-17; 17:1-8; Deuteronomy 7:9)

CHAPTER FIVE

Negative Values: Overvaluation and Undervaluation

I. CVP and RVP Part I, Transpositions (Negative Value Combinations)

An abundance of negative and evil trends continues to flourish year after year in our modern society; these include: the escalation in murder, violence, rape, and robbery; abusive and exploitative relationships in the home, the church, and the wider community; growing numbers of young people addicted to drugs and alcohol; and the adverse effects upon children from the high proportion of marriages ending in divorce. The list of evil trends could go on and on. These problems are not by nature inevitable, and none are due to any lack of knowledge. When we think carefully, we can see that all these problems have a major ethical component. They reflect our understanding of what is right and wrong, positive and negative, appropriate and inappropriate, acceptable and unacceptable. Our external and internal problems cannot be resolved until we address the underlying neglect of our inner spiritual dimensions. We need a spiritual revolution, and an important part of it must include identifying and avoiding ugliness or evil.

I. Kings 3:5-10 says that the Lord appeared to Solomon in a dream and asked him what he wanted to be given. Solomon asked for an understanding heart: *to discern between good and bad*. It pleased the Lord that Solomon did not ask for a long life, or riches, or for his enemies to be slain, but that he asked instead for a wise and understanding heart.

Currently, many popular concepts are floating around that may act as blocks to living a righteous life and to discerning the difference between right and wrong. The first is "relativity"; many people say there can be no absolute truth, it's all relative. Albert Einstein, the physicist who created the physical theory of relativity, had this to say: "Relativity is for physics, not for ethics." Our message in this book is that spiritual Goodness is absolute, and there is never a time or place where it is out of place.

Another concept being widely discussed is "tolerance." This means putting up with people who have different views, beliefs, or lifestyles. Within very broad limits, this is a wonderful thing, but clear cut evils should not be tolerated. If we embrace moral evils, this could be very dangerous to everyone's quality of life and to life itself. Tolerating legitimate differences must always go hand in hand with taking a firm stand for that which is righteous and godly.

In addition, the concept of "discrimination" may confuse many people. Discrimination as injustice or unfair treatment is a very bad thing, but discrimination in another sense is very good. Good discrimination consists in the mental clarity to distinguish between similar and dissimilar things, including the difference between good and evil. If you lose your ability to tell right from wrong, if you cannot distinguish between them, then you will be unable to recognize and resist temptation. Our society may have taken the concept of "politically incorrect" somewhat too far. When we change language itself in order not to offend some special interest group, we may be covering up evil and making things appear less bad than they actually are.

The Christian and Religious Value Profiles include familiar items and phrases having religious significance, and they call forth your religious knowledge, discernment, and involvement. Each item or phrase to be ranked involves both a thinking and an emotional response. The DIS score on your Result Form indicates your capacity to distinguish between good and evil, right and wrong. The Profiles consist of nine compositions (items having degrees of goodness), and nine transpositions (items having degrees of badness). If you ranked a good value item (a composition) as a bad one (a transposition), or vice versa, you may be somewhat confused in your thinking or understanding, or you may have had a strong emotional reaction to one or more of the items that blocks discernment, at least temporarily. Emotions and thoughts cannot ultimately be separated. Your overall state of mind and heart at the moment is the key to your actions. If powerful negative thoughts, hatred, or anger grip you, your mind and heart will be in turmoil. This can cause you to lose your sense of perspective and proportion and do things that have negative impacts on others and yourself. When your disposition is calm and compassionate, your thinking will be clearer; and your actions will likely contribute to the well-being of others and yourself and thus be ethically appropriate.

This section will help you to understand and distinguish more clearly between varying degrees of badness, just as the preceding chapters helped you to better understand varying degrees of goodness and Godliness. Let understanding guide you in avoiding evil; as you grasp the meaning of "badness," you will also become more aware of spiritual goodness.

1. Negative Devotional Triad
(Social Intrinsic)

The negative or transpositional intrinsic value items in Part I of the RVP and the CVP are as follows:

CVP
Absolutely rejecting Jesus
Despising Christian living
Maliciously perverting religious teachings

RVP
A person's eternal separation from God
Loathing righteous living
Utter contempt for the idea of God

Spiritual Development Opportunity: Negative values or transpositions in the devotional triad are *intrinsic* disvalues (things undesirable for their own sakes) that can express the absence or negation of an intimate or personal relation with God and with everything God loves. The disvalues on the Profile(s) involve varying degrees of badness or evil. If you ranked other values below these such that your "Intrinsic Orientation" score, line 3 on Results Form 1, fell into the "average," "fair," or "weak" column on the result graph, you could benefit from bringing this dimension into clearer focus. The main goals of this chapter are to provide conceptual clarification and mental exercises that can help raise your awareness of transpositions, of items that involve badness or evil. You have a significant opportunity to improve your awareness of negative intrinsic values if you study the discussions in this chapter. Two kinds of potential problems involve overvaluing or undervaluing the items on the Profile(s).

Overvaluing *positive* items, as in Chapters Three and Four, means that you see them as *better* than they really are; but overvaluing the *negative* items, as in this chapter, means that you see them as *worse* than they really are, that you attribute more badness to them than they actually have.

Unlike undervaluing positive items as worse than they really are, undervaluing negative items means seeing them as better than they really are.

Overvaluation

In most cases, overvaluation is not possible for negative intrinsic values, since they represent the worst possible items for religious and Christian believers. In a spiritual context, nothing is worse than these. In a forced ranking of 18 items, there is no possibility for a "19." The above items are the most extreme negative values on the Profile(s), so we will deal here mainly with undervaluations, with seeing the items as better than or not as bad as the mathematical norm specifies. In rare cases, people will rank something in the list as worse than it really is. They may see "despising Christian living" as the worst thing, "18," and they may rank "Absolutely rejecting Jesus" as "17." This can result in an overvaluation of the group or the triad as a whole. The people who mis-rank these items do not see the relative badness of each item in the triad as clearly as they should. If they rank "Absolutely rejecting Jesus" as a positive value (1-9), this is a distortion or confusion between good and bad, and they are either very confused or not religious or Christian at all! If you overvalued this triad, perhaps you are so sensitive to badness or evil in the world around you that you tend to overcompensate and label any and all degrees of badness as extreme, even though some things are really not all that bad objectively. Such misjudging can cause needless conflict with others who do not push every negative evil to an ultimate extreme.

Undervaluation

An undervaluation exists if your percentage score on line 3, "Intrinsic Orientation," on the Result Form, is *excessively* negative. For example, on the RVP, if you ranked "Eternal separation from God" as other than "18," this means that you see something else as being even worse. For sincerely religious persons, nothing is worse than being eternally separated from God! With only 18 items in the entire list, assigning it a "19" is not possible; this number falls outside the ranking system. A person must either rank "Eternal separation from God" exactly right as an "18" or else rank it with a lower number. If you ranked it as a "14," this means you see less badness in this item than you actually should. The value items contained in the devotional transposition triad represent the *worst* possible values for religious people, including Christians. Look at the three value items above, read them over again, and see if you don't "see" that these value items are instances of badness or evil and that some are worse than others. To rank something else in the lists as worse than these three is to underestimate the badness of the negative items in the devotional triad. Trying to think of other spiritually evil or bad values items not on this list would be a good exercise for you.

If your score for "Intrinsic Orientation," line 3 on Result Form 1, is more negative than positive, this means that you may not be as sensitive as you should be to badness or evil and the destruction it can bring. Perhaps you tend to ignore evil, but this could be very dangerous for you and to others around you. Perhaps you had an automatic and powerful negative emotional response to some other item that is actually less bad than the worst negative intrinsic items. For example, "Telling lies" or "Burning a cross" may have triggered an extreme reaction due to some previous unpleasant experience in your life, and you may have ranked them below the intrinsic evils. No matter what, badness or evil really does exists; and it can harm us and those we love, especially if we are not alert to it and constantly aware of it. Resolve to understand better and to acknowledge the sort and degree of negativity that these items represent.

The following explanation designed for all readers should help you better understand degrees of badness or evil, including the most extreme intrinsic evils.

Social Intrinsic Evils

The court systems in most countries differentiate between degrees of murder. Try to rank order from bad to worst the following three options.

a. an intoxicated driver hits another car head-on, killing its driver.
b. a wife shoots her husband to death during a heated argument.
c. a man keeps a woman prisoner in his basement and tortures her to death.

These are all very bad deeds, but "a" is not as bad as "b," and "c" is the worst of the three. Discuss these options in a group or with a friend, guide, or counselor, and try to identify the valuational differences between them. Look at a Biblical distinction between intentional killing and unintentional killing in Numbers 35:9-34.

Although death results in all three instances, in the U.S. court system, option "a" would probably be classified as "manslaughter," option "b" as "2nd degree murder," and option "c" as "1st degree murder." Each exemplifies a different degree of evil or wrongdoing. How are they different?

Option "a" is not as bad as the others because the killing was not planned, but it was an unintended indirect consequence of behavior well known as likely to be harmful. The deadly extrinsic deed was done without any systemic understanding of or anticipation of doing it and without any intrinsic intent to kill. That the man was so drunk that he could not drive well is truly regrettable, but people who inadvertently harm other persons do not *intend* the harmful consequences. However, if the behavior itself, drunk driving, is likely to have harmful results to others or self, it should be avoided. The drunk driver definitely caused the other driver's death and is indirectly accountable for it because he knew the perils of driving when intoxicated. The court will likely render a "guilty of manslaughter" verdict, sentence the drunk driver to several years behind bars, but not give him a death sentence.

Option "b" is somewhat worse than "a." Here, the wife temporarily "lost her mind," so to speak, due to the intensity of the argument. Her passions clouded both her systemic or conceptual understanding of what she was doing extrinsically as well as her intrinsic intentions, but she still knew right from wrong. Perhaps the husband was abusing his wife. Whatever provoked her, the wife suddenly devalued her husband to "non-person" status, to a "thing" to be stopped and destroyed. After the heat of passion was over, she probably had deep remorse over killing her husband. If she had no remorse, the court's sentence would likely be more severe, but her penalty would not be execution.

Option "c" is clearly the worst case. Here the extrinsic deeds of kidnaping, torture, and murder were done with full systemic understanding and with gruesome negative intrinsic intentions to torment and kill—a hideous intrinsic disvaluation of another intrinsically valuable person. This murder was planned, intended, and executed. The perpetrator meant to harm his prisoner, to torture her and eventually to kill her. This killer's sentence, proportional to the greater evil inflicted, would likely be life imprisonment or execution if allowed by that state's laws. This kind of behavior is hard to understand and very unpleasant to think about. But we have to consider such very evil deeds occasionally in order to make sure that we are sensitive to what we must avoid as morally, religiously, and spiritually committed people.

So what should we avoid as religious and Christian people? In the first case, we should avoid impairment of both body and mind likely to result in harm to or the death of another. Clearly, we should avoid impairments of our minds and bodies like those resulting from drugs or alcohol. We should value being in knowing control of what we do. We should also avoid circumstances of passion, as in the second case, where we could lose our grip on the intrinsic value of another person. Impassioned arguments, hostility, and hatred must be resisted.

We should never knowingly and deliberately treat another person, an intrinsic value, as merely a thing, an extrinsic value. Finally, as in the third case, malice, fervently intending the suffering and/or death of another, must be avoided. The intrinsic disvaluation of an intrinsic value is the worst evil of all.

In many discussions of ethics, a basic rule concerning how to treat another person is, "Above all, do no harm." We should focus on the beautiful and the good and avoid, as best we can, what is ugly and hurtful. If we have done something wicked or evil, or even if we contemplate doing it, we should have a guilty conscience. How can we avoid doing harmful deeds and evil? Religion provides one good answer: our relationship to God and/or Jesus can help us. Let God or Jesus guide your thoughts, actions, and feelings toward goodness and away from evil. To quote the 23rd Psalm, "Yea, though I walk through the valley of the shadow of death, I will fear no evil: for thou art with me . . . . Surely goodness and mercy shall follow me all the days of my life: and I will dwell in the house of the Lord forever." Godly goodness and mercy can and should be both within us and without us.

You may deepen your understanding of negative devotional values by looking up, reading, and reflecting on the following *Old Testament* and/or *New Testament* references.

Old Testament References

"A person's eternal separation from God," Psalms 1; 9: 15-17; 36; 37:1-2, 9-10, 38;

"Loathing righteous living," Deuteronomy 9:4-24; Isaiah 28:14-15; Ezekiel 20:5-32;

"Utter contempt for the idea of God," Job 2:9; 21:14-15; Psalms 14:1-4; Jeremiah 28:15-16;

New Testament References

"Absolutely rejecting Jesus," I. Corinthians 12:3; Hebrews 6:4-6

"Despising Christian living" II. Timothy 3:1-5

"Maliciously perverting religious teachings" Romans 1:18-22; II. Timothy 2:23-26; 3:1-7:4:1-4. See also: Isaiah 5:20; Jeremiah 28:15-16

2. Negative Practical Triad
(Social Extrinsic)

Please consider the following negative extrinsic value items that are in Part I of the RVP and the CVP:

CVP
Persecuting Christians
Burning a cross
Doing what we know is wrong

RVP
Oppressing God's people
Defiling a house of worship
Mocking sacred teachings

Spiritual Development Opportunity: *Practical negative religious values* (extrinsic transpositions) are actions or behaviors that oppose religious activities, rituals, and righteousness. If you ranked other values above or below the above items so that your score on Result Form 1, line 5, "Extrinsic Orientation," fell into the "average," "fair" or "weak" column, you could benefit from bringing this dimension into clearer focus. You have a significant opportunity for improvement if you read over and study the following. Two kinds of potential problems involve overvaluing or undervaluing the items.

Overvaluing *positive* items, as in Chapters Three and Four, means that you see them as *better* than they really are; but overvaluing the *negative* items, as in this chapter, means that you see them as *worse* than they really are, that you attribute more badness to them than they actually have.

Unlike undervaluing positive items as worse than they really are, undervaluing negative items means seeing them as better than they really are.

Overvaluation

If you overvalued the above items, as disclosed by a positive bias result score on line 5, "Extrinsic Orientation," you doubtless realize that when people do such bad things, they are really, really bad. You may see such undesirable actions as the worst possible things that anyone could do. Clearly, "Persecuting Christians" and "Oppressing God's people" are very bad acts; and they should be ranked relatively low on the scale. However, if you look again at evils in the preceding devotional triad, you will realize that "Absolutely rejecting Jesus" and the other items in that intrinsic devotional group are even worse. After due consideration, you should also recognize that the items in the conceptual triad below are not quite as bad. You should strive to achieve a correct ranking of all of these negative spiritual value items, one in which all the negative value items are ranked at or close to the norm.

Look again carefully at the items above. You should recognize that all of these items are indeed bad, but some are worse than others.

Undervaluation

If you ranked other items on the Profile(s) (besides the intrinsic devotional ones) as worse than the extrinsic evils above, these other items will be ranked as worse than they should be. Perhaps you do not clearly see the badness of these negative extrinsic religious values and their degree of seriousness in relation to the other bad items.

If you ranked any or all of the above extrinsically bad items positively as good things (that is, if you ranked them in the 1-9 range), this distortion indicates that you lack intellectual discernment and sensitivity concerning evil actions; you confuse evil with goodness. Certainly, no one should want to go around "Burning crosses" and no one should ever consider "Defiling a house of worship." Some people actually do these bad things; but they probably do not have genuine moral, religious, or Christian convictions or a very clear understanding of bad or negative practical actions. Yet some things of religious concern are not as bad as, and others are worse than, the three above items.

You can improve spiritually if you develop a clearer understanding and proper ranking of these practical negative values (disvalues), especially as related to the devotional and conceptual items.

If your positive percentage score on line 5, "Extrinsic Orientation," is low, then the following explanations, designed for all readers, may be of help you.

Social Extrinsic Evils

Destructive things and actions that result in extrinsic ruin are all negative values. They are not positive values at all; they involve less value, value loss, disvalue, or evil. If an old building is destroyed in order to build a new one, this is not necessarily a bad thing, all things considered, even though bulldozing the old building is a negative for it. By contrast, consider destroying and ruining a good building out of revenge, malice, envy, or hatred. Try to rank the following three options from bad to worst.

a. As a prank, a person cuts the electric wires and the phone lines to a business.

b. A disgruntled employee of the business comes back at night and sets fire to it, burns it to the ground, and destroys the business.

c. A gang kidnaps and holds a child for ransom at a business, and they wreck the building to show they are serious.

Alternative "a" is not as bad as "b," and "c" is the worst of the three. For option "a," destructive pranks by definition have bad consequences. The above prank is certainly bad for the business and the business owners because they lose contact with their paying customers and they must spend time and money to get the problems repaired. Also, the person playing the prank is harmed on the inside; the deed depreciates him or her as a person. This extrinsic devaluation (the prank) of extrinsic values (the electrical and phone lines) also devalues persons (the business owners and the prankster). In addition, if the prankster is caught, he or she will be arrested and may have to serve jail time. Pernicious pranks are evil and must be avoided. If we desire to develop our spiritual potentials, we can not even think of destroying property as a prank.

Alternative "b" is clearly bad and even more destructive evil than the prank. Destroying an entire building is clearly worse than the above prank because a much greater quantity of valuable property is obliterated. Very few people would actually burn down a building out of anger, but this sort of thing does happen, and when it does, the extrinsic devaluation of property and persons is even greater than the damage done by the prankster. Obviously, malicious arson will be avoided by good and godly people.

Alternative "c" is the worse evil in two senses. Kidnaping a person is a serious crime in itself, clearly an evil deed. The kidnaped child is terrorized, emotionally harmed, and deprived of her or his freedom. In addition, to show their seriousness, the kidnappers destroy a good building. Serious intrinsic evil is here compounded by serious extrinsic evil. Such compound evils will definitely be ranked as very bad and avoided by people who want to live godly and Christian lives.

You may deepen your understanding of negative practical values by looking up, reading, and reflecting on the following *Old Testament* and/or *New Testament* references.

Old Testament References

"Oppressing God's people," Deuteronomy 24:14; Proverbs 14:31; Isaiah 1:17; 10:1-3; Micah 2:1-2

"Defiling a house of worship," Ezekiel 22:8; 23:38

"Mocking sacred teachings," Exodus 32:1-10; II. Chronicles 36:15-16; Psalms 14:1-4

New Testament References

"Persecuting Christians," Matthew 5:11, 44; Acts 7:44-8:3; 9:1-5; Galatians 1:13; II. Timothy 3:12

"Burning a cross," This modern perversion did not occur during the Biblical era.

"Doing what we know is wrong," Romans 7:15-25

3. Negative Conceptual Triad
(Social Systemic)

Please consider the following three negative systemic value items from Part I of the RVP and the CVP:

CVP

Religious doctrines that depreciate women, minorities, or outsiders
Telling lies
Misunderstanding a Bible verse

RVP

Doubts about God
Actions condemned by a religious belief
False religious doctrines

Spiritual Development Opportunity: Negative conceptual value items are *systemic* negations of such religiously desirable things as doctrinal truths, theological knowledge, and religious laws and principles. If you ranked other values much higher or lower than these, and your score on Result Form 1, line 7, "Systemic Orientation," fell into the "average," "fair" or "weak" range, you could benefit from bringing this dimension into clearer focus. You have a significant opportunity to improve if you read over and understand the following explanations. Two kinds of potential problems are overvaluing or undervaluing the items.

Overvaluing *positive* items, as in Chapters Three and Four, means that you see them as *better* than they really are; but overvaluing the *negative* items, as in this chapter, means that you see them as *worse* than they really are, that you attribute more badness to them than they actually have.

Unlike undervaluing positive items as worse than they really are, undervaluing negative items means seeing them as better than they really are.

Overvaluation

If you ranked the above conceptual spiritual items very low on the scale (close to 18), you judged them to be worse than the norm specifies. This is an *overvaluation* that attributes more badness to these items than they actually have. For example, by comparison with intrinsic evils, "Telling lies" is a relatively mild negative value; it could be more seriously negative depending on its consequences, that is, when combined with additional negative values. If you think that lying is always a very seriously bad thing, you may overestimate its badness and place it toward the bottom of your rankings. "Misunderstanding a Bible verse" is another relatively mild negative, though it too at times could be rather serious when combined with additional bad consequences. If you consider lying or misunderstanding a Bible verse as such to be a very seriously bad thing always, you may rank them toward the very bottom of the 18 point scale. However, this would overestimate their badness relative to the other very bad things on the Profile(s).

Overvaluation of conceptual transpositional items is very common. Many people make such mistakes, and they are fairly easy to understand and correct. Read again the negative or undesirable conceptual spiritual items above. Then compare them with the bad things in the devotional and practical spiritual value dimensions. Consider this until you are clear about their differences and degrees of badness. Which values really have the worst bad-making properties?

Undervaluation

If you ranked any or all of the above conceptual spiritual items higher (closer to 1 on the 18 point scale) than you should have, then you see them as less negative or bad than they really are. Your ranking indicates that you do not perceive the degree of badness contained in these items and may not see them as bad at all. According to the mathematical norm, these items express the least degrees of badness relative to the other negative items. None of the above conceptual spiritual disvalues are positive; they are all negative; they all have some degree of badness. They are all disvalues, but you need to understand just how bad they are in relation to the other value items on the entire Profile(s).

Imaging a neutral line between the 9 positive items and the 9 negative ones on the Profile(s) might help you to understand. The conceptual spiritual items above fall slightly on the negative side, just below the imaginary line. The negative practical spiritual items represent a greater degree of badness and fall even lower, and the negative devotional items are the worst of all, illustrate the greatest evils, and fall lowest on the scale.

Undervaluation of the negative conceptual spiritual items will produce a "distortion" because a slightly bad value is ranked as at least slightly good. All distortions are undesirable because they confuse good and bad value items. Distortions may result because of the forced ranking procedure. That is, if you first ranked most of the other value items, you may then be forced to position one of the remaining slightly negative value items as positive.

Read over all of the conceptual spiritual items above, and then compare them with the devotional and practical spiritual items. Do this until you are clear about their differences and degrees of badness. If your score on line 7, Result Form 1, shows a very weak positive percentage, then you undervalued something in this group, and the following explanation written for all readers may benefit you.

Social Systemic Evils

Concepts or ideas can be used to negate other ideas, to depreciate various objects and activities, and to depreciate other persons. All such cases involve negative conceptual values or systemic evils. These evils are not very well articulated in most ethical and religious writings; but to make strides in developing your spiritual potentials, understanding these differences is important. Try ranking the following three alternatives from bad to worst. Do you know why you so ranked them? Which has the most undesirable or bad-making properties? Which has the least? Which falls in between the extremes?

a. Someone steals money from a bank and replaces it with counterfeit bills.

b. A person yells, "fire" in a theater when there is no fire.

c. Someone promotes the ideas that women are by nature subservient to men and that people of other races are less than human.

Alternative "a" is not as bad as "b," and "c" is the worst of the three. Why is this true? Alternative "a" involves financial theft and passing counterfeit money. This occurs often, even with trusted bank employees. Although the bank's money is insured and will be replaced by the insurance company, the deed still causes the bank a lot of trouble, and if the counterfeit money is not found in time, it may be passed on to bank customers in transactions. This can harm the bank as well as its customers, other businesses, and all of us taxpayers. Clearly, this immoral deed is a crime and is punishable in our court system. It involves harming the established monetary system with the falsity of counterfeit money, but its harms extend far beyond that. Established systems are often harmed with or by a false system. These days, identity fraud, where someone steals another person's credit cards, driver's license, bank account number, *etc.*, is a growing problem. The innocent person suddenly finds that identity theft results in enormous debt. Systems crimes facilitated by computers and the Internet are on the rise. More and more computer viruses are being introduced into the Internet system, and hackers often get into a widely used website, shut it down, or commit other "white collar crimes." The example of "Misunderstanding a Bible verse" in the Christian Value Profile is usually only a slightly bad thing. Its evil is very subtle, but it can also lead to bad consequences, and that new value combination makes things worse. All of us misunderstand the Bible at times. Bible verses from the book of *Revelation* are often misunderstood, and such misunderstandings can lead to even greater misunderstandings. All instances of a system disvalued by another system are bad; they are small evils that can become great evils when compounded with additional bad things or consequences. These evils are to be avoided and not tolerated. In religion, only the love of God with our minds stands between us and many such evils

Alternative "b" is slightly worse than "a," at least in its consequences. It may be a "joke" to the one screaming "fire," but it could easily cause some patrons of the theater to be injured or trampled to death. The immoral crime involves using the language system to mis-describe the facts, the external circumstances, in situations where people are likely to act and react in panic. Such bad deeds are sinful, clearly evil. Using words to frighten people literally to death is much worse, both legally and morally, than passing counterfeit money. Can you think of other instances where the wrongful use of language causes people to be alarmed, perhaps to panic, and to make choices that they otherwise would not make, to their great harm?

Is alternative "c" is the worst of the three alternatives? It seems to be because of the magnitude or scale of its evil consequences. Racial slurs and negative comments about women and minorities do great harm to them and often result in their persecution, exploitation, humiliation, physical abuse, or murder. Victims of prejudicial language may suffer economically, physically, and personally for many years. Prejudicial speech both harms minorities and spiritually degrades the people who promote and identify themselves with such undesirable ideas. Those who wish to clarify and develop their spiritual potentials cannot bear false prejudicial witness. (If you think that "b" is worse than "c," make a case for it.)

You may deepen your understanding of negative conceptual values by looking up, reading, and reflecting on the following *Old Testament* and/or *New Testament* references.

Old Testament References

"Doubts about God," Psalms 53:1; 107:11

"Actions condemned by a religious belief," Exodus 20:3-17

"False religious doctrines," Psalms 119:128; Jeremiah 5:30-31; 29:30-32

New Testament References

"Religious doctrines that depreciate women, minorities, or outsiders," I. Corinthians 14:34-35; Ephesians 4:22-28; 5:22-24; 6:5, 9; Colossians 4:18, 22; Galatians 3:28. See also Genesis 3:16.

"Telling lies," Galatians 1:6-9; Acts 5:1-11; Revelation 21:8. See also Exodus 20:16; 23:1, 7; Psalms 120:2

"Misunderstanding a Bible verse," I. Corinthians 13:8-12; James 3:1-2. See also: Isaiah 55:7-9

II. RVP and CVP Part II, Transpositions (Negative Value Combinations)

1. Negative Being/Feeling Triad (Personal Intrinsic)

Please consider the following three negative being/feeling intrinsic value phrases from Part II of the RVP and the CVP:

CVP
I feel that God could never forgive me.
I hate doing God's will.
I despise religious rules.

RVP
I blame God for all the evils people suffer.
I detest organized religion.
I despise religious dogmas.

Spiritual Development Opportunity: Negative or transpositional being/ feeling religious values are *personal intrinsic* values that negate or indicate the absence of a personal relationship with God and/or with other people. Taken together, the above value phrases express personal rejection of spiritual values in almost all segments of life. If you ranked other values so far below these that your scores were "average," "fair" or "weak" on Result Form 2, you could benefit from bringing this dimension into clearer focus by reading and studying the following discussions. Two kinds of potential problems here are overvaluing or undervaluing the items.

Overvaluing *positive* items, as in Chapters Three and Four, means that you see them as *better* than they really are; but overvaluing the *negative* items, as in this chapter, means that you see them as *worse* than they really are, that you attribute more badness to them than they actually have.

Unlike undervaluing positive items as worse than they really are, undervaluing negative items means seeing them as better than they really are.

Overvaluation

The above intrinsic disvalue phrases represent badness or evil, and nothing is worse, given all the phrases on the Profile(s). Overvaluation means placing *more* badness on these phrases than they actually have. Logically, this is not possible with the above items since they represent the very worst possible values for religious and Christian people. In a forced ranking of 18 value items, there is no possibility for a "19." With such items we usually must deal with undervaluations where people see less badness in these phrases than they really have; some people see them as better than the mathematical norm specifies.

Some people may rank one of the intrinsic spiritual disvalue or disvaluation items above lower than where it should be, judging it to be worse than it is. People who are burned out with following all the rules may thus rank "I despise religious rules" as the phrase they most disagree with, as "18." They may then rank "I feel that God could never forgive me" as "17." This can result in an overvaluation of the intrinsic spiritual negatives as a group. When this happens, people do not see the badness of each phrase above as clearly as they should.

Read over the above phrases, then compare them with the other negative doing/acting and thinking/believing phrases. Try to grasp the extreme evil that these items reflect. If your "Intrinsic Involvement" score, line 3 on Results Form 2, showed either a very weak or a highly positive percentage, then the following discussion of personal intrinsic evil may be of help to you.

Undervaluation

Problems are always associated with overlooking or not recognizing badness or evil for what it is. One kind of undervaluation occurs when a negative phrase is ranked as positive, resulting in a *distortion*. If a person ranks "I feel that God could never forgive me," so high on the scale (between 1 and 9) that it is a positive value, he or she very much agrees or identifies with this negative phrase. This indicates that the person is in great spiritual and personal distress and feels enormous guilt.

In most cases, slight undervaluations occur as a result of judging these phrases as *less bad* than the norm. This means that the person does not see all the evil that these phrases actually express. People who identify or agree with "I blame God for all the evils people suffer" and rank this phrase much higher on the scale than they should are not likely to be very religious, and they may openly rebel against religion and religious believers. This undervaluation reveals a severe block to their spirituality. They probably need help.

Read and study the being/feeling spiritual phrases above. Compare them with all the other evils on the Profile(s), and try to grasp the varying degrees of evil expressed by these phrases. The study below should help to elevate your awareness of degrees of badness and to make you more open to internalizing goodness. If your "Intrinsic Involvement" score, line 3 on Results Form 2, shows an extreme negative percentage, then the following discussion written for all readers may help you.

Personal Intrinsic Evils

On this personal section (Part II) of the Religious and Christian Value Profiles, you were asked to rank order the value items or phrases from most agreement to greatest disagreement. Earlier, we discussed different kinds of murder to clarify social intrinsic evil. Of course we do not believe that our readers are actually committing such evils as murder! From time to time, however, even religious people may bring about intrinsic evils. One such intrinsic evil is hatred. Hatred has the same general value structure as murder, the intrinsic disvaluation of an intrinsic value, and both represent evil in the extreme. We hope that no one actually hates anyone else for any reason; but if you happen to hate, you as a person are harmed, and hatred can ruin all your joy in life. Hatred is a very painful or miserable emotional state. Your hatred probably makes you much more uncomfortable than it does the people you hate!

Please consider the following three options, and try to rank their degrees of evil from bad-for-me to the worst-for-me.

a. Hating another person due to her or his different race or creed.
b. Hating another person due to social conflicts.
c. Hating another person totally and absolutely.

These options are listed and ordered from bad to worst. Option "a" is not as bad as option "b," and options "c" reflects the greatest evil. Can you see the differences? Read over the following explanation, and try to understand how such degrees of evil could negatively impact your own life.

Option "a" probably reflects a programmed emotional response due to such cultural habits as labeling people, name calling, or simply prejudice. Most social groups label other groups as "foreigners," "outsiders," "inferiors," or "undesirables." People in the labeling group try to elevate themselves by putting down the members of the other group. Many of us participate in this evil because as members of certain social groups we were taught these prejudices very early in our lives. As the song from *South Pacific* tells us, we have to be carefully taught to hate all the people our relatives hate! Some religious believers and Christians adopt such prejudices as a part of an ethnocentric cultural world view and confuse them with real religion or real Christianity. "Ethnocentric" means that your positive attitudes and beliefs are centered only in your own social group, and you are not able to embrace anything beyond your own limited social horizons. For authentic religious and Christian believers, this evil is to be avoided and condemned. Our God is the God of all. God does not approach human beings through prejudicial labels. God sees through all human social roles and linguistic labels to the heart and soul of each individual. At one time or another most Christians sing a hymn having these words: "Red and yellow, black and white; ALL are precious in His sight." We should embrace the words of this song!

Option "b" can take many forms. One person may hate an ex-spouse due to battles over money and child custody. Another person may hate competitors in the constant struggle to gain a better job, higher social status, or a better social position. A child may hate a schoolmate due to competition on the playground, or because he or she gets better grades or more recognition and praise in class. The list could go on and on. When David came to Saul and told the King, "I will go and fight Goliath." Saul looked at young David and said, "You are not able to do much against this giant. Let me provide you with a sword and a shield so that you can fight better." David tried on all the armor, then threw it off in favor of his trusty slingshot. When David relied on the talent God gave to him uniquely, he was able to kill the giant. If he had relied on what Saul wanted him to do, he probably would have failed. We should do as David did and rely on our own God-given resources and talents. God made each of us precious and unique. We cannot and should not always do what others want us to do. We have to do the best we can with what God has given to us specifically. There is no need to be jealous of someone else or to covet what they have. When we are authentically ourselves and true to what God has given us, we can shine to others and be at peace with them, with ourselves, and with God.

Option "c" is indeed so evil that it amounts to the same thing as actual murder, the intrinsic disvaluation of an intrinsic value. If we hate another person enough to kill him, then we have killed him in our own hearts. As we are in our hearts, so are we. Hatred eats us up inside, making the quality of our own lives miserable; and it gets expressed in deplorable deeds. Hatred makes people sour, irritable, stagnant, hostile. Hatred prevents us from seeing the goodness that exists in the people we hate. We cannot flow with the river toward God when hatred keeps us walled up in a pond. This kind of evil should be avoided, with God's help; it will definitely block us from developing our spiritual potentials.

You may deepen your understanding of negative being/feeling values by looking up, reading, and reflecting on the following *Old Testament* and/or *New Testament* references.

Old Testament References

"I blame God for all the evils people suffer," Job 16:6-17

"I detest organized religion," Deuteronomy 31:24-29; Ezekiel 20:10-13, 21

"I despise religious dogmas," Leviticus 26:14-17; Ezekiel 20:13; Amos 2:4

New Testament References

"I feel that God could never forgive me," Matthew 6:12; 18:21-22; Ephesians 1:7: See also: Psalms 86:5; 103:3

"I hate doing God's will," Matthew 6:24; John 15:18-25; Romans 1:28-32

"I despise religious rules," Romans 8:7; I. Timothy 8-11, III. John1:11. See also: Psalms 78:56-57; 107:11; Isaiah 59:12-15;

2. Negative Doing/Acting Triad (Personal Extrinsic)

Please consider the following three negative doing or extrinsic value phrases from Part II of the CVP and the RVP:

CVP
My actions dishonor Christ.
I work hard to undermine the church.
I do what I know I shouldn't do.

RVP
I curse God.
Serving God is a waste my time.
My actions often conflict with my religious beliefs.

Spiritual Development Opportunity: Personal negative doing- or action-based religious values, extrinsic disvalues or transpositions, negate or block taking an active role in religion or Christianity; they express non-participation in and negation of religious or church activities and good works. If you ranked other values so much lower or higher that your "Extrinsic Involvement" score, line 5 on Result Form 2, fell into the average, fair or weak range on the result graph, you should try to bring the above negative values into clearer focus. Reading and studying the following discussions may help. Two kinds of potential problems are overvaluing or undervaluing these extrinsic spiritual disvalue items.

Overvaluing *positive* items, as in Chapters Three and Four, means that you see them as *better* than they really are; but overvaluing the *negative* items, as in this chapter, means that you see them as *worse* than they really are, that you attribute more badness to them than they actually have.

Unlike undervaluing positive items as worse than they really are, undervaluing negative items means seeing them as better than they really are.

Overvaluation

Overvaluation occurs when negative value phrases are ranked as worse (closer to 18) than the norm specifies. Overvaluation is seeing *more* badness in these spiritual disvalues than they actually have. Overvaluing these doing/acting negative phrases shows that you see one or more of them as very, very bad, as maybe the worst thing possible. To understand the relative badness expressed by these phrases, compare them to the being/feeling disvalues above and to the thinking/believing disvalues below.

Just why "I curse God" should be ranked very low on the scale is easy to see; most religious people would never think of doing something like this. The directions in the Profile(s) instruct people to rank all the given value items according to their own agreement or disagreement. Most people would not agree with "I curse God," so they are likely to rank this very low, thereby indicating disagreement. This may be an overvaluation. The same is true for "I work hard to undermine the church." Very few if any people would identify or agree with this, so most people will rank this very low on the scale. But how low is low enough, and how low is too low? To improve and increase your spiritual sensitivity you must acknowledge that some things are even worse, that some phrases on the Profile(s) express even more badness or evil than these. Also, some things are not as bad.

Read over and study the above phrases until you gain a better or clearer understanding of their relative badness. You may benefit from reading the discussion below on personal extrinsic evils.

Undervaluation

An undervaluation occurs when people rank these doing/acting negative religious items better (higher on the scale) than the norm specifies. This means that they do not see as much badness in them as they should, that they agree with them to a higher degree than they should. For example, "I do what I know I shouldn't do" may get some agreement, and thereby an undervaluation, because most people at one time or another actually do something they know is wrong. Of course, when this happens, a religious person should seek God's forgiveness and should also seek forgiveness from those harmed by her or his action. If this happens very frequently, the person must agree that the item applies to his or her own life. This type of undervaluation indicates that the person is having great difficulty with certain aspects of his or her behavior. Help from God and from a religious or psychological counselor or guide may be needed.

The goal here is to raise your awareness of negative or undesirable doing/action items and to help you avoid them. Compare the negative items in the doing/acting list above to the negative spiritual being/feeling items, the very worst ones. Then compare them to the negative thinking/believing items below, the least bad. Read and study the differences and your awareness of degrees of badness and evil will be raised to a higher level. You may benefit from reading and thinking about the discussion below, written for all readers.

Personal Extrinsic Evils

Doing something that you may later regret is very common. We all want to avoid doing something that would bring not just regret but *remorse*. Extreme remorse is similar to hatred; it eats away at you continually, infects your thinking, depresses your life, and makes you miserable. To avoid remorse, we must become more aware of the disvalues associated with doing bad deeds. Realizing what evildoing means and understanding its consequences may help avoid it. We are not suggesting that a reader of this book would actually do the bad deeds listed above. However, any religious person may, at times, do some rather bad things. Try to rank the following deeds from bad-for-you to the worst-for-you, and try to understand the grounds of your ranking in terms of degrees of bad-making properties.

    a.   making a promise you know you will not or cannot keep.
    b.   ruining someone's work to make him or her look bad.
    c.   taunting or mocking another person.

Alternative "a" is not as bad as "b," and "c" is the worst of the three. Let us explore the meaning and possible consequences of these bad deeds.

Alternative "a" means doing something untruthful—acting extrinsically to make public a systemic disvalue. It means telling someone you will do something when you know you can or will not do it. This gives false hope and expectations to the other person, and thereby it harms her or him. It also harms you, the promise-breaker, due to the corrupt inner intent of the deed itself. Making lying promises is to be avoided and condemned because it harms all concerned, and it can and often does lead to larger evils. Allowing seemingly small evils to creep into your life will make you weaker spiritually, not stronger.

Alternative "b" is worse than "a." Here an extrinsic act destroys an extrinsic good to degrade an intrinsically valuable person. Maybe the doer of this evil deed is jealous of the other person or of his or her social or professional status. He or she may have done good work on a project, but the competitive doer of this destructive deed does not want the success of the rival to be recognized and praised, so the good work is ruined. Clearly, this kind of deed should be avoided and condemned as an evil thing.

Alternative "c" is the worst of these three options and perhaps the most subtle. We all "kid" others occasionally, and that's OK; but taunting or mocking others goes far beyond kidding in its harmful purpose, intent, and results. Here an intrinsically valuable person directly intends and acts to degrade another intrinsically valuable person. Suppose that this happens to a child in school who is overweight or who doesn't wear the best or most fashionable clothes. Clearly, the abused child will feel unworthy and rejected. If the snobbish and disrespectful mocking continues, the abused child may not even want to go to school, may seek horrifying revenge, and may even be driven to suicide. This very bad deed, extremely evil and subtle, should be avoided and condemned. Engaging in this kind of behavior, or allow your children to act that way, blocks spiritual development and sets a very bad example. Snobbish and disrespectful mockers are well down the road toward juvenile delinquency and adult criminal behavior. We should always treat others respectfully and teach our children to do the same.

You may deepen your understanding of negative doing/acting values by looking up, reading, and reflecting on the following *Old Testament* and/or *New Testament* references.

Old Testament References

"I curse God," Exodus 20:7; 22:28; Job 2:9; Psalms 62:4

"Serving God is a waste my time," Ecclesiastes 3:1-13; Malachi 3:14-16

"My actions often conflict with my religious beliefs," I. Kings 21:20-26; II. Samuel 11-12:14; Psalms 51; 78

New Testament References

"My actions dishonor Christ," John 8:49; Romans 2:12-24; Galatians 5:16-24

"I work hard to undermine the church," I. Corinthians 10:31-33; Galatians 1:6-14; I. Timothy 3; III. John 1:9-11

"I do what I know I shouldn't do," Romans 7:15-25

3. Negative Thinking/Believing Triad
(Personal Systemic)

Please consider the following negative thinking/believing personal systemic value phrases from Part II of the RVP and the CVP:

CVP
I have doubts about Jesus.
I don't always know the right thing to do.
I am confused about God's plan.

RVP
I have doubts about God.
God's commandments are too hard for me to keep.
Some of my religious beliefs contradict each other.

Spiritual development opportunity: Personal negative spiritual values in the thinking/believing dimension involve the negation or disvaluation of personal involvement with such things as doctrines and beliefs about God and his laws and principles. If you ranked other values so much lower or higher than the ones above that your systemic involvement score fell into the average, fair or weak range on line 7, "Systemic Involvement," on Results Form 2, you could benefit from reading and studying the following. Overvaluation and undervaluation are two possible kinds of ranking errors.

Overvaluing *positive* items, as in Chapters Three and Four, means that you see them as *better* than they really are; but overvaluing the *negative* items, as in this chapter, means that you see them as *worse* than they really are, that you attribute more badness to them than they actually have.

Unlike undervaluing positive items as worse than they really are, undervaluing negative items means seeing them as better than they really are.

Overvaluation

An overvaluation occurs when people rank any of the negative thinking/ believing religious phrases above as worse (closer to 18) than the norm specifies. This means that they do not agree that the item applies to their own spiritual lives, and they see *more* badness in or disagree more with it than is appropriate. If people have very little or no doubt(s) about Jesus, and their faith is strong, they will not identify or agree with the "I have doubts about Jesus" phrase. If they rank it too very low, this overvalues it, makes it worse than it really is. If people are not at all "confused about God's plan," they will not agree that this item applies to their spiritual life, and they may rank this item much lower on the scale than it should be.

Very little is wrong with most overvaluation as such; however, in a forced ranking system, overvaluation will push other disvalue phrases higher on the scale than they should be, and this may reveal problems that should be explored.

Read and study the negative thinking/believing spiritual phrases above and compare them to both the being/feeling and doing/acting negative phrases. You should gradually become more aware of the relative degrees of badness expressed by all these phrases. This new awareness will lead to an expansion of your own spiritual potentials.

Undervaluation

Undervaluation occurs when any of the religious phrases above are ranked as better (closer to 1) than the norm specifies. Those who undervalue the above phrases agree to some extent that the phrase applies to their own lives. This is easy to understand. Many people have some doubts about God or Jesus, and it is fairly common for people to think at times that this applies to their own spiritual life. If their doubt is very deep and persistent, then they may rank this phrase rather higher than they should, indicating that they agree with it and perhaps do not see the badness in it. More than likely, however, they do see the badness expressed by the phrase, and they are suffering because it really does apply to them to some degree. If their undervaluations become more numerous, these people are likely feeling great anxiety and stress with regard to their spirituality and faith.

If people agree with "I am confused about God's plan," ranking it fairly high on the scale (closer to 1), they are expressing a cry for help. Other undervaluations involving the thinking/believing spiritual phrases express a similar condition.

Read and study the negative phrases in the thinking/believing triad above and compare them to the negative being/feeling and doing/ acting phrases. Gradually, you will become more aware of varying degrees of badness expressed by all these phrases. This will help you to develop a much higher level of sensitivity to both bad and good spiritual values. With practice, you will be better able to overcome evil and allow more positive goodness to enter your spiritual life. For further clarification, please read over the discussion that follows, written for all readers.

Personal Systemic Evils

This section covers the least bad spiritual things that people can do. These disvalues are not terribly severe; as milder, they reflect less evil and have fewer bad-making properties. Most of these disvalues occur quite often, and many people fall into the trap of doing these things, which could have bad consequences and lead to even worse things. Religious and Christian people may not fully realize that these items are also sinful and should be avoided. Try to rank order the following three alternatives from bad-for-me to the worst-for-me and to understand why you make your rankings.

a. subtracting when you should add on your tax return, hoping the IRS will not catch it.

b. lying to avoid a meeting or to get out of work

c. spreading a rumor about someone when you know it is not true.

Option "a" is not as bad as option "b," and option "c" is the worst of the three. Think over these options and try to explain why this is so.

Option "a" is clearly cheating, and cheating is wrong. In this example, not as much value is lost as in options "b" or "c." The IRS may catch the intentional error, but they may not. The cheater may get away with it. Nonetheless, the cheater can never get away from himself or herself, and the act of cheating itself internally disvalues the cheater. The cheater develops a pattern of cutting corners for fictitious reasons. Using a fiction or falsehood to alter or to invert established rules or the truth, a systemic disvaluation of systemic value, is dishonest and should be avoided.

Option "b" is very common. It involves spreading systemic misinformation to avoid fulfilling extrinsic obligations. Almost every day someone may ask you to attend an important meeting or some other event. Perhaps you have something else that you would rather do. Instead of responding truthfully with, "I have a conflict, something else scheduled," you may say "Yes, I will come to the event" knowing full well that you will not. Misleading others should be avoided. On the job, lying is very common. Often a person feels in fine health, but he or she may call in to work and say, "I am really sick today." On the face of it, this "little white lie" is not so bad. But think about it. The liar risks becoming habitually untruthful about "small things" (in the liar's estimation) that inevitably spills over into larger things. The consequence is that others who count on what the person says are likely to be harmed; but the harm done is not only to others; the liar is also harmed spiritually and morally. Any enduring vice is sinfulness that degrades the sinner. You do not want to develop very bad habits.

Option "c" is the worst of these three options. It involves systemic misrepresentation for the purpose of directly degrading another intrinsically valuable person who should be treated as intrinsically valuable. The "tale-bearer" in this instance deliberately damages another person who does not deserve it. This bearer of false witness also devalues himself or herself through the act. Such bad deeds are spiritually and morally corrupting and block spiritual development. Spiritual excellence allows no place for spreading malicious rumors or gossip.

You may deepen your understanding of negative thinking/believing values by looking up, reading, and reflecting on the following *Old Testament* and/or *New Testament* references.

Old Testament References

"I have doubts about God," Psalms 52:7-9; 78:21-22; Isaiah 45:11

"God's commandments are too hard for me to keep," Psalms 119; Proverbs 24:7

"Some of my religious beliefs contradict each other," This is a problem for *you*.

New Testament References

"I have doubts about Jesus," Matthew 14:30-32; John 20:24-29; Jude 1:22

"I don't always know the right thing to do," Mark 12:24; Luke 23:33-34

"I am confused about God's plan," Romans 13:8-10; Hebrews 8:10-13

CHAPTER SIX

Being and Becoming All that
We Can Be Before God

All of us can, do, and should want to live more abundantly, to be all that we can be, to live the very best life that we can possibly live. Jesus expressed this idea when he suggested that we could and should live more abundantly, but this is not a distinctively Christian belief. All believers in one God agree that we live out our lives "before God" and that God wants every one of us, his children, to live the best lives we can in his presence. The trouble is, most of us do not know what living abundantly means, much less how to achieve it or our need for God's help in doing so; these issues must be explored in some depth. We do not have a concept of "our total human development," but most religions, and even some secular sources, emphasize the importance of ongoing self-development. You may remember that for many years the United States Army used "Be all that you can be" as its recruiting slogan. Similar expressions of this ideal are commonplace; it has universal religious and human appeal.

Religious people include spirituality within the idea of "being all that we can be," recognize that we live out our lives "before God," and acknowledge that without God our lives are immensely if not infinitely impoverished. Often this is only "lip service," but we would all live very differently if we really took the idea of existing "before God" very seriously. In principle if not always in practice, Christians, Jews, Moslems, and all believers in one God share this belief; and it can and should be a key element in the highest forms of personal and spiritual development. It should be profoundly felt and lived as well as believed. This chapter will try to explain how to live more abundantly in several value dimensions. When, with God's help, we realize our potentials in all these dimensions and keep our confidence in God and His promises in our hearts and thoughts, we will both be and become all that we can be before God. If and when we fail to be and become all that we can be before God, we are moral and spiritual underachievers, that is, "sinners," and none of us really want that! There are many ways to fail, as we sinners know at least dimly; but we need to understand more clearly what succeeding and failing before God really mean. And then, by and with God's grace and help, we need to do something about it. We need to achieve a clearer comprehension of "abundant living, of "all that we can be," of "our total personal development" before God. Then we need to do our part as God does his part; we need to do whatever it takes to reach this high mark, this high calling of God. In order to find the mark, or to fall short of it, we have to have the mark, the standard, the goal; and to achieve it we have to think, choose, feel, and act effectively.

I. A Believable Concept of "All that We Can Be Before God"

In thinking about "our total personal development before God," we must first consider the idea of "development." This dynamic concept is relevant to our situation because we live in time; we have a present now with us, a past behind us, and a future before us; and we can recall the past, directly experience the present, and anticipate the future. If this were not true, we would have no personalities at all and would not be concerned with our spiritual growth and development![8] Think of one of your own ongoing projects—like trying to become a better person. You were doing it in the past, are working on it in the present, and will continue it in the future. This particular project may never come to an end! Striving in God's presence and with God's aid to complete our projects, to achieve our objectives, is an important part of being and becoming all that we can be before God.

Being all that we can be is really not enough to describe us; we cannot afford to ignore *becoming* all that we can be. What and who we are now are important, but so are what and who we could become. This means that we must know who and what we were and are and envision and choose what we could and should be. We don't exist merely in static space as material beings; we are much more than just "matter in motion." We are *unfinished* individual conscious spiritual becomings in need of further development—toward God and toward our own personal godliness. If we are not moving toward God, we are denying our destiny and wasting our lives. We need to avoid becoming spiritually and morally stagnant or stuck where we are.

Our human reality is mainly dynamic becoming, not static being. Time perpetually perishes and perpetually creates. Much of what we *are* at this moment is simply given to us by our heredity and environment; but some of what we are is due to partly self-creative choices or decisions that we made in the past. Our past and present decisions can imprison us, or they can free us and propel us towards God, who is our ultimate environment and destiny. What we will *be* in the future depends largely on what and how we decide right now to *become* because we create who we will be through the choices that we make in the here and now. Our reality *includes and largely is* our becoming; it is realizing our possibilities through our receiving, striving, willing, and aspiring. Time is a key factor in our lives; just *killing time* can waste or destroy who and what we are. Some people "die" at twenty and are buried decades later. We want to escape time's emptiness and meaninglessness. We want to live in the "*fullness* of time," to fill our time with the richest possible meaning and worth. If we kill the time of our lives, we waste it; but we can learn to consecrate it, to fill it full, to live more abundantly.

As our real selves grow, partly through our personal striving, choosing, and aspiring, our lives become more certain and definite; some of our real possibilities decrease while others increase. As we make life's choices, we eliminate some possibilities while opening up new ones. If each of us marries one spouse, we cannot marry all the other possibilities, but we open up new possibilities for living concretely, intensely, intimately, and devotedly with our "dearly beloved one and only." If we take one job we cannot take the alternative jobs, or if we join and participate fully in one religious group we cannot join and participate fully in the others. Eliminating some options makes our lives more definite and opens up new possibilities for fulfilling ourselves distinctively in our chosen mates and work and in our selected communities and congregations. If we choose to do the right thing, the moral thing, we cut off the immoral possibilities; but we also find new and fulfilling possibilities for righteous, godly, and abundant being and becoming before God. Sometimes, spiritual development and moral integrity require us to make hard choices. We cannot serve both God and mammon!

A. Some Help from Hartman's Theory of Value

We cannot make much sense our of "our total human development" without doing some thinking about values. One of the best things about Robert S. Hartman's formal value theory is that it can tell us very clearly what an abundant life is. It can tell us how to be and become all that we can be and how to understand and measure such things.[9] In showing us what it is like to be as good as we can be, axiology also shows us what it is like to be less than the best, what it is like to underachieve. By fulfilling certain standards, we can live better and thus more abundant lives. If we fail to fulfill the appropriate norms, we thereby become axiological and spiritual underachievers. Axiology or value theory can show us both how to meet and also how to fail to fulfill the standards that give meaning to the very notion of being and becoming the best individuals that we can be before God. We have to be very careful what we think about and dwell upon. Things like greed, envy, pride, hatred, and jealousy can block our moral and spiritual development and deny us the joy or happiness that comes from being in harmony and touch with God.

Robert S. Hartman's value theory, applied to us, says that our ideas, concepts, and beliefs are very important, but they are not the most important things in the world. Ideas can be contemplated and enjoyed, and we can do many things with them. We can create ideal standards of value that may be fulfilled and used to measure degrees of worth or degrees of worthlessness and unworthiness, of fulfillment or non-fulfillment. The procedure of measuring things by standards of excellence can be applied to almost anything, including "our total human development," which seems to mean the same thing as "having a full life," "living the very best life we can possibly live," and "having a truly abundant life" before God. None of us will ever live a perfect life, but whether very religious or not we want to live as abundantly as we can. Spiritually, we want to live as fully and faithfully as we can before God, and this involves having a constant awareness of God's presence with and to us and of God's concern for us and for all creation. It involves godliness without ceasing!

"Good" things fulfill the names, concepts, or standards that we apply to them; "bad" things do not measure up. Fair, average, and poor things measure up (or fail) by degrees. Some things are better or more valuable than others, depending on (1) the degree to which they include or illustrate the features expressed in our standards or concepts, and (2) on the degree of goodness or richness in and of the standards themselves.

Morally and spiritual, we yearn and strive to bring our value standards into harmony with those of God. We can and do hope that our most deeply considered human judgments about good or evil, right or wrong, better or worse, coincide with God's. We implore God's help in making it so. If we don't succeed, we are idolaters who confuse God with the relative goods of our own limited time and place. We must always proceed cautiously and pray earnestly that in the depths of our souls we are in tune with God. Axiology or value theory can be extremely helpful in keeping us on the right track. Some valuable things are better than others, and some are the very best of the lot that is available to us. Axiology can tell us what our value judgments mean and how best to apply them. It can tell us what it means to be and to become the very best persons we can be, to live the richest and most meaningful lives that we can possibly live, before God.

The concept "value" can be applied to different *kinds* of value. This means we can both recognize and prioritize different kinds of value. By now you are familiar with the differences between intrinsic, extrinsic, and systemic values. Value theory can help us to get our priorities straight. *Some kinds of value are richer than others in both quantity and quality of what philosophers call "good-making" traits or properties. Value objects* are the ideas, things, and people to which we attach some degree of goodness or badness; we measure how much goodness or badness they have by applying our *value standards* to them and checking to see how they measure up. Just as inches or feet compose our measuring rods for distances, so sets or groups of ideas compose our standards or measuring rods for value. The realities to which we apply them are good or less than good according to the degree that they measure up to or fulfill their measuring rods. We can rationally measure the value of anything by comparing it to the ideal elements that compose our relevant value standards and by discerning the degree to which it fulfills those standards. Some things are better or more valuable than others, depending on the degree to which they exemplify the good-making traits contained in the standards or ideals of value that we apply to them.

If the standard by which we measure a certain kind of thing consists of five good-making traits—A, B, C, D, and E—then an instance of that kind of thing will be good if it actually has all five of these traits; and it will be less than good (fair, average, poor, no good) to the degree that it lacks some of them. An example may help. Let us say that "good preachers" A. know the Bible; B. can explain its messages well to their congregations; C. can use language that most people understand; D. can present their messages in an appealing way; E. and can show the relevance of their messages to people's lives. Then, if Rev. Doesitall satisfies all these conditions, he is a good preacher. To the degree that he fails to fulfill this ideal set of standards, he is less than good, maybe only fair or average. Of course, being a good preacher involves a lot more than this, which means that we really need a richer set of value standards for "good preacher," one that contains more than five ideal elements.

Different *kinds* of value standards and value objects can be placed into hierarchies of value where some are better (or worse) than others because some *kinds* of value are richer in both quantity and/or quality of good-making traits than others. Robert S. Hartman believed that intrinsic value objects have more worth than extrinsic value objects, which in turn have more worth than systemic value objects. Thus, they form a hierarchy of kinds of value. In simpler words, in application this hierarchy of value says that *people as unique individuals are more valuable than things, but things are more valuable than mere ideas of things or of people.* Thus, we ought to value individual persons (including God as the Supreme Person) more than things, and things more than mere ideas, and live accordingly. This needs more explaining, but in one way or another, this hierarchy is affirmed by the world's major religions, and many recent studies now show that the majority of people all over the world agree with this hierarchy, at least in their more reflective moments.[10]

Why should we believe that some *kinds* of value are better than others? This is another place where Hartman's theory of value is illuminating. "Better than," is defined as "having more good-making qualities than," and this is the key to understanding and applying the hierarchy of values. Things are better in good-making traits than mere ideas; and people are richer in both quantity and quality of good-making traits than both things and ideas. "Best," means "richest in good-making traits or qualities," so to live the best lives that we can possibly live before God, we must live lives that are richest in good-making qualities. Just what that means will now be explained.

Valuable *thoughts or ideas* are *systemic "blueprints" or mental tokens that point to certain realities and function in our thinking as substitutes for them*, and they are less valuable than (have fewer good-making qualities than) the objects toward which they point. Scientific value theory thus shows us that things are more valuable than mere concepts of things. If anything has more good-making traits than an idea, it is more valuable than an idea. Material or physical things, processes, and activities, including human behaviors, are very valuable extrinsic realities; and they are always richer in good-making qualities than the merely systemic ideas or concepts that we have of them. Actually doing God's will is far better than merely thinking about it, but just thinking about it is itself a good thing! Extrinsic realities are always better than systemic concepts. Innumerable words about a good car never add up to a real car, especially not a good one! Doing the word is more valuable than merely thinking about it. Almost everyone, except Plato, would rather have a real peach than the mere idea of a peach, a real vacation instead of the mere idea of a vacation, a real trip to Mexico instead of a flight of fantasy, real material assets like money and property rather than mere ideas of such, real moral commitment and action instead of only nice thoughts about them, and real salvation instead of mere talk about it or "lip service" to it!

In this hierarchy of value, applied to creation, why are *people* at the highest level, the grade of reality having the greatest value? Individual persons like us are composed of (A) our good-making thoughts, (B) our highly desirable physical, social, and moral processes and activities, and (C) our inner conscious souls with all of their capabilities—our unique dynamic, active, and constantly flowing "stream of consciousness." All these together make up our total selves. As *unique, integrated, embodied persons*, we contain all these kinds or dimensions of value within ourselves; so we are much more valuable than any one particular kind or dimension of value in isolation. As unique individuals, inclusive of all other kinds of value, we are richer in good-making qualities than all other valuable entities (on this earth). Within earth-bound creation, we belong at the top of the hierarchy of value. In this sense, perhaps, we are made in the "image of God," for God is "that being than whom none greater or richer in good-making qualities can be conceived," as St. Anselm suggested; or, as he put it, God is "that being than whom none greater can be conceived." This is the clearest concept we have of a supremely worshipful Reality, of a God who fully deserves not just our "whole-hearted" but our "whole-personed" devotion.

Unique persons, whether human or Divine, are immensely more valuable than mere things or mere ideas; that is the most essential practical application of Hartman's hierarchy of value. With respect to our own personal worth, our thoughts and ideas really are good; our physical and social realities and behaviors are also good; but our bodies and social roles are better than our thoughts about them; and our total intrinsic reality, which includes the totality of our unique conscious awareness as well as our thoughts, bodies, and social actions and roles, is best of all. To be the most valuable individuals we can be before God, we must actualize within ourselves as much as possible of all three dimensions of value in balanced proportions. That is what it means to live on this earth in the *fullness* of time, to live *more abundantly, more richly* in overall goodness. Being a "saint" and "living abundantly" ought to be connected. "Sanctification," the process of becoming a saint or a holy person, is the lifelong process of spiritual development—which is what this book is about. "Conversion," whether sudden or gradual, may begin the process, but it is only the beginning, not the end. Some people seem to believe, mistakenly, that conversion is both the beginning the end, that there is nothing more to do, that nothing else has to change, after you have been initially "saved;" but as one evangelical television evangelist succinctly put it, "When you got saved, you didn't get it all!"

Understanding Hartman's hierarchy of value can help us know who we are as unique individual persons. It can help us appreciate, accept, and positively value who we are, choose who we wish to become, and express who we are and will become in the way that we live and move and have our being in and before God. Axiology says that *as unique persons, we are the sum of all our properties or traits, both good-making and bad-making.* Both our goodness and our badness, our virtues as well as our sins or vices, are essential parts of who we are. To deal effectively with our *bad-making* qualities, we need to repent, change our ways, make amends where possible, and accept forgiveness from and be reconciled to ourselves, others, and God. We must learn not merely to accept ourselves but actually to like, even to love, ourselves so that it will make sense to love others *as* we love ourselves. Being fully redeemed involves the full realization that before God our unique personal existence is something intrinsically good, something made in God's supremely valuable image, something that deserves to exist for its own sake, and that we have and are something worth giving to others, including God. Ultimately, *to God* we give all the positive value that we are and that we bring about or create within our own lives and the lives of others.

Whatever our present stage of spiritual development may be, we want to know, "How can I 'be somebody' and not just 'a nobody' before God?" Well, we already are a "somebody," for God loves and redeems us just as we are, with all our faults, immaturity, and insecurities, long before we come to love God, repent, and receive God's forgiveness, and often before we come to love and forgive ourselves. At our worst, God loves us! Even if we know this "with the top of our heads" (systemically), we still may not know it "deep in our hearts" (intrinsically).

Some people feel so worthless they can't believe that God could love them or that God could ever forgive them for who they are and what they have done. Much "terror preaching" is designed to make us feel like worthless sinners before God, but far too many of us do not need terror preaching to make us feel worthless. We are deeply troubled by guilt and by anxieties about our own unique value or worth; we lack self-respect, self-confidence, and the courage to be, to do, and to give, all of which are parts of self-love. Just why we feel worthless or unworthy before God varies greatly from person to person, as results from the Religious and/or Christian Value Profiles indicate.

If living abundantly is done before God; so is living sinfully. We know what we should do and don't do it; and often we do what we know we shouldn't do. Knowing what is good does not guarantee that we will actually do it. We have *standards* of how we *should* be living before God; and, measured by these standards, we are found wanting, sometimes severely, but we are never utterly worthless. We all have our deficiencies, but before God there are no "utterly worthless" sinners. God knows realistically that even sinners have both good-making as well as bad-making qualities, and being loved by God is everyone's most significant good-making property. We are all sinners, yet God loves us, saves us, and wants the best for us, even in our sinfulness. God wants to build upon our existing goodness, no matter how small it is, and to bring goodness out of our shortcomings. God wants us to be better than we are and to live more abundantly than we do right now.

Before God, we all have our strengths and our weaknesses. As *good* persons we are the sum of all our good-making qualities, the fulfillment to some degree of our deepest self-concepts or ideals; but *what are our good-making qualities, and how can we understand and further actualize our good-making potentials?*

In being and becoming all that we can be, we must come to know, cherish, create, and express ourselves as fully and as positively as we can in all three dimensions of value, without seriously neglecting any of them. Spiritually and otherwise, we must *both conceive of and actually develop and apply* ourselves systemically, extrinsically, and intrinsically, as fully as possible. Then, the glory of God will shine through us to others, and we can become more effective in carrying out God's work. If we do not, we will be less abundant and productive persons; we will not live as completely or fully as we can before God. By failing to develop ourselves in, or not giving due worth to, any one or more value dimensions, we will be less than the best that we can be. Next, three-dimensional spiritual self development will be discussed in more detail.

II. Achieving Three-Dimensional Self-Development

Our personalities are organized around our values in three dimensions, so we have systemic selves, extrinsic selves, and intrinsic selves. These are explored in some depth in Chapter Seven. To truly live abundantly in the fullness of time, we must fully develop, use, and appreciate our systemic selves, our extrinsic selves, and our intrinsic selves—all of them in proper balance. What does this involve? What strategies for living abundantly in three value dimensions has God made available to us?

A. Our Systemic Selves

Our systemic selves are our mental selves. Our systemic selves engage in such mental activities as thinking, reasoning, conceiving, classifying, analyzing, defining, inferring, knowing, assenting or believing, and doubting or disbelieving. Through our systemic selves we relate to formalities and to formal systems of every kind, including definitions, laws, rules, rituals, creeds, logic, mathematics, computer programs, *etc*.

i. Systemic Value Objects

Systemic value objects include thoughts, ideas, knowledge of all kinds, doctrines, ideals, reasons, concepts, classifications, definitions, inferences, beliefs, and doubts. All systemic value objects are constructed by our minds, though some but not all of them refer to things that exist outside of our minds. The word "churches" refers to actual churches; but "lines with length but no breadth" exist only in our minds. Systemic value objects like thoughts, ideas, and ideals, belong toward the bottom of the hierarchy of value, but we should not underestimate their worth or importance. Nor should we underestimate the value of our capacities for thinking and using ideas. We should take care not to over- or underestimate the value of anything. Although systemic value objects and mental capabilities are immensely valuable, we should never forget that other realities like people and things are even more valuable because they are richer in good-making qualities.

Theologians have often insisted, perhaps at the expense of other dimensions of value, that we are made in the rational (*i.e.*, the systemic) image of God. In the beginning was the Word, the *logos* . . . and the *logos* was God. God knows everything that there is to know, so God values knowledge, ideals, ideas, rules or laws, doctrines, wisdom, and so on. No doubt, to be and become all that we can be in a Godlike way, we must develop and use our minds, our thinking capacities— all of them, or at least as many as practically possible in our lifetimes. Expressed axiologically, we ought to develop our systemic selves, but without neglecting our extrinsic and intrinsic selves. Expressed religiously, we ought to love God with all of our minds. Curiosity, wonder, the desire to know, and the ability to value ideas, ideals, guidelines, and beliefs, are among God's most precious gifts to us. Since minds and brains are inseparably connected, this thought can also be expressed as, "We ought to develop and use our brains." (For the moment, of course, we are considering only the conceptual, rational, or systemic parts of our brains.) We know that most of us use only a fraction of our brain capacity for thinking, learning and knowing—and for everything else, including morality and spirituality. What we affirm or think mentally is an important part of what and who we are, and to the extent that we fail to develop and "use our brains," we thereby fail systemically to live as abundantly as we can. Learning is a lifelong adventure; what we can learn if we try is practically unlimited. To become Godlike, we cannot afford to be "brain dead at age 20," not if we really want to be and to become all that we can be. Education—all continuing education, especially ongoing religious education—enriches us; it fills us with good-making systemic qualities and objects of value; and failure to educate ourselves throughout our lives restricts our growth and keeps us from realizing our potentials.

Religiously, we must learn how to think and believe in spiritually fruitful and faithful ways and how to help others do so. God made us to be knowers and learners as well as doers and lovers. Yet, we must be careful to avoid reducing everything to conceptual systems, especially religion, for religion is not just an intellectual game. It is not just an opportunity to stick up for our own beliefs or knock down the beliefs of those who disagree with us. It is not a mere arena for theoretical discussions of topics of religious interest. That really is a part of it, but there is so much more! Although this is the way we usually talk about them, religious people really shouldn't be called "believers" because such talk is misleading. It gives the impression that the mental acceptance of religious doctrines is the very essence of religion, that systemic value objects are the most important values in religion. But this is not so. Religion at its best involves conceptual beliefs, loving God with our minds; but this is only a very small part of the story. A good religion is a total way of life, an intrinsic, extrinsic, systemic, holistic walk through life with Ultimate Reality, not just a mental journey with systemic thoughts or beliefs about It.

Thou shalt not live by thoughts and doctrines alone. A contemporary anecdote says that one day some traditional Christians and less traditional Unitarians were walking down the same road. Eventually they came to a fork in that road and found signs giving directions and destinations. The sign pointing to the right said "Heaven," and the sign pointing to the left said "Discussions of Heaven." As the story goes, all the traditional Christians went to the right, but all the Unitarians went to the left!

Most of us can readily discern that and why these fictional Unitarians made the wrong choice. Why? Because they preferred systemic conceptual images of spiritual reality to that reality itself, and because desirable realities are always better than, richer in goodness than, the thoughts and beliefs we have about them. So it is with spiritual development. Religious beliefs and doctrines are only signs or symbols that point beyond themselves. Systemic values (thoughts and beliefs alone) are not adequate substitutes for The Real Thing!

ii. Systemic Valuation

To live abundantly in the systemic dimension, we must have systemic value objects (ideas, beliefs, doctrines, *etc.*) *and* use our capacities for *systemic valuation*. Value objects are *what* we value; valuation is *how* we value. Both are essential parts of every dimension of value and of religion. By now we know that systemic value objects are beliefs, doctrines, ideas, *etc*; but what exactly are our capacities for *systemic valuation*? They are our capacities for valuing objectively, fairly, and disinterestedly, quite apart from considerations of personal, material, or social gain or profit. They are our capacities for seeking the truth objectively, *i.e.*, without bias, prejudice, pre-judgment, or distortion, even if the quest for truth requires us to give up some of our most cherished personal convictions. When we become adults we put away childish things, usually with some anxiety and distress. God wants us to strive for truth, even if the outcome of questioning and learning is unpleasant and distasteful, and even if we have to learn to understand, tolerate, and appreciate the religious beliefs of those who disagree with us. Our unfolding spirituality must make an important place for mental growth as well as for profound extrinsic and intrinsic involvement and commitment.

A systemic truth-seeking attitude does not mean a total absence of all desires and feelings, but it minimizes those particular appetites and emotions that interfere with intellectual honesty and integrity. It is a willingness to be fair-minded in dealing with ideas, theories, doctrines, dogmas, and ideals, even religious and axiological ideals. It is a willingness to engage in honest discussions and to follow arguments and new thoughts and insights wherever they may lead, even if they take us into uncharted or uncomfortable territory. Religious people definitely need to learn how to be more honest with themselves and with one another, and how to reason together with God and before God.

Proper systemic valuation makes a place for thinking in *black* or *white* categories, but only when the issues, including the religious ones, are so truly simple that they really are black or white, but we must be willing to stop "all or nothing," "black or white" thinking when the issues before us are truly more complicated. We shouldn't oversimplify. Most of us are underdeveloped with respect to our capacities for systemic valuation, but if we really want to live more abundantly, we must increase and use our capacities for objective and fair-minded learning, thinking, and reasoning. For most of us, tolerating uncertainty is difficult; yet, life is full of uncertainties, so we might as well get used to it! If we really want to live more abundantly, we must cultivate and use all our capacities for intellectual fair-mindedness, honest, and modesty. We cannot neglect our systemic selves. God wants us to study, think, and develop and use the minds that He gave us. If we want to live abundantly, we cannot fail to love God with all our minds, as well as in so many other ways.

B. Our Extrinsic Selves

Our extrinsic selves are our practical selves, our capacities for relating to and dealing practically with the public world in which we daily live. To be all that we can be, we must also develop, use, and properly appreciate our bodies, our senses, our physical environment, and the practical physical and social skills that we use in our jobs and in other social roles.

i. Extrinsic Value Objects

Extrinsic value objects are *things* and *actions* that involve things and processes in our common sensory world. "Things" is understood broadly to include all the physical objects, processes, and activities that we encounter in normal sensory experience. Extrinsic value objects include all the physical goods, social services, and events in the public world around us—all the things we need for survival, comfort, enjoyment, entertainment, experiencing, and "doing our thing." A very large part of our own reality and value is extrinsic. We are embodied souls, and "extrinsic value objects" includes our own bodies, their workings, the social roles we play through them, and all our physically expressed and facilitated activities. Our extrinsic reality is an absolutely essential part or aspect of our total reality.

Worldly individuals, as well as some religious and Christian people, tend to overvalue extrinsic realities and often make them the greatest goods in life. Worldly people live primarily for *things* and *social status*; this way of life, when successful, is what Jesus called "gaining the world"; but in gaining the world, people who live primarily for "material goods" lose their moral and spiritual souls. Loving mainly "the world" makes people greedy; it makes them believe that greed is good. Worldly people notice mainly sense objects, not their own souls; they try to dominate and control other people, other human bodies; and they can be very aggressive. They tend to overvalue their bodies, all bodies—what they own, how they look, how physically and socially competitive and competent they are, how often they win (and others lose), how well they fulfill the social roles that make them "top dogs," how thoroughly they dominate those who are "beneath them" in wealth and social status. Systemic-bound ideologists (most "absent minded" professors as well as religious dogmatists for whom ideas, ideals, and beliefs are the greatest goods) tend to undervalue bodies and social dimensions, their own as well as others'. They live primarily in the world of ideas, in "ivory towers" of their own making, and they are largely *"absent"* from normal physical, social, and moral realities and responsibilities, even though no one can escape these completely.

To live truly abundantly, we must neither overvalue nor undervalue the things of the world, including our bodies, our social actions, practices, roles, stations, responsibilities, and status, our physical and social being and becoming. Instead, we must learn to value them properly, not too much, not too little, but just right, and live accordingly.

So how should we value ourselves? "Objectively," that is, according to the hierarchy of value, our extrinsic selves are very valuable; they are more valuable than our systemic selves but less valuable than our total unique intrinsic selves, including our distinctively intrinsic "stream of consciousness." We should learn to value ourselves in all three dimensions of value; all three of them together are more valuable than any one of them taken separately. We should learn to attach appropriate worth to physical and social realities, including our own personal physical, social, and moral reality, while not forgetting that our *total intrinsic selves* have even greater worth. Our total intrinsic selves contain far more good-making qualities than our systemic or extrinsic selves taken separately. All are God-given, but the goodness of the whole outweighs the goodness of each of the parts.

To live abundantly, we should attach balanced objective significance to the mental, physical, and social worlds in which we live and to the mental, physical, and social aspects of our own total reality. Without supporting physical and social environments, we cannot live at all, for in large part we are physical and social beings. We are far more than our thoughts or our inner consciousness. According to the Biblical view, we are essentially *embodied* or *incarnate* souls, not essentially disembodied immaterial (non-spatial) spirits that are temporarily imprisoned in spatially extended bodies. We become fully human and fully individual only if we have supportive *physical* and *social* surroundings. We live and act bodily for better or for worse. Rightfully appreciating but not overvaluing our bodies and what we are and can do through and with them is an integral part of our spiritual development. Our informative bodily senses are good, not evil; as Proverbs 20:12 tells us, "The hearing ear and the seeing eye, the Lord has made them both." Our bodies and physical senses are created by God and are good and precious gifts from God. They are dwelling places of God, so we must learn how to treat them as holy temples. This includes not abusing our bodies and giving them proper rest, exercise, nutrition, and care. We can and should dedicate our bodily existence, presence, and actions to God. Love to others, even to God, must be publicly communicated and expressed somehow, for example, in public worship of God or in many small acts of kindness to others. Not so much what we do but the spirit in which we act counts the most, but doing definitely counts. Inner and spiritual graces stand in need of outer and physical expression. We are known by our fruits.

In considering survival after death, Christianity and many other monotheistic religions emphasize *the resurrection of the body* and *the communion of the saints.* Thereby they reject, for both this world and the next, the idea that we can or should exist and live abundantly as disembodied souls or in complete social isolation. Counterparts for this can be found in many other world religions. The *Koran* clearly presupposes the resurrection of the body in a social environment, and many Jews today agree with the ancient Sadducees in affirming it, even though there is very little of it in the *Old Testament*. Our extrinsic reality is an essential part of our total reality. Our bodies are not evil things that we should aspire to escape (as many Greek thinkers believed); they are good things, God-given things, that we must take good care of and not abuse. They are an integral part of who and what we are, not an extraneous impediment. Religiously understood, they are temples of God, and we should not desecrate sacred temples. We do not always realize it, but God is "omnipresent." God is everywhere, including within our own bodies, so whatever we do to our bodies we do to God, and whatever we do through our bodies we do with and for God. God's living spirit fills the earth, the heavens, and the entire universe, which many people believe to be the body of God. To the child's simple question, "Where is God?" the profound answer is, "everywhere." Our own lives are far richer and more meaningful when we fully understand and appreciate how God pervades and is present within everything, including us.

Similarly, our social memberships, roles, and involvements with other people are not bad things that we should avoid or try to escape. They are good things, divine things, religiously considered, that make up a very large part of living abundantly and being all that we can be, together with others, before God. We cannot be or become all that we can be without our minds, our bodies, other people, or God. Without our physical "temples" and God-filled social bodies, there could be no communion of the saints, no social incarnation of God, no body of God or Christ.

We are by nature social beings with a deep need for social belonging. By nature we all seek to be understood, accepted, appreciated, and loved by others. When others are indifferent to us, misunderstand us, reject us, or even hate us, we always experience some degree of "hell on earth." We long deeply for a community of saints, a kingdom of ends, a fellowship of love, where every person recognizes, deeply internalizes, and passionately affirms the equal intrinsic worth of every other person and in turn has his or her own intrinsic worth profoundly validated and affirmed by all.

Of course, we must take care not to rank extrinsic goods higher than intrinsic goods, as worldly people do. Yet, to live abundantly *we really do need things having extrinsic value*—healthy bodies, adequate (but not extravagant) material resources, and supportive physical and social environments—*the things of the world*. God created such things and judged them to be good even before we came along. We should not seek them first and foremost; but as essential parts of life they must be "added unto" us if we are to live truly abundantly (Matthew 6:31-33; III. John 1:2). You and God both know that you need the basic necessities of life, but they can't be your highest priority. They can't be "first." The scriptures definitely rank human values!

We should not confuse being competent and accomplished in managing business and the affairs of the world with placing too much value on extrinsic things and social roles, with loving such things with all our souls. As religious people, we need to be and should be capable and clever. We must be wise and good caretakers of all in our charge. We are always *in* the world, but we need not be *of* the world. The children of God should be as worldly-wise as serpents and as innocent and harmless as doves (Matthew 10:16). We should use the world without abusing it (I Corinthians 7:31). We should regard our work in the world, our vocation, whether clerical or secular, as a calling from God. Some of us may have to change jobs to find a vocation that really is a calling from God suitable for us as the unique individuals we are. The *world* that God created is good (Genesis 1:31), including our social and physical roles, jobs, and hopes—in their proper place. Our bodies are good, all bodies are good. God created the entire physical universe and found it to be good (Genesis 1).

ii. Extrinsic Valuation

This section will focus on *extrinsic valuation*. To live most abundantly, we must develop our capacities for extrinsic valuation. What does that involve? Extrinsic valuation includes (1) *establishing, assessing, and refining standards of excellence or goodness* that apply to our everyday needs, interests, desires, and feelings, (2) *measuring the values* of perceived actions, objects, bodies and processes against these standards of excellence, (3) *comparing value objects and processes* in the world with respect to their degrees of goodness, (4) *identifying effective ways or means* to reach our goals, whether these means are our own personal behaviors or natural and social processes, and (5) *choosing and actively pursuing* what is practically the best.

Extrinsic valuation is ordinary, everyday, practical, or pragmatic valuing and living. Our most basic survival skills involve extrinsic valuation. We have to make a living, provide the necessities of life for ourselves and our loved ones, and find or make a place for ourselves in various social groups. We need to function competently within the world without being an excessive burden to others and without conforming completely to the materialistic value standards of the world.

A grasp of axiology can help us to become more capable and polished in our practical skills. To do so, we must reflect carefully upon both traditional and conventional, both old and new, *standards or concepts* of practical goodness. Some of these are received or derived from human nature, some from society, some from trend-setting celebrities, some from our religious institutions, and some we have created for ourselves. Thoughtfully, we must either accept, amend, or replace the good-making standards received from others or from our past experience and inventiveness. Without clear standards, we cannot value effectively in *any* dimension of value, including the practical extrinsic dimension. Without clear standards, we do not know where or how to begin to identify a good deed, a good job, a good car, a good house or apartment, a good book, a good meal, a good shirt, a good cactus blossom (like the one on the cover of this book), a good song, a good toothpaste, a good education, a good politician, a good teacher, a good priest, a good employee, a good employer, a good church, a good religion, or a good anything.

Every aspect of extrinsic valuation has an important place in religion and in personal spiritual development. For God's people, all places can and should be viewed as holy places; all things can and should be regarded as holy things. Everything that we do can and should be sanctified, as done before God, and as offered to God. Of course, God is already there in all times and places; we only need to be come conscious of it.

We may not be saved by good works, but faith without works is dead, and we are known by our fruits. Good works have a vital place in complete, abundant, spiritual lives; but good works are impossible, they cannot even be identified, without standards of goodness. To be "doers of the word" we must have "wisdom," "the word," the *"logos,"* that is, conceptual *norms* for telling right from wrong and good from evil. Ideally we must distinguish what God loves from what God hates. Our wisdom should be Wisdom from God. Getting any job done right for God requires that we learn how to be practically effective. God's hands are often our hands; again and again God works through us, but God's hands should not act blindly.

In living religions, rituals and ceremonies are much more than mere formalities, though they are at least that. Systemic religious forms can be acted out extrinsically in communion with others to establish, affirm, reaffirm, and celebrate unions of family, faith, brotherhood, sisterhood, and godliness. Often, ritual enactments are occasions for profound personal intrinsic devotional experience. Formal, repeatable, systemic patterns of religious rituals, ceremonies, and sacraments can be and often are acted out extrinsically in public, usually in a religious community, though sometimes in private. When religious music is performed, hymns are sung, prayers are said, liturgies are reenacted, and God's words are studied or preached, forms are combined with actions. When deep intrinsic devotion and religious sensitivity are added to these systemic patterns and extrinsic behaviors, devotional practice includes all dimensions of value. When rituals, sacraments, liturgies, ceremonies, music, preaching, and so on, are experienced as "empty," the intrinsic dimension is lacking. Religious leaders who conduct devotional practices and services should do all they can to create an atmosphere in which the presence of God and the union and communion of the saints are profoundly experienced in all dimensions of value, systemic, extrinsic, and intrinsic.

To be effective religious workers, we must become proficient men and women *in* the world, but not *of* the world. We must be and become *good observers, careful perceivers, and capable comparers.* We must learn to use our God-given senses to verify the presence or absense of good-making qualities in things, processes, social activities, and moral conduct in the whole of life. Especially in interpersonal relations and roles, we need to develop our capacities to recognize good-making and bad-making qualities. Within our "secular" social groups, we have to decide whether or not what we call "going along with the crowd" is good or bad. When shopping, we have to compare and select among many possibilities, and we want to be sure that the objects we buy have the good-making qualities we seek. On the job, we must know how to offer good products and services to our customers. When we hire anyone—carpenters, mechanics, professors, college presidents, or clergy—or when we promote or re-train employees, we must know the candidates well enough to predict accurately that they are likely to do their jobs well and that they can be retained after they are trained or re-trained. They should exemplify the good-making qualities required for performing their jobs effectively and with lasting loyalty. When compared to other candidates, they should be the best person(s) for their job(s).

To get better at judging practical worth, must be or become good at experiencing and comparing. We must be skilled at telling the difference between things and people that "measure up" and those that don't. In many cases, we must rely on the experiences of others to inform our own judgments, so we need trustworthy references when dealing with people. When selecting the best consumer products and services, we often need real expertise like that offered by consumer magazines or capable consultants. Even for devout religious people, a great deal of worldly wisdom is required for effective and abundant living! All too often saintliness is ineffective in getting things done for God because religious people do not develop and use their practical talents in the service of God. Robert S. Hartman wondered why bad people like the Nazis are so good at organizing evil, while good people are so bad at organizing goodness.[11] The richest possible spiritual life is *not* one that dwells upon religious ideals but never puts them into practice. It is rather a life in which, as very skilled extrinsic valuers before God, our practical talents and actions are dedicated wholeheartedly to God.

To become excellent extrinsic valuers, merely perceiving, conceiving, and comparing are not enough. We must also *choose and act* according to the best practical knowledge that we can get. We have to be doers of the word and not thinkers only. Faith without works is dead. Another kind of knowledge comes into play in effective acting: *we must know about causes, effects, and probabilities.* We must be able to identify those courses of action, as well as those natural and social processes, that are likely to bring about the results that we judge to be best, or less than the best. We must know how to distinguish between effective, less effective, and ineffective *means to our ends* or ways to reach our goals, and we must act on that information. We must know what is likely to cause what in the world and act on the basis of that knowledge. Too much of the time, we really don't know what we are doing, but God gave us minds with the expectation that we would use them to learn and recognize what we are doing and to know how to do it as well as possible. Even with the best knowledge available to us, we will not always succeed. Sometimes even good deeds have unexpected and unintended bad results. In practical matters, we always have to act on the basis of probabilities, not absolute certainties. But our chances of doing God's work effectively and well are greatly increased if we are properly informed and act carefully and knowingly.

Our extrinsic talents, like almost every other good thing, can be used or misused; they can be used for good or for evil. Good religious practices encourage and enable us to use all our talents for good purposes. Our extrinsic talents should be used to express and promote cooperation instead of excessive competition, conservation instead of extravagant consumerism, community rather than narcissistic individualism and egoism, the common good rather than narrow self or group interest, equality rather than domination, justice instead of injustice; peace instead of war-imposed resolutions of human conflicts, human rights instead of human wrongs, good causes instead of bad ones.

Doing presupposes the courage to be, to do, to act, to practice what we preach. Doing God's will often involves the courage and strength to do what is right even in the face of resistance and powerful opposition by the powers and principalities that be. Pray for the courage and the strength to be who and what you are and to do what you ought to do.

Clearly, if we are informed, competent, deeply loving, and religiously devoted doers, we are much more likely to have richer and more abundant lives; and the world is likely to be much better for our having lived.

C. Our Intrinsic Selves

Most important of all, if we wish to live as abundantly as we can, we must fill our lives as completely as possible with intrinsic values and valuations. We cannot be or become all that we can be as long as we are stuck merely or primarily in the systemic or extrinsic value dimensions, though, sadly, many worldly and ideological individuals get stuck there. We cannot live by beliefs or by bread and circuses alone. We must develop and actualize our intrinsic potentials. We must bring as many intrinsic value objects and as much intrinsic valuation into our lives as we possibly can. This great lesson is taught by the founders of all the major world religions.

i. Intrinsic Value Objects

Robert S. Hartman maintained that *intrinsic value objects* are unique individual persons. If we want to extend this notion beyond the human realm, perhaps to God or to non-human animals, we could say "consciously experiencing, feeling, thinking, choosing, acting, and valuing beings." Rem B. Edwards, the author of this chapter, confesses that he did not at first agree with Hartman's answer to the question, "What things are intrinsically good?" but when he finally saw Hartman's point, his whole outlook on life was revolutionized. Like many others, for years he sought the answer to this question *in abstractions* that can be repeated over and over again like pleasure or happiness—both qualitative and quantitative, or contentment, desire-fulfillment, thoughts, knowledge, truth, beauty, freedom, creativity, love, conscientiousness, moral and religious virtues and actions, and the like. He now realizes that these abstract good-making qualities have no awareness of their own; they cannot exist *for* themselves;

they can exist and have worth only when conscious individuals are aware of them and attach value to them in their own lives. We cannot even assess their worth *merely* "in themselves," that is, entirely apart from our own unique awareness. They cannot exist or have worth "in isolation"; their true significance is that they enrich the experience of conscious individuals like us with good-making qualities.

These abstractions are *intrinsic value enrichers or enhancers.* Real intrinsic values, in Edwards's present view, are *combinations* of embodied conscious individuals with such intrinsic value enrichers. Intrinsically valuable realities are unique and *unrepeatable* conscious individuals exemplifying within themselves such *repeatable* value-enriching universals. Neither individuals nor these value-enrichers have any intrinsic worth in complete isolation or separation from one another. Beings valuable in themselves and for their own sakes are individual conscious beings whose lives are filled as much as possible with pleasure or happiness (both qualitative and quantitative), contentment, desire-fulfillment, thoughts, knowledge, truth, beauty, freedom, creativity, love, conscientiousness, moral and religious virtues and actions, and the like. Quality as well as quantity of life is important.

To live the richest and most abundant lives that we can, we must embrace, include, and create as many of these intrinsic-value-enriching qualities as possible. Happiness or enjoyment, physical and emotional fulfillment, knowledge, beauty, freedom, creativity, and so on are essential for abundant living; so are the individuals who experience them. Abundant living also includes self-creativity, a sensitive conscience, and moral and religious virtues and actions like self-control, justice, courage, temperance, wisdom, gratitude, forgiveness, faith, hope, and love. Most important of all, abundant living includes nurturing and using our talents for intrinsic valuation, for identifying ourselves with others, for being compassionate, empathetic, and loving. Through such virtues, at their best, we are able to become completely one with what we value most deeply and intrinsically.

ii. Intrinsic Valuation

To be all that we can be, we must consciously develop and nurture our intrinsic capabilities. If real intrinsic values are conscious individuals living value-enriched lives, then if we are to live a life that is as rich as possible in goodness, especially intrinsic goodness, must include the value richness of other conscious individuals within ourselves—and the more the better. We must learn *to make their value our own value*, but how can we do this? This brings us to *intrinsic valuation*, where the intrinsic value of a unique self merges psychologically and valuationally with the intrinsic value of other unique conscious beings, and with all beings in the best conceivable case. Intrinsic valuation can spill over into all dimensions of value. Anything and everything can be valued in every dimension. In intrinsic valuation, the valuer becomes one with what he or she values, as lover and beloved are one, as mystic and the Ultimate are one; but what does this mean, and how can we concretely experience and live it?

To be and become all that we can be, *we must become competent intrinsic valuers*. Mentally or conceptually, intrinsic valuation involves *measuring ourselves by and living up to our self-standards or self-ideals*, and the richer our self-ideals, the better. It involves being who we really are and aspire to be before God, being true to ourselves, being authentic persons. But it is more than that. We have the fascinating capacity *to identify ourselves fully with valued objects*, to become completely united psychologically and valuationally with them. Our capacities for systemic, extrinsic, and intrinsic valuation exist on a continuum. In systemic valuation, we are only minimally involved with valued objects. In extrinsic valuation, we have a more intense "everyday interestedness" level of involvement with valued objects. In intrinsic valuation, we identify ourselves so completely with valued objects that the differences between us and them don't matter anymore, although they still exist. When lover and beloved identify fully with one another, each still fully exists as a unique person with all their good-making and bad-making traits, but they merge so completely valuationally and psychologically that everything (both good and bad) that happens to and in one also happens to and in the other. Many people will recognize their own capacity for intrinsic self-identification-with-other if they think about how they relate to their favorite athletic teams. When their team wins, they win; when their team loses, they are losers; when their team is "number one," they are number one! Most of us experience identification-with-other in profound patriotism. When our nation prospers, we prosper; when our nation is attacked, we take it very personally; we are attacked; and we become "one nation," hopefully "under God." Our national motto is "unity in variety," "out of many, one," *E Pluribus Unum*; and this is a matter of personal experience for us in our moments of profound patriotism.

When we fully identify ourselves with (a valuation) something or someone (a value), the differences between us and what we value are still very real, but they are resolved into an almost mystical experiential unity. In more detail, here is what intrinsic identification involves for us.

1. We feel a deep and powerful sense of union with those (people, animals, things, etc.) being valued. "That" and "thou" are one.
2. We want this union and communion to continue indefinitely.
3. The differences between us as valuers and those valued still exist, but they no longer matter, and we may no longer pay any conscious attention to them.
4. We experience the goodness of those with which or whom we identify as our own goodness. Their good-making qualities become an internal part of us. Their goodness becomes our goodness.
5. We experience the good things that happen to those with which we identify as happening to us. Their good fortune becomes our good fortune.
6. We experience the evil or badness of those with which or whom we identify as our own evil or badness. We may respond to it with sorrow, guilt, remorse, regret, and forgiveness.
7. We experience the bad things that happen to them as if they were happening to us. We may respond with sorrow, sadness, pity, and compassion.
8. We are deeply moved to act to help them, to promote their well-being, and to relieve or prevent their being harmed. We act as if we and they were one.
9. We take great joy in their very existence as well as in their happiness and well-being. Their life is our life, their existence

is our existence, their happiness is our happiness, their well-being is our well-being.

10. We experience great sorrow when they are harmed, killed, or destroyed. Their hurt is our hurt; their death is our death.

Intrinsic identification occurs in what Abraham Maslow called the "peak experiences" of life. In intrinsic valuation we find ourselves by losing ourselves, by giving ourselves over completely to and fully identifying ourselves with whatever we value intensely. Empathetic intrinsic valuation is the ultimate solution to the religious paradox of finding ourselves by losing ourselves, and to the philosophical paradox of overcoming the infamous "subject-object" distinction. This is what God requires of us—to find ourselves by losing ourselves completely in loving God, loving neighbors, loving ourselves, and loving all creation.

In human experience, peak experiences of total self-identification with a value object can occur in many circumstances, such as:

intimate, loving, interpersonal relations with friends, loved-ones, neighbors, strangers, anyone, everyone,
empathetic self-projection into the shoes of others,
all absorbing concentration and creativity in all fields of human endeavor,
participation and delight in natural and artistic beauty and creativity,
compassion toward and with those who suffer,
complete forgiveness, reconciliation, and acceptance between offended and offenders,
moral commitment and action,
the wholehearted consent of being unto being,
mystical union, ecstasy, and bliss, and
the joy and rapture of many-splendored religious experiences.

Peak experiences of self-identification with another happen to us mainly in our loving relations with those who are closest to us—our spouse, our parents, our children, our brothers, sisters, and closest friends. Self-identification-with-other is often experienced in intellectual and artistic creativity where we are so intensely concentrated that we have no self-awareness, and what we are creating becomes our experiential universe. With such close but restricted intrinsic identifications as a starting points, growth in divine grace can and will gradually extend our ability to identify ourselves fully with everything and everyone.

If the scope of our love never expands or extends beyond our most intimate kin and friends, we are in deep trouble religiously. Jesus suggested that loving only those who love us is without reward or merit (Matthew 5:46-47)! This is the limited love of those who have not grown in grace, not the limitless love of grace and godliness.

Even if only a few (the true saints) find The Way, interpersonal intrinsic intimacy definitely *can* happen in our relations with other if not all human beings. This means that we can intrinsically value other, perhaps all, people as neighbors, family, brothers, sisters, and children. A good religion helps us to realize in our own experience that all of God's children are our brothers and sisters, not literally, but metaphorically. Metaphors are words that can help us to bridge the gaps between the familiar and the unfamiliar. To help us broaden the scope of our loves, words like "neighbors," "family," "brothers," "sisters," and "children" are often used metaphorically rather than literally to expand our moral and religious horizons and our sense of spiritual union with others. All of God's children are our brothers and sisters, and we all belong to the family of God, we are often told. Hartman was convinced that metaphorical or poetic speech is the language of intrinsic valuation, that metaphors both express and facilitate the process of intrinsic self-identification with other people, or with anything else to which we give ourselves completely like works of art, hound dogs, and pickup trucks. The scriptures are loaded with metaphorical, not just literal, language. If we are to live truly abundantly, we must have a great deal of metaphor, of poetry, in our lives and in our souls! And the more souls, the more intrinsically good beings, we embrace and unite with in our own souls, the richer and more abundant our own lives become, and the more we live in that joy and peace that passes all ordinary human understanding.

Faithfully and fully loving all of God's children and extending this love to all of God's creation is not losing ourselves; it is finding ourselves. Our lives are poorer precisely to the extent that anyone or any being exists that we don't love, even our enemies. Loving others unselfishly as ourselves does not make us poorer or smaller; it enriches us and makes us bigger and better! *Their good becomes our good*, but not in a selfish way. Their good-making qualities become our good-making qualities when we take them into ourselves and intensely identify ourselves with them. To live the best lives that we can possibly live, we must learn to broaden the scope of the individuals who we are prepared to love and with whom we fully empathize and personally invest ourselves. This takes us far beyond family and community, beyond kin and tribe, beyond race and nation, even beyond species—to all things that have breath or life. Ultimately, in religious experience and devotion, we identify ourselves with all things that have being and becoming, including God. As St. Augustine, said, "Whatever is, is good." As the mystics say, "That art thou." No one and no thing is excluded from the communion of saints, even if some people defiantly exclude themselves. The universal Kingdom of God knows no borders or boundaries.

Only by giving ourselves away can we find and become truest and deepest selves that we can be before God. The more of reality we can take into ourselves and fully invest ourselves in, the more abundant and blessed our own lives become, the more we experience and live in salvation here and now. This is true in all value dimensions, mentally (systemically), practically (extrinsically), and personally (intrinsically). The best life is all of the above—loving wisdom and knowledge, loving all creation, loving all persons equally, and loving God with our whole being. By losing, transcending, or moving beyond our narrow and imperfect "natural" selves, we can be reborn as much richer, more loving, and more abundant souls. Loving God and all that God loves with all our hearts, minds, souls, and strength, is the richest, the most abundant, fulfilling, and blessed life that we can possibly lead. Then, everyone's intrinsic worth becomes our intrinsic worth! But not in a selfish way!

Every world religion emphasizes moving beyond or transcending our imperfect "natural" selves. Religious teachers are not always clear about how to do this or what the final result would be like, and self-overcoming is often mixed in with and confused by conflicting messages.[12] Yet, a Way or path of spiritual self-development that leads beyond selfishness is found in all major world religions.

Religious people do not always put their deepest insights and beliefs into practice. Most historical religions have taught us both to love and to hate. Consider the lack of goodness in your own life when you are aggressive or indifferent toward others (animals included), hate others, and don't fully identify with others. Then, their goodness is not your goodness, and you *could* be living much more abundantly. If we love too narrowly and bury our intrinsic talents, we are poor souls, spiritual underachievers, so think about what you might be missing if you heed small-minded religious messages. How inclusive are your religious convictions, and how exclusive are they? Who do you personally love to hate? Who does your religious outlook exclude from the scope of God's love and your own love? Who does your religious congregation teach and empower you not to love, perhaps even to hate? Your enemies? Wicked people? Unbelievers? Foreigners? Members of other races? Christians? Non-Christians? Jews? Non-Jews? Moslems? Non-Moslems? Liberals? Conservatives? Outsiders? People who think too much? People who think too little? Anyone who believes, looks, acts, or loves differently? Who? We must guard against the sin of pride. Too many religious groups say that their own beliefs, practices, and attitudes are the only ones sanctioned by God, and all others are condemned, along with the people who subscribe to them; but isn't this an instance of the sin of pride? The more inclusive you are, the more abundantly you live, witness, and reflect God's love; the less inclusive you are, the poorer is your life before God. The choice is yours to make.

What is true of you as an individual may also be true of religious organization and communities. What is the mission to the world of your religious group? Should it be something like this: systemically— to seek, comprehend, and bring profound religious understanding to the world; extrinsically—generously to minister physically, socially, morally, and spiritually to everyone in the world, especially to the "least of these," persons who lack social standing and material resources; intrinsically—to love and to express and promote love and devotion to God and to all the world that God loves, including every person, every animal, every living thing, and all of God's glorious handiworks? God himself so loved the world! We will embrace that love and move deeper and deeper into it as we grow in spiritual grace.

Academic courses on religion tend to concentrate on its doctrinal or systemic aspects. They leave the impression that agreeing with or assenting to a worldview is the very essence of religion, but we have seen that religion is far richer than beliefs alone. As St. Paul indicated in *I. Corinthians* 13, faith, hope, and love abide; but the greatest of these is not faith (affirming doctrines); it is love. When relating to people who are very different, shouldn't we be more loving, more tolerant, and less insistent on religious formalities and the doctrinal aspects of faith? Love is the more excellent way. Can you think of any religious beliefs, rituals, or practices that might interfere with love, with interpersonal understanding, respect, justice, cooperation, acceptance, forgiveness, and reconciliation? If so, which ones in particular? And which ones are *yours*?

Loving those who think, look, act, and worship differently may first involve only systemic toleration, then sincere extrinsic practical acceptance, and finally wondrous intrinsic delight in them just as they are. The most valuable spiritual gift is not doctrinal or ritual conformity; it is a communion of hearts. As St. Paul said, "If I speak in the tongues of men and of angels, but have not love, I am only a resounding gong or a clanging cymbal. If I have the gift of prophecy and can fathom all mysteries and all knowledge, and if I have a faith that can move mountains, but have not love, I am nothing. If I give all I possess to the poor and surrender my body to the flames, but have not love, I gain nothing" (*I. Corinthians* 13:1-3). As non-dogmatic John Wesley said, "If your *heart* is as my heart, give me your hand." (Compare *II. Kings* 10:15). Shouldn't humility or "poverty" of spirit influence the way we hold our doctrines, especially in light of how little we really know for sure? Yes, all three—faith, hope, and love— have immense spiritual value; nevertheless, "the *greatest* of these is love." The heart (intrinsic unity) is far more valuable than the head (systemic conformity). *Religious doctrines and observances that are really most important and truthful may simply be those that enable us to be more loving, more intrinsic!* John Wesley said that "there is nothing higher in religion" than the "love that is described in the thirteenth of *Corinthians*," that "there is, in effect, nothing else," . . . and that "you are to aim at nothing more." Can you think of some intrinsically constructive or positive religious beliefs and observances? Can you think of any unloving or negative religious beliefs and practices? And which of these are *yours*?

About any religious doctrine, belief, practice, or attitude being considered for adoption, it is always worthwhile to ask, *Would accepting this make me a more loving person, or a less loving person?* Or would it just make no difference at all? Would it make me a better traveler, and guide me well along the pathway of spiritual development? Shouldn't we ask such questions about any business, professional, political, social, educational, *etc.* doctrine, practice, or attitude we are considering? Remember, no matter what or how intensely we believe, our believing amounts to (almost?) nothing if we do not have love. (To emphasize a point, even the scriptures exaggerate a bit at times!)

Loving people who are well-developed morally and spiritually in all three value dimensions are on the right road. No one else can walk it for us. It might be a rocky road, but because of "the communion of the saints" it need not be a lonely road, even if it is less traveled. Being accompanied and assisted by more experienced travelers can and will make the trip a lot easier. This road is worth traveling for its own sake, not just for the sake of its ultimate destination. It is a very long road, a lifelong road; not even the most spiritually developed saints ever reach the end of it; even the best saints have their imperfections. But this is the only road that can give us the most worthwhile and meaningful life that we can possibly live, before God.

III. Hartman's Own
"How to Develop Our Self"

In an unpublished monograph, *The Individual in Management*,[13] Robert Hartman himself addressed the topic of "How to Develop Our Self." Now we will consider *his* answers to our questions about self-development and self-enrichment (even if at times some of his words seem a bit sexist by today's standards!). "How do we do it?" Hartman asked. He answered, "There are, as far as I can see, [a number of] ways in which we can develop":

I. The first is through *Crisis*. In crisis, as in a deep sickness, the loss of a beloved, or a horrible experience like a concentration camp, we are forced to delve into the depth of ourselves and there find our strength. This is a pretty rough way to self-development. It cannot be voluntarily brought about. And when a crisis strikes we may just as well go under than triumph. It may break us rather than make us. One of the greatest examples of self-development through crisis is the ordeal of Franklin D. Roosevelt, the thirty-four months from the day he was stricken with infantile paralysis at Campobello, on August 10, 1921, to the day, June 26, 1924, when on the platform of Madison Square Garden, he nominated Al Smith as the Presidential Candidate for the Democratic Party—standing on his two legs, holding the podium with his left hand, and waving with his right hand to the screaming and cheering crowd—a man triumphantly and almost miraculously emerged from the depth of despair to a new life.

II. The second way is through *conscious effort*, the always continued *sensitizing of our Conscience*, the continuous refinement of our sensibilities. Our conscience is the organ of the self. It is, so to speak, the barometer of the soul, the measure of its spiritual pressure. In the degree that we register normal sensitivity, especially compassion, our conscience is sensitive; in the degree that we do not, it is insensitive and undeveloped. We have to register in our conscience all the twenty properties of the self-test, check ourselves almost every moment as to how we measure up. [These "twenty properties of the self-test" will be given shortly in Hartman's discussion of "Intrinsic Faith" versus "Intrinsic Fear."]

III. The third way of improving ourselves morally is to *follow the Example of Sensitive Persons*, especially our wives. A wife who loves is usually more mature than a man. Women, having to deal with the creation of life, are usually more sensitive to the true values than men. Men are often lured by their intellectual and social power to insensitivity and disregard of the moral. To women both the intellectual and—if they are true women—

the social play a relatively small role, and love and compassion play the main role.

IV. However, women value intuitively and do not articulate their value pattern consciously. If we can do this we may be able to use our *intellectual power* to develop ourselves morally. This is the fourth way to self-development. One can develop himself [or herself] morally *by intellectually learning about the Self and growing in step with one's knowledge.* This is the way it happened to me, although it must be said that I was helped by a previous experience of crisis which expanded my awareness at one almost shattering stroke. Yet, it was my life-long endeavor to find a rational account for this experience, and I did find it eventually in the precision of formal axiology. In the same way the learning of axiology has helped others who have steeped themselves in this new science . . . we can change our lives by consciously applying our knowledge of value, either in existing situations or abroad—in concerts and church, museums and lecture halls, in reading a book or walking through the woods.

V. This leads us to the fifth way of self-development: through *the conscious pursuit of Peak Experiences.* Peak experiences, in the terminology of Abraham Maslow who has studied these experiences experimentally, are experiences in which we feel ourselves at the peak of life, in the fullness of our powers and the maximum depth and width of our awareness—as in love, in musical and other aesthetic experiences, in experiences of creation and inspiration, and of religious insight and rapture. People who are able to make their whole life into a peak experience are called by Maslow "self-actualizing" people. Such people live in the depth and width of their consciousness, and throughout their lives strive to deepen and expand their awareness. They work at their *Being*, and not primarily at their doing, their awareness rather than their activities. Their cognition gradually becomes sharper for the things that matter and weaker for the things that do not. They fulfill the prayer that Kierkegaard put as motto to his book *The Sickness unto*

Death: "Lord! Give us weak eyes for things that matter nothing, and eyes of clarity for all thy truth."[14]

At this point, Hartman describes Peak Experiences in some detail following Abraham Maslow, but we will not now go into that any further.

Hartman explained the "twenty properties of the self-test" mentioned in Section II above through the following contrast between "Intrinsic Faith" and "Intrinsic Fear." In reading this, consider how the qualities of "Intrinsic Faith" positively enrich us and how those of "Intrinsic Fear" diminish us. By becoming intrinsically faithful or intrinsically fearful, we can increase the *number* of our qualities either way, so the difference between them is not *quantitative*; it is *qualitative*. Both approaches to human existence involve individual conscious beings plus the good-making or bad-making qualities that enrich or diminish their lives. Hartman claimed that "Intrinsic faith is the fundamental property of the morally good person," and "Intrinsic fear is the fundamental property of the morally insecure person." People with intrinsic faith are "well born" and have "trust in the world." People with intrinsic fear are riddled with "suspicion, insecurity, world-wariness." He contrasted these two character types in the following twenty ways.[15]

1.

Faith: **Humility**—They do not need defiance; they are cradled within the universe as a child in the arms of his mother. They trust God as does the child. They are "poor in spirit;" they "bend humbly to the spirit." They are the meek, the gentle, who shall inherit the earth. They are the pure in heart who will see God. They are humble in spirit toward God, and gentle toward people.

Fear: **Defiance, Spitefulness, Superiority**—They cannot trust the world. They can only trust themselves. All they have are themselves, their own power. They have to be in command for otherwise everything would go awry. They have and need a feeling of superiority and indispensability for they are the only ones who can make order in the universal chaos. They cannot delegate authority; if they did everything would go wrong; the world itself would fall apart. God was just lucky that they came around.

2.

Faith: **Serenity**—They feel a deep joy at being alive and around. They make everyone around them feel good. Nothing touches them. They are spiritually happy. They are transparent within themselves.

Fear: **Aggressiveness, Defensiveness, Combativeness**—Fearful people are aggressive, defensive, and combative. They have to be because everything depends upon them.

3.

Faith: **Cooperation**—To them, their fellows are helpers in a cooperative world. Everyone is a friend.

Fear: **Competitiveness**—To them everyone is a potential enemy who has to be overcome.

4.

Faith: **Expansive**—Their spirit is as large as the whole world and it takes in everyone. They are continuously in love with the world and with everything in it. As God has his arms around them so they have their arms around everyone and everything.

Faith: **Restrictive, Narrow**—Fearful people are like the fellow in Steig's organ box who is cowering in that box and gasping "People are no damn good." They are narrow. They want to shrink the world; they want to shrink themselves. They want to be nothing, in order not to be touched by anything.

5.

Faith: **Humaneness**—They love people. They help them. They never say a bad word about anyone, no matter who. They give everyone the benefit of the doubt. They always build others up;

they always find something good in everyone. They see the human in everything.

Fear: **Cynicism**—They tear down everyone and everything. The word "cynic" comes from the Greek word "*kyon*" or "dog." Fearful people feel themselves to be dogs, and they make a dog out of everyone—although I don't want to offend dogs. They see everything and everyone as evil.

6.

Faith: **Magnanimity**—Since they see the best in everything and everyone, they are magnanimous. They have great souls. They praise with full hearts; every praise is a praise of God's creation and thus of themselves.

Fear: **Sanctimoniousness, Holier-than-thou Attitude**—They pretend at greatness of soul, but their praise is tinged with superiority. They are condescending, talking down to everyone, even when they praise. For them, every building up others means tearing down themselves. Thus, when they praise they have to do so with condescension so that their own merit will not be obscured. They praise rarely since few things or people appear to them praiseworthy. They have the Holier-than-thou attitude of the dogmatic and the fanatic.

7.

Faith: **Generosity**—They can afford to give because they know that when they throw their bread on the waters it will come back to them manifold. Money and indeed all material goods mean little to them; yet, they value them in their place and are not prodigal or wasteful. They respect the economy of the world.

Fear: **Greed**—Unless they take theirs, somebody else will take it from them. They have to keep piling it up, lest they may starve one day.

8.

Faith: **Unpretentiousness**—They don't try to call attention to their appearance. They don't have to try to pretend they are anything but what they are. This is their world, and they belong. They may be a little sloppy, but they will never be dirty. They follow nature in their outward appearance and do not force nature to follow them. Vanity is outward appearance, the ornament of pride; humble persons who are gentle and natural cannot be vain.

Fear: **Vanity**—They have to improve on creation, including their own appearance; thus they have to squeeze themselves into things and tie themselves down to forms that their nature may dislike. They use their handsomeness in order to be effective and beat others who are not similarly endowed. Thus they build up themselves. They look at themselves in the mirror, and their finery makes them feel good.

9.

Faith: **Not Easily Hurt, Self-Possessed**—They never expect anything extra from the world, but they take whatever they receive as grace, as a gift from the bounty of God's goodness, for which they are grateful.

Fear: **Easily Hurt, Touchy**—They're so insecure, and they have great self-pity. They have to struggle so hard, and everything is against them. They're concerned only about their own suffering, not that of others. They are spiritually thin-skinned. They are not overly sensitive generally but only where themselves are concerned. They think the world owes them a living and, more importantly, owes them loving. They are love-starved. Since they did the world a favor in being born, much against their will, the world ought to reciprocate and pamper them. Thus anything that goes against them is exaggerated because it is so unjust, and anything that goes for them they take for granted.

10.

Faith: **Boldness, Courage**—Nothing to them appears impossible, every problem resolvable, every deed achievable, every difficulty superable. They know they are on the right track so they aren't afraid to move ahead. They take everything in stride, never getting overly agitated either in failure or in success.

Fear: **Cowardice**—They are scared in their spirit, thin-skinned. They are born, so to speak, without a spiritual skin against the world, but they are sensitive only about themselves. They are spiritual crybabies; few things appear possible to them. They try to hoard what they have—like the unfaithful servant in the Parable of the Talents.

11.

Faith: **Forgivingness**—With their great hearts, they are forgiving. They know that vengeance is the Lord's. They pity rather than hate the malefactor.

Fear: **Vengefulness**—They will not rest until they have wrought their revenge. Since they are the navel of the universe, anything done against them is done against the world itself; and it is up to them to righten this cosmic evil.

12.

Faith: **Light Touch**—They are blessed with the light touch. They bounce through life, having with them the powers of infinity. They play on the instrument of the world like a virtuoso on a piano, seemingly without effort; yet behind this light-handed and light-footed performance is their effort of acquiring the power of eternity.

Fear: **Heavy Touch**—They are burdened with the heavy touch. Everything is very, very difficult for them. They have to work so hard, harder than anyone else, and nothing comes of it. Hitler always said he worked day and night for the German people and they did not thank him.

13.

Faith: **Uncomplicated, Purity, Innocence, Common Sense**—They have an innocence of spirit and purity of heart that sees through the chaos of a situation to its very core. Such persons are Billy Budd in Melville's novel; St. Bernadette in the novel of Franz Werfel, who winds all the great theologians around her little finger; and such persons are the true scientists, the people of genius who see the simple solution of the complicated. They can see things as they are and not as they would like them to be.

Fear: **Complicated, Lack of Common Sense**—They regard complication as a virtue and a sign of profundity. As they are deficient in spirit, they are also deficient in mind.

14.

Faith: **Relevance, Sense of Proportion**—They are prone to see the relevant. They have a sense of proportion, see things in their true relation to each other. They are able to differentiate. They take the important seriously and value it accordingly, and they take the unimportant not seriously and disvalue it accordingly.

Fear: **Irrelevance, No Sense of Proportion**—They are prone to see the irrelevant. They lack a sense of proportion, make mountains out of mole hills, or *vice versa*. Since they have little direction, they take everything to be equally important. They thus confuse the important with the unimportant, giving importance to the unimportant and no importance to the important. They exaggerate trifles and dismiss weighty matters with a wave of their hand.

15.

Faith: **Rationality**—They use reason in conformance with the structure of the world itself. Therefore, true science, although nothing but a construction of the human mind, can yet account for what is going on in the world.

Irrationality—Fearful people are at bottom irrational. Their defective selves interfere with the clarity of their vision. They use systems in order to bolster themselves.

16.

Faith: **Spontaneity, Flexibility**—They play upon and with systems as a virtuoso with and upon his instrument. They are sovereign above systems; the system is not sovereign over them.

Fear: **Systemicness, Rigidity**—They use systems as a crutch and are lost without them—as was Adolf Eichman. The system is sovereign over them

17.

Faith: **Relaxed Dynamic**—They are relaxed; their dynamics is quite like that of a noiseless Cadillac and therefore much stronger than that of the bustling busybody who sputters like a scooter and takes extrinsic activity for intrinsic dynamics.

Fear: **Tense, or Frantic, Business**—They exhibit bustling busyness. Their activity is like that of children squirting water pistols.

18.

Faith: **Perseverance, Patience**—They know they're on the right road and if they persist, they will reach their goal. They feel within themselves the strength of the universe. They never stop for a moment on their way, but they are never obtrusive. They are the still waters that run deep.

Fear: **Inconstancy, Hesitancy, Impatience**—They lack enough faith and inner strength to move toward their objectives consistently. They may seem persistent, but they have a certain deep hesitation about their actions and their work. Since they do not have enough faith and enough strength for the whole universe, they only go up to a certain point and then stop, looking for another direction.

19.

Faith: **Awareness, Vision, Warmth, Wisdom**—They have complete awareness, wide vision, warmth and wisdom. They are wide awake to everything that the world offers them. The world is right, and God is in His Heaven watching it. They are cosmic optimists. There are many bad things in the world, but they are flaws of the design, or the execution of the world, but they are not its essence. They belong to the realm of contingency, and this realm is a small part—a statistically calculable small part—of the grand design. The pessimist does not see the whole for the parts, and thus . . . is a little crazy.

Fear: **Non-awareness, Myopia, Dullness, Coldness, Trifling Acuteness, Fastidiousness**—Since they lack complete awareness, they have a certain dullness of vision and of feeling, a coldness of heart which, coupled with their trifling acuteness and fastidiousness, their attention to detail without seeing the great line, makes them deadly bores. Lacking vision, they must exaggerate the small and denigrate the big. Their dullness, coldness, and fastidiousness are consequences of the irrelevancy of their actions. They do not have faith in either God or the world.

20.

Faith: **Compassion**—Compassion is their deepest trait. They suffer with the sufferers. Every suffering is their own suffering. They manifest within themselves the intrinsic oneness of all creation. Compassion, as we said, is the touchstone of morality; this is the most important difference between moral types.

Fear: **Indifference, Callousness**—They are indifferent toward what really counts, especially toward the infinite greatness of human beings. Since they are weak inside and hate to be touched by anything unpleasant, they are indifferent to suffering.

Certainly, persons who are all that they ideally can be will have the twenty virtues of "Persons of Faith" and will avoid the twenty vices of "Persons of Fear."

You should have read enough by now to have a clearer concept of "our total human development," as well as a better understanding of *your own* personal total human development and what you must do to achieve it. One final point will now be emphasized. To be and become all that you can be, *you must be willing to be and become what **only** you can be before God.* You must develop your systemic self, your extrinsic self, and your intrinsic self all that you can; and through it all you must intrinsically valuate, develop, and express your own uniqueness. You must be willing to be yourself, to be who you are and who you might become, before God. You must learn to love yourself, not only because you are worth it, but also because God loves *you.* You must fulfill your own unique self-concept or self-ideal and know and identify yourself fully with your given reality and with your own personal ideals or norms of becoming. No one else since God created the universe has been *you*, and no one else ever will. After God created *you*, he threw away the pattern! You have you own uniqueness rights: to exist, to have your own totally unprecedented perspective on the universe, to have and develop your own personal interests and talents, to assume your own special moral commitments and responsibilities, to fulfill your own self-ideals, to be true to yourself, and to become yourself, before God. Being and becoming *fully* ourselves isn't easy and won't come instantly or effortlessly. As the actress Tallulah Bankhead once said, "No one can be exactly like me, and sometimes even I have trouble doing it!"[16] But you can better understand who you are and choose who you want to become if you comprehend your own reality and your own values in the three dimensions recognized by Robert S. Hartman. Hartman correctly discerned that our values are the real keys to our personalities. They are also the keys to being and becoming all that we can and should be, before God.

CHAPTER SEVEN

The Structure of the Religious and Christian Value Profiles

Our values are the real keys to our personalities. This should be just as true in religion as anywhere else. Expressed religiously, our present values are the real keys to the states of our souls, to our present stage of spiritual or religious development. To use another metaphor, our values are the windows into our souls. If we could measure our values accurately, we should be able to get a clear picture of our present spiritual condition. This is something that religious thinkers have wanted for centuries. Much needed is a spiritual "thermometer of the soul" that measures our spiritual temperature. Most people probably believe that such things can't be measured at all because we lack, and always will lack, a proper instrument for taking such measurements, but this is no longer true!

Accurate information about what and how we value religiously should be immensely helpful to people who really want to understand religious development and maturity, especially their own. Certainly most ordinary religious people, religious "followers," want to understand and improve their own religious development, and so do most religious "leaders"—counselors, clergy, teachers—all dedicated persons who want to understand, guide, and help themselves and/or others to mature personally and spiritually. The Religious and Christian Value Profiles measure present stages of religious growth through the way that people order their values. They help people understand their present spiritual development through they way they rank their values.

A "spiritual thermometer" that really works should help people to know themselves better. It should increase *self-knowledge* and help people to identify their *strengths*, as foundations upon which to build, as well as their *weaknesses*, as projects on which to work. Such instruments are now available in the Christian Value Profile (CVP), for Christians in particular, and the Religious Value Profile (RVP), for religious people who center on One God.[17]

I. A Bit of Value Theory

Three kinds of value and valuation, as identified by Robert S. Hartman,[18] are exemplified in the Christian Value Profile (CVP) and the Religious Value Profile (RVP). These Profiles are sensitive both to *what* we value and *how* we value. *What* we value (value objects) we will call "values," and *how* we value will be spoken of as "valuations."

1. Three Kinds of Valuable Things or Value Objects (*What* We Value)

The three kinds of values and/or valuations represented in these Profiles are:

(1) *Systemic Values*, (S): conceptual constructs that exist in our minds.

Examples: definitions, ideas, ideals, norms, rules (*e.g.*, the Ten Commandments), beliefs, truths, doctrines, ritual forms, musical notations, mathematical and logical systems, and the like.

(2) *Extrinsic Values*, (E): actual or potential means to ends located in and observable in our common world of space and time.

Examples: physical objects and processes, bodies, books, houses, cars, human actions, behaviors, social memberships, roles, conventions, groups, established institutions, and a lot more.

(3) *Intrinsic Values*, (I): things that have value in, of, and for themselves; things that should be valuated intrinsically because they are ends in themselves, desirable or valuable for their own sakes.

Examples: unique centers of conscious experience, choice, thought, and valuation such as human persons, non-human animals, angels, and God. (Many philosophers have suggested things like knowledge, pleasure or happiness, freedom, dutifulness, and desire fulfillment, but these only exist within and enrich the lives of those unique conscious individuals who exist *for* themselves).

2. Three Kinds of Valuation
(*How* We Value)

From the very murky beginning, people have been attaching value to things in many different ways. All valuations include cognitive or mental elements—value standards or concepts by which objects of value are measured. Valuations involve judgments by persons about objects of value, judgments that they measure up or fail to do so in some degree. Valuations also include feelings, affections, emotions, and desires that range on a continuum from minimal (systemic), through ordinary (extrinsic), to maximal (intrinsic) personal involvement.

(1) *Systemic Valuations*, (S): black or white, all or nothing, oversimplifying, and dispassionate or "objective" feelings and judgments.

Examples: "2 + 2 = 4"
"This class will dismiss at 10:35 a.m."
"If you are not with me, you are against me." (Thought in a cold, calculating way)
"Race is all that counts." (Thought in a cold, calculating way)

(2) *Extrinsic Valuations*, (S): commonplace practical motives, involvements, activities, and judgments.

Examples: ordinary everyday practical feelings, likes and dislikes, emotions, appetites, needs, interests, actions, vocations, value judgments, classifications, and comparisons.

(3) *Intrinsic Valuations*, (I): complete self-identification with valued objects; intense personal involvement with, concentration upon, or investment in value objects. This kind of valuation includes all the ways in which conscious individuals like us combine or unite ourselves totally, intensely, and passionately, (either positively or negatively), with objects of valuation, so that distinctions between self and valued other cease to matter or to be noticed, and "the subject/object distinction" is overcome psychologically and valuationally.

Examples: love, empathy, intense delight and joy, conscience, creativity, deep religious devotion, worship, communion, and mystical union.

The Religious and Christian Value Profiles focus primarily on systemic ideas, extrinsic things, and intrinsic persons—human and divine—and the ways in which people react to and evaluate them. They are based on Robert S. Hartman's value theory called "formal axiology."

3. The Hierarchy of Value

The above three kinds of value and valuation form *a hierarchy of worth*. Extrinsic things and processes are more valuable than mere ideas, and unique centers of personal consciousness are more valuable than mere things. The richest form of valuation is intrinsic valuation; the poorest is systemic. This is all intuitively obvious to most people, at least in their more reflective moments, as confirmed by statistical results derived from administering the Hartman Value Profile (HVP)[19]—the original value-based personality Profile—to many people all over the world.[20] Many philosophical considerations also support this hierarchy.

The philosophical justification for the hierarchy of value, as developed by Hartman and others, are (1) that "good" or "value" means "concept or standard fulfillment." Value objects have degrees of value to the extent that they fulfill the conceptual standards we set for and apply to them. These conceptual standards consist of lists or sets of good-making properties or qualities. Degrees of value or goodness may be compared rationally. One thing is better (or worse) than another to the extent that it has more (or less) of the properties contained in its normative concept. Thus (2) "better" just means "richer in good-making qualities" and "best" means "richest in good-making qualities." Things are richer in good-making qualities than mere ideas, while people and other unique conscious beings are richer in both quality and quantity of good-making properties than mere things. Similarly, intrinsic valuations differ with respect to the degrees of personal involvement, ranging from the minimal involvement of systemic disinterestedness or objectivity, through everyday pragmatic or practical extrinsic interestedness, to total personal intrinsic identification. The best or richest *values* are intrinsic values, but the richest or most abundant *lives*, the best lives we can possibly live, are those that are *richest in good-making qualities in all three dimensions*.

II. The Composition and Structure of the Profiles

Profile takers rank the eighteen items on the RVP and CVP from best to worst. Some items in the middle may seem of little significance, perhaps almost neutral in worth. All eighteen items are instances of *combinations* of Systemic, Extrinsic, and Intrinsic Values and Valuations. Values and Valuations in these three dimensions may be combined positively or negatively, to enhance or to degrade or damage. Combinations that sustain or enhance value are *compositions*. Combinations that degrade, decrease, or destroy value are *transpositions*. The eighteen items on the RVP and CVP are either compositions or transpositions of values and/or valuations, nine of the former and nine of the latter, some better, some less good, some worse, than others. The task for those who take the Profile(s) is to rank all eighteen items from best to worst according to their own present value insights. In taking the Profile(s), people reveal the present state of their own spiritual development, including their moral development. Profile takers should not consult with others about how to rank the items. Their rankings must express their own values, not someone else's.

Compositions and transpositions of value and valuation occur in all of life, including religion. In selecting items and phrases to be included in the RVP and CVP, the following criteria were employed. Profile items should be:

1. theologically well-informed,
2. relevant to the religious lives of great numbers of people,
3. familiar and not offensive to typical Christians and others committed to One God,
4. expressed in language that is easily understood,
5. expressed in language that is as clear and unambiguous as possible,
6. indicative of a person's state of soul, kind of religiosity, or stage of religious development.
7. Compound items or phrases (compositions and transpositions) should normally *state both value-elements* quite explicitly and not leave too much to be guessed or added by the profile taker.
8. Compound items or phrases should be linguistic expressions that fall within and are ranked according to the hierarchy of value, as identified by Robert S. Hartman's scientific framework.

Both the RVP and the CVP come in two parts. *Part I* of each Profile deals with religion in the social world, in your broad social environment. The Results from Part I show how you understand and respond to elements of religion or Christianity outside of yourself—in the world, in other people, in other groups, in other cultures, and the way that you present your religious self to others in public. *Part II* of each Profile deals with your own personal involvement with the values of Christianity or other religions centered on One God. The Results from Part II show the kind of relationships you have personally with values in your religion. *Part I* is a Religious World Profile, and *Part II* a Religious Self Profile. No absolutely sharp distinctions exist between the two parts, but the difference in emphasis or orientation is much more personal in Part II. You used the Internet to take and score your Profile(s). Just what the score numbers on your Result Forms mean is explained in Chapters One and Two. Due to limitations of time, most people will take only one of these Profiles; but where time and religious orientation permit, we recommend taking both the RVP and the CVP. We also strongly recommend taking your Profile(s) again after you have worked through this book to see if your results have changed and how you have developed spiritually.

Profile items that you ranked very far from the norm should receive special attention in personal reflection and/or in counseling or group discussions. In fact, much relevant information about specifics may be obtainable only in personal and/or group or class interviews, discussions, or counseling sessions. These Profiles can have at least one important use; they can open up opportunities for in-depth discussions with others of your religious beliefs, practices, personal orientation, and involvement. Of course, you may have such dialogues only with yourself, but you are much more likely to avoid blind spots and much self-deception if you also discuss your results with others. We all need to be understood, accepted, and affirmed by others in the presence of God, as well as by ourselves, alone, before and with God. The perspectives of other people such as trusted religious leaders, guides, or counselors may be immensely helpful to you.

1. Ordering the Profile Items

The immediately following framework gives the value formulas, their proper rank order according to Hartman's hierarchy of value, each of the composition and transposition items that illustrate them, and their random position from top to bottom in each part of the CVP and the RVP.

Column 1 (on the left) gives the proper rank order of each of the 18 value items, as based upon the hierarchy of value.

Column 2 gives the value formulas—9 value compositions expressed as superscripts, and 9 value transpositions expressed as subscripts.

Column 3 gives the value combination items, with each component value item in parentheses, and with its S, E, or I value written just above it.

Column 4 identifies the actual random position of each item in each Profile.

Part I of both Profiles combines *two* instances of the three kinds (I, E, S) of value/valuation. The nine positive compositions and nine negative transpositions, ranging from best, to almost neutral, to worst, represent all logically possible formal combinations. Items that could illustrate them are practically innumerable.

Part II of each Profile actually combines *three* kinds of value/ valuation, the self ("I," "my," "me") with two others, but since the self, the intrinsic value (I), is constant throughout Part II, we keep track only of the two others that are combined with it. In Part II, value/valuation combinations always modify the personal self of the individual taking the Profile.

THE CHRISTIAN VALUE PROFILE

Part I, Christian World

Proper Rank	Formula	Items	Actual Random Position
1	I^I	(Jesus)^I (our)^I Redeemer	11
2	E^I	(Rejoicing)^I in Christlike (living)^E	13
3	S^I	(Loving)^I (scriptural truths)^S	17
4	I^E	(Personal salvation)^I expressed by (good works)^E	10
5	I^S	(Learning)^S about (Jesus)^I	6
6	E^E	(Participating)^E in (church activities)^E	1
7	S^E	(Witnessing)^E about (the Gospel)^S	18
8	E^S	(Actions)^E guided by Christian (principles)^S	15
9	S^S	(Christian beliefs)$^{S, S}$ that support one another	2
10	S_S	(Misunderstanding)^S (a Bible verse)^S	3
11	E_S	(Telling)^E (lies)^S	4

12   S_E E   S
              (Doing) what we (know) is wrong   9

13   E_E E   E
              (Burning) a (cross)   5

14   I_S S
              (Religious doctrines) that depreciate   14
                              I
              (women, minorities, or outsiders)

15   I_E E   I
              (Persecuting) (Christians)   16

16   S_I I   S
              (Maliciously perverting) (religious teachings)   8

17   E_I I   E
              (Despising) (Christian living)   7

18   I_I I   I
              (Absolutely rejecting) (Jesus)   12

THE CHRISTIAN VALUE PROFILE

Part II, Christian Self

Proper Rank	Formula	Items	Actual Random Position
1	I^I	I (love) (Christs) with my whole heart, soul mind, and strength.	11
2	E^I	(Christ's love) is expressed in (everything I do).	13

3   S^I $\overset{I}{\text{(My life)}}$ is centered around Christian   17

$\overset{S}{\text{(principles).}}$

4   I^E To me, $\overset{E}{\text{(the heavens)}}$ declare the $\overset{I}{\text{(glory of God).}}$ 10

5   I^S My Christian $\overset{S}{\text{(beliefs)}}$ help me to understand   6

$\overset{I}{\text{(myself and others).}}$

6   E^E I $\overset{E}{\text{(support and attend)}}$ my $\overset{E}{\text{(church)}}$ regularly.   1

7   S^E I $\overset{E}{\text{(practice)}}$ $\overset{S}{\text{(what I preach)}}$ 18

8   E^S In religion, I $\overset{E}{\text{(put my money)}}$ 15

$\overset{S}{\text{(where my mouth is).}}$

9   S^S I $\overset{S}{\text{(understand)}}$ God's $\overset{S}{\text{(covenant).}}$ 2

10   S_S I am $\overset{S}{\text{(confused)}}$ about God's $\overset{S}{\text{(plan).}}$ 3

11   E_S I don't always $\overset{S}{\text{(know)}}$ the right thing $\overset{E}{\text{(to do).}}$ 4

12   S_E I $\overset{E}{\text{(do)}}$ what I $\overset{S}{\text{(know)}}$ I shouldn't do.   9

13   E_E I $\overset{E}{\text{(work hard)}}$ to undermine $\overset{E}{\text{(the Church).}}$ 5

		S I	
14	I_S	I have (doubts) about (Jesus).	14

		E I	
15	I_E	My (actions) dishonor (Christ).	16

		I S	
16	S_I	I (despise) religious (rules).	8

		I E	
17	E_I	I (hate) (doing) God's will.	7

		I I	
18	I_I	I feel that (God) could never forgive (me).	12

THE RELIGIOUS VALUE PROFILE

for One-God Religions
Part I, Religious World

Proper Rank	Formula	Items	Actual Random Position
		I I	
1	I^I	(God's love) for (us)	11
		I E	
2	E^I	(The glory of God) in (creation or nature)	13
		I S	
3	S^I	(Total devotion) to religious (truths)	17
		E I	
4	I^E	(Helping) needy (people)	10
		S I	
5	I^S	The (principle) of forgiving (others)	6

6   E^E (Attending) a (house) of worship   1

7   S^E (Living) according to God's (laws)   18

8   E^S (Health and healing) resulting from religious (beliefs)   15

9   S^S (Knowing) God's (commandments)   2

10   S_S (False) religious (doctrines)   3

11   E_S (Actions) condemned by a religious (belief)   4

12   S_E (Mocking) sacred (teachings)   9

13   E_E (Defiling) a (house) of worship   5

14   I_S (Doubts) about (God)   14

15   I_E (Oppressing) God's (people)   16

16   S_I (Utter contempt) for the (idea) of God   8

17   E_I (Loathing) righteous (living)   7

18   I_I (A person's) eternal separation from (God)   12

THE RELIGIOUS VALUE PROFILE

for One-God Religions
Part II, Religious Self

Proper Rank	Formula	Items	Actual Random Position
1	I^I	$\overset{I}{I}$ am (fully devoted) to $\overset{I}{(God)}$.	11
2	E^I	$\overset{I}{I}$ (love) doing the Lord's $\overset{E}{(work)}$.	13
3	S^I	$\overset{I}{I}$ (love) the $\overset{S}{(words)}$ of God.	17
4	I^E	My (love for others) is enhanced by my religious (group).	10
5	I^S	My religious (beliefs) strengthen (my soul).	6
6	E^E	I (actively help) my religious (group) to grow.	1
7	S^E	My (actions) reflect and support my religious (beliefs).	18
8	E^S	I try (to live) by God's (commands).	
9	S^S	My (mind) is in harmony with God's (plan).	2

10   S_S Some of my religious (beliefs)   3
            contradict each other.

11   E_S God's (commandments) are too hard for me   4
            (to keep)

12   S_E My (actions) often conflict with my religious   9
            (beliefs).

13   E_E (Serving) God is a (waste of my time).   5

14   I_S I have (doubts) about (God).   14

15   I_E I (curse) (God).   16

16   S_I I (despise) religious (dogmas).   8

17   E_I I (detest) (organized religion).   7

18   I_I I blame (God) for all the evils (people) suffer. 12

The Religious Value Profile (RVP) may be fruitfully taken by both non-Christians and Christians, by anyone who takes the reality of one God seriously. Very likely, only Christians will want to take The Christian Value Profile (CVP), though anyone is welcome to try it. Christians are encouraged to take both Profiles and compare the results.

III. Axiologically Structured Selfhood

Our values structure our selves or personalities in three dimensions. As explained in what follows (taken with a few modifications from Rem B. Edwards, *Religious Values and Valuations*,[21]) we all have or are Systemic Selves, Extrinsic Selves, and Intrinsic Selves; and each of these may be developed to varying degrees and ordered in relation to each other in an immense variety of ways. Where knowing, doing, and individuality are present in each part of the self, the value dimensions merge and are not sharply differentiated. They are, in Hartman's words, "within each other."

1. The Systemic Self

*Systemic value applied to individual persons shows
the individual as a system . . .* Robert S. Hartman[22]

Our *systemic self* is our conceptual or thinking self. It consists of our actual and potential:

a. knowledge and application of mathematics, logic, computer programs, rules, regulations, laws, symbols, the formal aspects of music and the arts, and the formal aspects of the sciences, including the natural sciences and value science or axiology;

b. knowledge of and obedience or conformity to ideal constructs, rituals, institutional regulations, laws, moral rules, and social action-guiding principles;

c. our self-ideals, the conceptual aspects of conscience;

d. offices, memberships, and positions in institutions and organizations;

e. non-empirical, formal, theoretical, philosophical, theological, and religious concepts, beliefs, doctrines, dogmas, ideologies;

f. capacity for systemic valuation, for measuring things objectively with constructed concepts, for using "all or nothing" logic, for reducing things to minimal essentials, and for combining systemic with other values.

2. The Extrinsic Self

> *. . . The application of* extrinsic *value to individual persons shows each person as a class of functions.*
> Robert S. Hartman[23]

Our *extrinsic self* is our public, practical, doing self, our actual or potential:

a. perceptions or sensations of and personal relations with perceptual objects, including our own possessions, our immediate physical environment, the world of nature, our own bodies, and the bodies of other living beings;

b. mastery of facts, including knowing and using means/ends, cause/effect relations;

c. bodily structures, functions, and behaviors or actions;

d. physical skills, talents, abilities, habits, hobbies, exercises, disciplines;

e. social skills, talents, abilities, habits, discipline—our abilities to relate socially to others;

f. knowledge of and conformity to the ideal demands or expectations of others such as parents, peers, and our broader society;

g. knowledge of and conformity to manners, customs, conventions, dress codes, and social morality;

h. social roles such as student, teacher, rabbi, minister, athlete, coach, parent, child, sibling, spouse, citizen, alien, high caste, outcast, employer, employee, producer, consumer, leader, follower, ruler, ruled, *etc.*

    i.   social memberships, status, ranks, reputation, roles; positions in social hierarchies;

    j.   management of practical affairs, career, work, ambitions, business, property or possessions, meeting physical needs, health habits, amusements, hobbies, athletics, and so on;

    k.   competitiveness with others;

    l.   comparisons between ourselves and others;

    m.   proneness to accidents, to good or bad luck;

    n.   analytic, empirical, factual, and social concepts and beliefs;

    o.   immersion in and absorption by the present moment; short range foresight.

    p.   capacity for extrinsic valuation, for measuring practically by empirical class concepts and standards, for manifesting ordinary human desires, emotions, interests, and for practically or actively combining extrinsic with other values.

3. The Intrinsic Self

. . . Intrinsic *value applied to individual persons shows the uniqueness of each person and its fulfilling or failing to fulfill its own self.* Robert S. Hartman[24]

. . . This is the important thing; you cannot fully be systemic or extrinsic unless you are fully intrinsic. In other words, the moral man will also be a better accountant, pilot, or surgeon. The value dimensions are within each other. The human contains the social, and the social the systematic. The lower value is within the higher. The systemic is within the extrinsic, and the extrinsic within the intrinsic. The more fully you are yourself, the better you will be at your job, and in your social role, and in your thinking. Out of your intrinsic being you summon the resources to be anything you want to be. Thus, the intrinsic, the development of your inner self, is not a luxury. It is a

necessity for your own being yourself in all three dimensions. Robert S. Hartman[25]

Our *intrinsic self* in the broadest possible sense is our total self with ALL its properties—our inner consciousness, our thinking minds, our bodies, our relationships that help to make us what we are, and all else. It is the sum total of all our properties—our qualities, and the relations that help to make us who and what we are, down to the very last detail. As such it is our richest self because *it includes our systemic and extrinsic selves*, but to these it adds the distinctively intrinsic *inner or primordial self.* Systemic and extrinsic self-development are immensely enhanced by intrinsic self-development. Our systemic beliefs and extrinsic behaviors ultimately express the inner intrinsic states of our souls.

Our *inner or primordial self* consists of our actual or potential:

a. experiential self-awareness, paying attention to our internal psychological states, processes, activities, and experiences;

b. awareness and appreciation of ourselves and others as unique centers of conscious activity, experience, and valuation;

c. capacities for attention, concentration, choice or decision, self-control, effort-making, free will, autonomy;

d. emotions, feelings, desires, interests, the most intense and focused of which belong to intrinsic valuation;

e. enjoyments, pleasures, delights, joys, happiness;

f. empathetic identification with and compassion for self and others; ability to take the perspective of others;

g. imagination and creativity in any field;

h. religious experience, devotion, spiritual union;

i. conscience, the most profoundly experienced ideal demands or expectations that we place upon ourselves and others, including our deepest moral sense of right and wrong, virtue and vice, good and evil;

j. authenticity, being true to ourselves;

k. moral virtues or moral dispositions like honesty, sincerity, truthfulness, courage, integrity, temperance, fidelity, gratitude, justice, wisdom, benevolence, harm-avoidance, harm-prevention, and so on;

l. self-acceptance, self-respect, self-esteem, self-love, and delight in our own existence;

m. acceptance of and respect, esteem, and love for others, delight in their existence and well-being, and personal identification with them;

n. acute aesthetic sensitivities and creativity;

o. faith (in Kierkegaard's sense of knowing and accepting ourselves as unique individuals trusting in, being faithful to, and living out our lives before God);

p. deepest hopes for ourselves and others, our long and short range objectives and plans of life;

q. cooperation with others;

r. sense of intrinsic unity with others, or with anything and everything;

s. singular and metaphorical concepts and beliefs, including our concepts of ourselves and others as unique individuals;

t. the capacity for intrinsic valuation, for the foregoing forms of self and other understanding, identification, and measurement; and the capacity for combining or uniting intrinsic realities with other value objects.

Now, all we have to do to know ourselves is work through the details of this outline of the value dimensions of selfhood, improve it where it is deficient, and apply each item to ourselves in detail and depth! The self has been portrayed positively in all of the above. Yet, our neglect and perversion of all of the above dimensions and elements also belong to the inner self and the total self. We are the totality of our properties, even the undesirable ones. The total person cannot be separated from his or her evil thoughts, dispositions, actions, or bad-making properties; we cannot simply love the person and hate his or her sinfulness. Our sinfulness is an integral part of who we are. All of us have a dark side that we cannot love, though we can forgive and reconcile and seek forgiveness and reconciliation. Religion says that we should not be satisfied with this dark, undesirable, sinful side of ourselves, a complication explored in some depth in Chapter 2 of Rem B. Edwards, *Religious Values and Valuations*.[26] Chapters 3, 4, and 5 of *Religious Values and Valuations* also discuss in some detail the three basic spiritual types briefly discussed next. Interpreters of the RVP and CVP will want to use this book as a more scholarly companion volume. So will anyone interested in character or personality types and in stages of religious growth.

IV. Axiological Stages of Religious Development

Systemic, Extrinsic, and Intrinsic Values and Valuations may be combined with one another in a vast number of ways. A differently structured and developed self corresponds to each of these possible combinations. Dr. David Mefford[27] identified 260 different personality patterns resulting from these value combinations—thirteen basic patterns that can be combined with twenty formulas for positive and negative temperaments. If strict account were taken of the distinction between value objects (what we value) and valuations (how we value), this number would double. Religious people can be incredibly complex!

Based on the hierarchy of value, axiology generates its own highly plausible and appealing account of stages of spiritual development. The axiological approach to spiritual development emphasizes three general patterns or personality types, *three basic stages of religious development*, under which all more particular types and stages may be subsumed. Individual persons will approximate to these general types and stages only by degrees and with an incredible variety of differences—hundreds of them, as indicated in the preceding paragraph. Yet, these stages loom large in the religious literature of all religions centered on One God, including Christianity. They are, from lowest to highest:

(1) *the ideological stage* in which personality and spirituality are dominated by systemic values such as beliefs or doctrines (that are usually valuated intrinsically);

(2) *the worldly stage* in which personality and spirituality are dominated by extrinsic practical values and valuations; and

(3) *the saintly stage* in which personality and spirituality are dominated by intrinsic values and valuations.

For real people in each of these stages, the two non-dominant dimensions of value and valuation are always present and developed to some degree. Human spiritual development is very complicated! Just how our systemic, extrinsic, and intrinsic selves are developed and ordered makes all the difference!

Systemically or cognitively dominated religious ideologists were traditionally called "dogmatists," and you may be familiar with them by this name. Predominantly extrinsic practical persons have been called "worldly" or "worldlings" since the beginning of Christianity and in other world religions as well. People whose lives are centered intrinsically are the "saints."

The process of growing spiritually in grace and the knowledge and love of God has traditionally been called "sanctification," which means "saint-making" or "making holy." Saints are made out of non-saints, out of sinners like us, out of people who start low and aim high. All world religions have their saints—and their non-saints.

At least two types of saints must be distinguished, intrinsic and holistic. William James made it clear in his chapters on "Saintliness" in *The Varieties of Religious Experience* that some people historically identified as saints are not truly admirable people.[28] Many were very gushy, sentimental, affectionate, and somehow deeply religious while being incredibly ignorant, unwise, and practically ineffective. Many overvalued (almost exclusively valued) the intrinsic while neglecting the systemic and extrinsic dimensions of value and valuation. Many had very little mental understanding of who they were, or what they were doing, or what they really ought to be doing; and many others were fundamentally incompetent and inefficient in organizing goodness and actually getting God's work done in the world.

Saintliness comes in both intrinsic and holistic varieties. Both focus primarily on intrinsic value objects or values. However, (a) *intrinsic saints* develop and use their intrinsic valuational capacities while neglecting their systemic and/or extrinsic capacities, while (b) *holistic saints* develop and utilize *all* their valuational capacities, systemic, extrinsic, and intrinsic. Holistic saints still acknowledge the validity of the hierarchy of values—that people are more valuable than things, and things more valuable than mere ideas.[29] In all three value dimensions, their valuational capacities are well developed and balanced, but their valued objects are hierarchical. In their value hierarchy, intrinsic value objects are dominant; but in their valuational capacity, all dimensions of value are as fully and evenly developed as possible without denying the hierarchical superiority of the intrinsic. The scope of their profound love extends not just to kin and kind but to everyone and everything that has being, to all of God's creation, and to God himself. By identifying fully with all other persons and creatures, they take all created goodness into themselves. When their intrinsic identification is extended or applied to God, they take the whole realm of reality and goodness into themselves. Axiologically, holistic sainthood is the very best kind of human existence; their goodness is for everyone; and they live the most abundant lives that it is humanly possible to live. Holistic sainthood is that stage of ethico-religious development that is richer in good-making properties than all others; but few there be that find or achieve it. The ideological personality type, where systemic norms and abstract doctrines matter immensely and all else matters very little, is the lowest and paltriest stage of human existence or development, the poorest in good-making properties, and so is ideological spirituality.[30] In between falls worldliness and worldly religiosity; but holistic saintliness is unsurpassed goodness.[31]

These three basic spiritual personality types do not necessarily succeed one another chronologically, that is, in time. Intellectual or systemic dominance is relatively rare and may develop later in life than practical or extrinsic dominance. Very little *axiological* work has been done thus far on the spirituality of children, though other researchers have said many meaningful things about it and about chronological sequences of faith development.[32] By the time most of us reach early to late adolescence, we have settled into a very natural worldliness where our lives, including our religiosities, are dominated by practical self-centered concerns for natural values like survival, success, resources for living; social belonging, acceptance, status, and dominance; sexuality and other so called "worldly pleasures"; pain-avoidance; revenge against actual or potential rivals or opponents; help to those (and only those) who help us (reciprocal altruism); and aggression toward others who have what we want. This is the "natural man" of the theologians![33] Spiritual thinkers through the ages believe that most people, including most members of institutional religion, are worldlings throughout their lives; and saints are few and far between. Broad is the extrinsic way!

More recently, building upon the insights of Robert S. Hartman and others, ideologists in religion and elsewhere are being explicitly recognized. They have always been present, but we have not always recognized their axiological distinctiveness. In their most extreme form, ideologists (e.g., "ivory tower" intellectuals, religious dogmatists, and authoritarians of every description) are like saints in being relatively few in number. Most of us have more worldly "common sense" than this; but all of us have deep ideological streaks within us. Our systemic capacities are developed and deployed to varying degrees and may distort our spirituality when overvalued. Our systemic capacities may begin to develop with toilet training, the first "rule" that we learn to obey, according to Sigmund Freud; and they continue to develop to and through the "age of reason." (Freud was probably mistaken about this; even before they are toilet trained, most very young children learn that it is wrong to hurt, harm, or injure others, with particular focus on their siblings and playmates. This is one of the most important moral lessons that they will ever learn.)

Our intrinsic capacities begin to develop prenatally or in early infancy with our attachments to our mothers or other primary caregivers. Attachment theory psychologists stress the fact that the earliest years of life really are the most important formative years. Good "mothering," whether by literal mothers or other capable caregivers, gives us our best chance for a good life, a life rich in intrinsic as well as other values and virtues. Mothers, fathers, and all caregivers, should be very careful. Not just their virtues, but also their vices and sins of neglect and abuse may be "visited upon" or learned and imitated by their children! God gave us all the capacity to love, but this capacity can be suppressed by others. Yet, it needs to be nurtured carefully, especially by mothers and intimate caregivers. We are empowered to love only by being loved first by others, including our mothers, intimate caregivers, and God. What is said here about parents must also be said about more extended families and whole communities. Their vices and their virtues will likely be visited upon upcoming generations, just as the Bible suggested. Hateful, abusive, or indifferent families and communities usually nurture and produce hateful, abusive, or indifferent people; loving and loyal families and communities typically nurture and produce loving and loyal people and communities.

Communities are composed of interrelated individuals having common experiences, activities, traditions, memories, beliefs, communications, loves, loyalties, and values. Communities begin to disintegrate when any of these are lost. In strong communities people share the right values, that is, they affirm and live according to the hierarchy of value; in weak communities they share the wrong values or very few values. Values are the real keys to understanding and developing communities as well as individuals. Valuationally inadequate communities (e.g., communities of thieves, or prostitutes, or the "kingdoms of this world") will and should disintegrate, self-destruct, and pass away. Finally, only the Kingdom of God, the communion of the saints, where each identifies fully with every other, the universal kingdom of mutually loving and respectful individuals, can and should remain and endure. Without ethico-spiritual development into a kingdom of mutual love and respect, the human species will eventually self-destruct.

For individuals, intrinsic growth is a lifelong enterprise of personal initiative and activity, with a lot of the grace of God thrown in; it is not just an inevitable product of genes, socialization, and early or later passive life experiences. It requires continuing active personal conceptual, practical, emotional, and devotional education and development. Only mature holistic saints fully cultivate and apply their capacities for intrinsic and all other kinds of valuation. Thereby they live the richest, best, and most abundant kind of human existence—a non-egoistic form of selfhood in which losing themselves is finding themselves and fulfilling their truest and deepest selves. Yet, even the best of human saints fall short of complete perfection. The hierarchical spiritual typology offered here ranks saintliness as the highest form of human existence; but this does not imply that anything is inherently wrong with being thoughtful or practical. These important human capacities *should* be developed and employed to their fullest, even by saints; but their respective degrees of worth must be rationally assessed and prioritized; and each should be given its proper place within the whole spectrum of human values. Thoughtful and practical people have their own significant and unique contributions to make to religion and to religious organizations, where reflective and effective people in positions of leadership and authority are greatly needed. They have immense strengths upon which to build; but they also have weaknesses and considerable room for spiritual growth. Ideas, ideals, doctrines, and truths have immense value; but they should be neither overvalued nor undervalued. Things, roles, actions, and processes also have immense value; but they too should be neither overvalued nor undervalued. Where systemic or extrinsic values and valuations prevail or predominate, these value dimensions should be "dethroned"(as Kierkegaard would say) and relegated to their proper place; but they can and should never be ignored or eliminated altogether. All are integral and desirable parts of God's creation. Religious people are never *completely* "done with lesser things," if for no other reason than that "lesser things" can be sanctified! On a deeply religious level, systemic and extrinsic realities can be brought up into the intrinsic![34] Every day can become a holy day, every place a holy place, and every thing a holy thing. You will know that you have arrived at this state of religious development when, evil excepted, every person, every living creature, every thing, and every thought becomes a sacrament. In the fullness of God's kingdom, God is all in all.

Many previous religious and psychological thinkers have produced theories of stages of moral and religious developmental. Significant among these are St. Bonaventure,[35] Jonathan Edwards,[36] Søren Kierkegaard,[37] Horace Bushnell,[38] Jean Piaget,[39] Lawrence Kohlberg,[40] and James W. Fowler.[41] If the present book were an academic treatise on stages of religious development, an axiological analysis of the place of systemic, extrinsic, and intrinsic values and valuations in the stages recognized by all of these thinkers could and would be given, but this will not be attempted here. You, along with your spiritual guides, counselors, clergy, and other interpreters of the CVP and RVP, are simply referred to these writers for additional background information. For more information about how spiritual guides, both clergy and laity, can help, take a look at the recent book edited by Gary W. Moon and David G. Benner, *Spiritual Direction and the Care of Souls.*[42]

Formal axiology provides a much more powerful, systematic, and more general applicable instrument and frame of reference for understanding spiritual development than anything previously available. We believe that this is shown in this book's discussions of scoring, interpreting, and applying the CVP and RVP. The Christian and Religious Value Profiles, based on the axiological hierarchy of value, should be immensely helpful to people who want to know who they are, where they are, and where they might go next in the realms of self-knowledge and moral and spiritual growth. They and the spiritual exercises and reflections presented in Chapters Three through Six point in the direction of a spiritually mature holistic saintliness where all value capacities are fully enhanced and people become as completely systemic, extrinsic, and intrinsic as they possibly can, each in her or his own unique way, before God.

ENDNOTES

[1]   Nels F. S. Ferré, *The Christian Fellowship* (New York: Harper & Brothers, 1940), p. 26.

[2]   Robert S. Hartman, *The Structure of Value* (Carbondale, Ill.: Southern Illinois University Press, 1967).

[3]   The formal structures of, instructions for taking, and system for scoring the CVP and the RVP are based on the HVP. To learn more about the HVP itself, its various uses, and the qualified consultants who currently administer it, go to the website of the Robert S. Hartman Institute: *http://www.hartmaninstitute.org*

[4]   Technically, Lines 2, 4, and 6 are absolute sums of differences from the norm, while lines 3, 5, and 7 are qualitative numbers that take into account only the **positive** deviations, as a percentage of the absolute sum. If you subtract the positive percentage from 100, the result is the negative percentage of the absolute sum.)

[5]   Robert S. Hartman, *The Structure of Value* (Carbondale and Edwardsville, Ill.: Southern Illinois University Press, 1967).

[6]   This measure tells us how significant the DIM_1 score is in relation to the overall sum of the differences (DIF_1). The DIM_1 score is calculated as a percentage of the DIF_1 score, to get a qualitative measure of the significance of the DIM_1 score.

[7]   Both DIF scores are summary scores of DIM I, DIM E, and DIM S. Refer to the next 3 sections to find out specifically which dimensions, Intrinsic, Extrinsic or Systemic, are causing disharmony. Then review and study the appropriate sections in Chapters Three, Four, and Five.

[8]   The American pragmatist, Charles Sanders Peirce, said that "reference to the future is an essential element of personality. Were the end of a person already explicit, there would be no room for development, for growth, for life; and consequently there would be no personality." Quoted in Charles Hartshorne and William L. Reese, *Philosophers*

Speak of God (Chicago: The University of Chicago Press, 1953), p. 261.

9   The Hartman Value Profile (HVP), as well as the Religious and Christian Value Profiles, can measure our valuational strengths and weaknesses. For more information about the HVP, please visit the web site of the Robert S. Hartman Institute, *http://www.hartmaninstitute.org.*

10   See Leon Pomeroy and Richard Bishop, "A Behavioral Axiology: Cross Cultural Studies of Values," in Rem B. Edwards and John W. Davis, eds., *Forms of Value and Valuation: Theory and Applications* (Lanham, Md.: University Press of America, 1991), pp. 315-327; Leon Pomeroy, *The New Science of Axiological Psychology* (Amsterdam-New York: Editions Rodopi, 2005).

11   Robert S. Hartman, *Freedom to Live: The Robert Hartman Story*, edited by Arthur R. Ellis (Amsterdam - Atlanta: Editions Rodopi, 1994), pp. 32-33.

12   In axiological self-losing and self-overcoming, intrinsic valuation and values such as love, compassion, self, consciousness, and unique individuality are positively valued. Their undeveloped forms are to be transformed, transcended, and expanded. As mature individual conscious beings, we grow toward including every kind and instance of consciousness and all creation within ourselves. By contrast, in some Oriental religions, self, consciousness, and individuality are often disvalued, and the ideal religious goal is self-extinction rather than self-expansion. Yet, alongside their negative themes, these same religions affirm intrinsic valuation in the form of compassion. Some mystics encourage eliminating or excluding all qualities whatsoever from conscious awareness, even the good-making ones, so that only pure consciousness that isn't conscious of anything (except bliss?) remains; but other mystics advocate including all good-making properties within religious consciousness. One religious ideal says that the form of awareness that is poorest in good-making properties is Divine and ultimately desirable; the other affirms that the kind of awareness that is richest in good-making properties is Divine and ultimately desirable. You must decide between them for yourself.

13   Robert S. Hartman, *The Individual in Management*, an unpublished manuscript available in the Hartman archives of the Special Collections Library at The University of Tennessee, Knoxville, TN. Now available through the "Research Topics" button of the website of the Robert S. Hartman Institute: *http://www.hartmaninstitute.org*. Quoted by permission of the Secretary of the Robert S. Hartman Institute. For "How to Develop Our Self" see pp. 55-61.

14   *Ibid.*, pp. 55-58.

15   The table of "twenty properties" is from pp. 49-50 of "The Individual in Management." The explanations above were abstracted from pp. 40-50. In describing the traits, Hartman used masculine words, but these are changed here to plural words that apply to both males and females. A few phrases are from Hartman's *Freedom to Live*, pp. 114-116.

16   Quoted in Rem B. Edwards, *Religious Values and Valuations*, p. 30.

17   At present, special Profiles for other religions like Judaism and Islam are not available, but the authors of the present value Profiles would be happy to work with religious groups or individuals who want to see such Profiles developed. After a little thought, anyone who knows much about the complexity of the world religions will realize the impossibility of creating a "Universal Religious Profile" that would cover them ALL. Any such Profile would be so watered down that adherents of particular historical religions would not be able to recognize themselves in it. For example, "God" could have no place, since many religions like Communism and the original and Hinayana versions of Buddhism are atheistic or non-theistic. Technically, no metaphysical concepts at all would appear in a Profile that covers Buddhism, which professes to be totally anti-metaphysical, even though Buddhism always sneaks in metaphysical concepts like reincarnation, karma, the universality of temporal change, and the likes of such. Of course, these central Buddhist concepts have no place in many religions, so they could not appear either on a "Universal Religious Profile." Serious problems of finding common family religious traits abound. We also have no "Atheist Value Profile" to offer, though Paul Tillich regarded atheism as a kind of

religion having its own ultimate concerns. Yet, atheists and non-theists could actually learn much about themselves from the standard "secular" Hartman Value Profile, which is religiously neutral.

18   Robert S. Hartman, *The Structure of Value* (Carbondale and Edwardsville, Ill.: Southern Illinois University Press, 1967).

19   To order copies of the original Hartman Value Profile, contact its publisher: John J. Austin, Research Concepts, 1368 East Airport Road, Muskegon, MI 49444; phone: 231-739-7401.

20   Leon Pomeroy and Richard Bishop, "A Behavioral Axiology: Cross Cultural Studies of Values," in Rem B. Edwards and John W. Davis, eds., *Forms of Value and Valuation: Theory and Applications* (Lanham, Md.: University Press of America, 1991), pp. 315-327; Leon Pomeroy, *The New Science of Axiological Psychology* (Amsterdam - New York: Editions Rodopi, 2005).

21   Rem B. Edwards, *Religious Values and Valuations* (Chattanooga, Tenn.: Paidia Press, 2000), pp. 26-29.

22   Hartman, 1967, p. 309.

23   *Ibid.*, p. 307.

24   *Ibid.*, p. 308.

25   Robert S. Hartman, "The Individual in Management," unpublished manuscript, 1962, p. 31. Available now on the Hartman Institute website (*http://www.hartmaninstitute.org*) under the "Research Topics" button.

26   Edwards, 2000, pp. 39-66.

27   David Mefford, "Self Knowledge and Self Development," in Edwards and Davis, eds., *Forms of Value and Valuation*, pp. 337-340.

28   William James, *The Varieties of Religious Experience*, (New York: The Modern Library, 1902), Lectures XI-XV, especially XIV and XV.

29   Edwards, 2000, pp. 169-222.

30   *Ibid*, pp. 125-164.

31   *Ibid.*, pp. 71-118.

32   Horace Bushnell, *Christian Nurture* (New Haven: Yale University Press, 1953); James Fowler, *Stages of Faith* (San Francisco: Harper, 1995), pp. 53-68.

33   Edwards, 2000, pp. 75-98.

34   *Ibid*, pp. 194-199.

35   St. Bonaventure, *The Mind's Road to God* (New York: The Liberal Arts Press, 1953).

36   Jonathan Edwards, *A Treatise Concerning Religious Affections* (New Haven, Yale University Press, 1959).

37   Søren Kierkegaard, *Stages on Life's Way* (New York: Schocken Books, 1967); *The Sickness Unto Death* (Princeton: Princeton University Press, 1980).

38   Bushnell, 1953.

39   Jean Piaget, *The Child and Reality* (New York: Penguin Books, 1976; *Six Psychological Studies* (New York: Random House, Vintage Books, 1967).

40   Lawrence Kohlberg, *The Philosophy of Moral Development: Moral Stages and the Idea of Justice* (San Francisco: Harper & Row, 1981); *The Psychology of Moral Development: The Nature and Validity of Moral Stages* (San Francisco: Harper & Row, 1984).

41   James W. Fowler, *Becoming Adult, Becoming Christian: Adult Development and Christian Faith* (San Francisco: Jossey-Bass Publishers, 2000); *Faith Development and Pastoral Care* (Philadelphia: Fortress Press, 1987); *Stages of Faith* (San Francisco: Harper, 1995). Fowler's second and third stages of religious development correspond approximately to what axiology identifies as "Worldly religion," (Edwards, 2000, Ch. 3). His fourth stage is axiology's "Ideological religion," (Edwards, Ch. 4). and his fifth and sixth stages are degrees of "Saintliness" (Edwards, Ch. 5).

42   Gary W. Moon and David G. Benner, *Spiritual Direction and the Care of Souls: A Guide of Christian Approaches and Practices* (Downers Grove, Ill.: InterVarsity Press, 2004).

ABOUT THE AUTHORS

REM B. EDWARDS, Ph.D., received his A.B. degree from Emory University in 1956, where he was elected to Phi Beta Kappa. During graduate school he was a Danforth Graduate Fellow. He received a B.D. degree from Yale University Divinity School in 1959 and a Ph.D. in Philosophy from Emory University in 1962. He taught for four years at Jacksonville University in Florida, moved from there to the University of Tennessee in 1966, and retired from there partly in 1997 and partly in 1998. He continues to be professionally active and kept an office on the University campus until the end of May, 2000. He was a U. T. Chancellor's Research Scholar in 1985 and a Lindsay Young Professor from 1987-1998.

His areas of specialization are Philosophy of Religion, American Philosophy, and Ethical Theory and Medical Ethics—with a special focus on Mental Health Care Ethics, Ethics and Animals, and Formal Axiology.

He is the author or editor of seventeen books including *Reason and Religion* (New York: Harcourt, 1972 and Lanham, Md.: University Press of America, 1979); *Pleasures and Pains: A Theory of Qualitative Hedonism* (Ithaca: Cornell University Press, 1979); with Glenn Graber, *BioEthics* (San Diego: Harcourt, 1988); with John W. Davis, *Forms of Value and Valuation: Theory and Applications* (Lanham, Md.: University Press of America, 1991); *Formal Axiology and Its Critics* (Amsterdam-Atlanta: Editions Rodopi, 1995); *Violence, Neglect, and the Elderly*, co-edited with Roy Cebik, Glenn Graber, and Frank H. Marsh (Greenwich, Conn.: JAI Press, 1996); *New Essays on Abortion and Bioethics*, (Greenwich, Conn.: JAI Press, 1997); *Ethics of Psychiatry: Insanity, Rational Autonomy, and Mental Health Care*, (Buffalo, NY: Prometheus Books, 1997); *Values, Ethics, and*

Alcoholism, co-edited with Wayne Shelton, (Greenwich, Conn.: JAI Press, 1997); *Bioethics for Medical Education*, co-edited with Dr. Edward Bittar, (Stamford, Conn.: JAI Press, 1999), *Religious Values and Valuations*, (Chattanooga, Tenn.: Paidia Publishing Co, 2000; *Dialogues on Values and Centers of Value* (Amsterdam-New York: Editions Rodopi, 2001), co-authored with Thomas M. Dicken; and *What Caused the Big Bang?* (Amsterdam-New York: Editions Rodopi, 2001). *What Caused the Big Bang* received the "Best Book of 2001" award from the Editors of the Value Inquiry Book Series. Edwards has also authored over sixty articles and reviews.

He is an Associate Editor with the Value Inquiry Book Series, published by Editions Rodopi, where he is responsible for the Hartman Institute Axiological Studies special series; and for a number of years he was co-editor of the Advances in Bioethics book series published by JAI Press. He also did significant editorial work on the following books published in Rodopi's Hartman Institute Axiological Studies: Frank G. Forrest, *Valuemetrics: The Science of Personal and Professional Ethics*, 1994; Robert S. Hartman, *Freedom to Live: The Robert Hartman Story*, 1994; Armando Molina, *Our Ways: Values and Character*, 1997; Gary Acquaviva, *Violence, Values, and Our Future*, 2000; Robert S. Hartman, *The Knowledge of Good*, 2002, co-edited with Arthur Ellis; Leon Pomeroy, *The New Science of Axiological Psychology*, 2005; Gary Gallopin: *Beyond Perestroika: Axiology and the New Russian Entrepreneurs*, 2005.

Edwards has been the President of the Tennessee Philosophical Association (1973-74), the Society for Philosophy of Religion (1981-82), and the Southern Society for Philosophy and Psychology, (1984-85). He is a Charter Member and Fellow of the Robert S. Hartman Institute for Formal and Applied Axiology and has served on its Board of Directors since 1987. Since 1989 he has been its Secretary-Treasurer. He is Webmaster for the website of the R. S. Hartman Institute at: *http://www.hartmaninstitute.org*. He is a lifelong Methodist.

DAVID MEFFORD, Ph.D., is a native of Morristown, Tennessee with 35 years of experience in formal axiology and its applications to business and to individuals. David attended a Christian college, Andrews University in Barrien Springs, Michigan, as part of his undergraduate education. David's career as a value theory practitioner began as a student and assistant to Professor Robert S. Hartman, the creator of scientific value theory, *axiology*. Professor Hartman created the foundations for a logic-based science of values and a system to determine personality differences based on their own values. Abraham Maslow's "hierarchy of needs" was an early application of Hartman's new science of value. Hartman's personality instrument is known as the Hartman Value Profile (HVP). As Hartman's commercial representative in Europe (1970-73), David conducted his first business development seminar at Garmisch-Partenkirchen in Southern Germany in 1971. He attended his first class in European axiology at the University of Paris, Nanterre, France and earned his Magister Artium (M.A.) degree in psychology, philosophy, and law at the University of Heidelberg, Germany in 1976. David's Heidelberg studies included graduate seminars with Professor Hans Tellenbach, M.D., the head of Psychiatry at the Heidelberg Medical College. While completing his Ph.D. degree at the University of Tennessee, David evaluated and counseled psychiatric patients under the supervision of Dr. John Wolaver, M.D., for a three year period. David's dissertation, *Phenomenology of Man as a Valuing Subject* achieved a comprehensive typology of personality based on value judgment patterns. This axiological personality model of 26 cognitive types and 40 emotional temperaments is currently in use by professional psychologists, counselors, and business leaders for individual and group assessments and counseling. David co-developed a "core values" model for excellence in officership for the USAF in 1997. (See: *www.usafa.af.mil/jscope*). In collaboration with Dr. Clayton Lafferty, former president and owner of Human Synergistics in Detroit, Michigan, David created a new series of values-based personality instruments known as VUE's (Values Usage Exercises). David is co-founder and Board member of the R. S. Hartman Institute, a non-profit professional organization. A prolific writer, David has authored several publications on the applications of axiological value science, and several articles have been published about his work.

Publications

The Hartman Value Profile for Professionals, 1984

Home Federal Trust Services Guide, 1985

The Hartman Value Profile for Tennessee Corrections, 1986

Values Management for the Security Industry, 1987

The Universal Value M.A.P., 1988

Phenomenology of Man as a Valuing Subject, (Doctoral Dissertation), 1989

Krebsforum (Cancer Forum), "Personality Values Test for Cancer Diagnosis," with Vera Mefford and Dr. Manfred von Luhmann M.D., Head Oncologist at the Habichtswald Klinik, Kassel, Germany; June, 1993, Synmed Verlag, Berlin, Germany

"Self Knowledge and Self Development," in *Forms of Value and Valuation*, Edwards and Davis, University Press of America, New York, 1991

"The Values Usage Exercise (VUE)," a model for officership excellence in the USAF, proceedings of the Joint Services Conference on Professional Ethics (JSCOPE), Washington, D.C., 1997

Values for Living (Self Development Course), 1990, currently being edited for 3rd publication.

Between 1977 and 2003, Dr. Mefford presented numerous papers at annual meetings of the Robert S. Hartman Institute held at The University of Tennessee, Knoxville, Tennessee.

VERA MEFFORD, M.A., is a native of Hamburg, Germany. She immigrated to the U. S. when she was 2 years old and has resided in Tennessee since 1976. She received her Bachelor's Degree from Houghton Christian College, New York (1973) and her Master's Degree from Schiller University, Heidelberg, Germany (1975) in Psychology and German. Vera also completed her Master's post-graduate anthropological studies at the University of Heidelberg, *Institut fur Ur-und Fruhgeschicte*. She is co-owner and Chief Operating Officer of AXCES Corporation (formerly, Value Measurement Technologies) since 1982, where she develops and markets axiological products and services for human resources, advertising, and corporate development. Her clients have included Chase Manhattan Bank, Oak Ridge National Lab, Alcoa Aluminum, State Farm, and Cellular One. She has served as a business consultant and executive coach for over 20 years, with a focus on organizational development, team-building, and achieving a balanced quality-of-life focus for executives.

From 1987-93, Vera trained medical staff in values-based assessment and counseling at the Habichtswald Cancer Clinic in Kassel, Germany. Research, assessment, and counseling continued over a 5-year period, and her suggestions for life changes and "will-to-live" scale showed exceptional accuracy and success on a group of 60 post-operative cancer patients. Her assessments were judged to be exactly parallel to that of the medical team after they conducted 12 weeks of psychotherapy. From 1989-90, she conducted staff evaluations for the Knoxville based Rescue Mission, and she conducted staff and student evaluations for the Knoxville-based, seven county JTPA project. This involved creating a simpler HVP version and output report for students to help determine their potentials and aptitudes. She continues to evaluate prospective adoptive parents for Dr. Bruce McCoy.

Vera also co-developed a core values model for excellence in officership for the United States Air Force and a series of self-scoring, values-based, personality instruments, VUEs (Values Usage Exercises), in collaboration with Dr. David Mefford and Dr. Clay Lafferty, previous owner of Human Synergistics in Detroit, Michigan. She co-wrote and edited "The Hartman Value Profile for Professionals," *Values Management* for the Security Industry, and authored "Uses of Axiology in Business," a benchmark chapter in *Forms of Value and Valuation*, Edwards and Davis, University Press of America, New York, 1991.

Vera has also been a consultant to the Christian music industry in the areas of promotions, band management, bookings, production, and tax shelters. She was previously Vice President and is now on the Board of Directors of the Robert S. Hartman Institute for Formal and Applied Axiology. She has authored several articles and registered numerous copyrights in the field of value science (formal axiology). She co-founded Proethics, a non-profit organization dedicated to raising awareness about ethics and ethical issues in 1993. She is currently developing communications and training programs for various special interest groups (relationships, parents, children, professional conduct, college ethics education, religious values, *etc.*) At AXCES Corporation, Vera is responsible for the venture capital division, which identifies promising start-up companies, develops business and marketing plans, and raises funds for these ventures.

BVG